The Age of Independence

The Age of Independence

INTERRACIAL UNIONS, SAME-SEX UNIONS,
AND THE CHANGING AMERICAN FAMILY

◆ ◆ ◆

Michael J. Rosenfeld

HARVARD UNIVERSITY PRESS
Cambridge, Massachusetts
London, England
2007

Library of Congress Cataloging-in-Publication Data

Rosenfeld, Michael J., 1966–
The age of independence : interracial unions, same-sex unions, and the changing American
family / Michael J. Rosenfeld.
p.   cm.
Includes bibliographical references and index.
ISBN-13: 978–0–674–02497–7 (alk. paper)
ISBN-10: 0–674–02497–4 (alk. paper)
1. Family—United States.   2. Interracial marriage—United States.   3. Same-sex marriage—
United States.   4. Young adults—Family relationships—United States.   5. Domestic relations—
United States.   6. Social change—United States.   I. Title.
HQ536.R658   2007
306.850973—dc22   2006046821

Contents

Acknowledgments

THIS BOOK STARTED OUT as a small-scale project to interview inter-racial couples in the summer of 2001. A few students suggested that I expand the project to also interview same-sex couples, which I re-sisted at first. As the interviews progressed over the next three sum-mers, I was struck by a few patterns. My interviewees almost all told stories of moving away from their parents and from their communities of origin. I started to wonder whether independence from parents was a historically new phenomenon, and whether more traditional types of couples were equally independent from their parents. I turned to the U.S. census for answers.

Studying the census, I discovered that the changes in intergenera-tional relationships over time were rather different from what the literature on the history of the family had led me to expect. At that point my modest project on intermarriage was growing into a full-fledged reassessment of the history of the family in the United States, and I knew I was going to need some help. Thankfully, many students, friends, colleagues, and no small number of strangers offered their assistance.

Stanford University graduate students Brian Colwell and Tahu Ku-kutai helped me conduct the interviews, while undergraduates Julie Walling, Jennifer Kong, and Andrea Alarcon interviewed participants and transcribed all the tapes. These students were funded by several small grants from Stanford's Vice Provost for Undergraduate Educa-tion and by Stanford's sociology department. I owe a special debt to individuals who volunteered to be interviewed, who let us into their homes, and who shared their stories with us.

Byung-Soo Kim worked diligently and thoughtfully with me on some of the early versions of the census data analyses, which were eventually published as "The Independence of Young Adults and the Rise of Interracial and Same-Sex Unions" in the *American Sociological Review*. I am grateful to the American Sociological Association for permission to reprint, in revised form, material that appeared in that article, and I am grateful to the Population Council and to Blackwell Publishing for permission to reprint material, also revised, that appeared as "Young Adulthood as a Factor in Social Change in the United States" in the *Population and Development Review*. The University of Chicago Press has kindly granted me permission to reprint table 1 from Duane Alwin's "From Obedience to Autonomy: Changes in Traits Desired in Children, 1924–1978," *Public Opinion Quarterly* 52: 33–52, © 1988 by the American Association for Public Opinion Research.

This book was written during a full year junior faculty leave generously provided by Stanford University. During this leave, the Hellman Foundation provided a grant that helped me finish this manuscript.

This project would never have been made into a publishable book without the thoughtful input of my mentors, colleagues, students, family, and friends. I hope they believe the final product justifies their efforts on my behalf. The following people read the manuscript in its entirety at some point in its development and provided wonderful comments: Brian Colwell, Kenny Dinitz, Paula England, David John Frank, Tahu Kukutai, Vivian Levy, Adrienne Lo, Douglas Massey, John Meyer, Bruno Navasky, Julie Walling, and Sharon Weiner. Dawne Moon introduced me to some of the literature on family studies, which helped orient this project. Doug McAdam and Mark Granovetter not only read the manuscript, but both patiently answered my questions about authorship and publishing. Emily Ryo read the manuscript twice, both times marking nearly every page with penetrating questions. I do not know where she finds the energy, but I am very indebted to her. Mordecai Rosenfeld also read the entire manuscript twice, but as my father he had more of an obligation. My wife, Vivian, read the manuscript once, but demurred when I suggested a second reading of a later version. "Once is enough," she said. Tony Fang and David Grazian provided assistance and support along the way. Several anonymous reviewers gave me the benefit of splendid and detailed suggestions.

This is my first book, which means this is my first opportunity to publicly thank some of the people who have helped me along the way. Massey and Denton's *American Apartheid* is the book that first made me want to be a sociologist. I was most fortunate to have Douglas Massey as an advisor in graduate school. Marta Tienda chaired my dissertation; her intelligence, energy, and open-mindedness still serve as an example to me. Roger Gould advised my dissertation and was perhaps the most erudite person I have known; his untimely passing was a tragic loss.

I dedicate this book to my own family: Vivian, Raúl, and Omara. Vivian is a truly independent spirit who has made me happy as long as I have known her. Raúl is old enough to ask complicated questions and wise enough to know that his father does not know all the answers. Omara is only one year old, so she cannot be held responsible for any remaining deficiencies in the text.

The Age of Independence

ONE

Introduction

IN THE 1990s, state courts in Hawaii and Alaska ordered their states to issue marriage licenses to same-sex couples, but both states changed their constitutions to prevent same-sex marriages.[1] In the winter of 2000, under pressure from its state court, Vermont granted same-sex couples the right to a new kind of legal status called civil unions. Civil unions gave same-sex couples some but not all of the rights that heterosexual married couples enjoy.[2] In 2003, the U.S. Supreme Court reversed itself and struck down long standing state laws that had criminalized gay sex between consenting adults.[3] In 2004, Massachusetts, following a state court order, began to marry same-sex couples on an equal basis with heterosexual couples, and several other localities began marrying same-sex couples in defiance of local laws.[4] In just a few short years the frontier of gay rights had moved into uncharted territory. The pace of political and legal changes to gay rights is so rapid that the leading legal texts cannot keep up with the changes.[5] To borrow a phrase from a leading historian of gay life, "the world turned."[6]

We certainly seem to be living in a time of precipitous social change, but reports of rapid and disorienting social change are as old as society itself. Are the changes in modern social and family life really as dramatic as they seem? If homosexuality has been part of human society since the beginning, why has the climate for gay rights changed so quickly in the last decade? Law and custom governing the family have changed so rapidly in the United States that it is easy to

1

forget that interracial marriage was illegal in much of the country until as recently as 1967. Before the Supreme Court finally struck down the laws against interracial marriage, the court had avoided the issue for years, fearing racial intermarriage was too controversial.[7]

In recent years the number of same-sex couples and the number of interracial couples have both risen sharply. In the post-1960 era, divorce has become much more common, heterosexual cohabitation has increased, and young adults are marrying later, to mention but a few of the important changes in family life. The family is a venerable institution, which, despite many claims to the contrary, has been rather slow to change in the past. How then, can we explain the current pace of change in the family system?

In this book I examine some of the underlying demographic factors that play a role in shaping the modern family. I focus on the life stage of young adulthood because that is the life stage when new families are made. Instead of living with parents until they got married, young adults in the post-1960 United States began to live on their own before settling down. During this new life stage, which I refer to as the independent life stage, young men and women go away to college, travel, and begin careers. Young adults experience the independent life stage as a period of social independence. Of course, young adults in the modern world are far from being completely independent of their parents. When young adults go away to college, the tuition bills are usually sent to their parents. And during the independent life stage, young adults may return to the parental nest several times. Even though the independent life stage consists of something less than full and complete independence, it represents substantially more independence than young adults in the United States have ever experienced before.

In recent years scholars have been paying increasing attention to the changing course of young adulthood.[8] Most of this research examines the order of life stage events: leaving school, getting married, starting full-time work, having children, and whether the passage through young adulthood is any less orderly than it used to be. My focus is different. I examine whether the independent life stage has an effect on the *type* of families young adults form. I argue that, by separating adult children from their parents, the independent life stage fosters a new diversity in the kinds of families young people form.

At a Stanford student panel on interracial dating in 2002, a black student told the crowd that he had a white girlfriend. If there was any disapproval on campus, he said he had not felt it and no one in the audience spoke up to disagree. Someone in the crowd asked him whether the parents of his white girlfriend had objected to the relationship. He looked a bit puzzled, as if he had not considered that question before. "It doesn't matter," he said, "because they're far away."

In the past when adult children lived with their parents, parents had much more control over their children's eventual mates. Adult children who were economically dependent on their parents could not easily form romantic relationships against their parents' wishes. Now, when young adults choose an interracial or same-sex partner, their parents are usually without recourse to prevent the match. Not only do parents no longer hold veto power over their children's mate selection, but also parents have increasingly come to believe that children have the right to choose whatever mate suits them. The demographic reality of looser intergenerational ties has changed the way we think about personal freedoms.

The decline of parental influence over adult children does not imply, however, that the young select mates without any regard to the social boundaries and norms of their parents. Prior to 1967, parents in many U.S. states who sought to prevent their children from marrying interracially had the law on their side. After the Supreme Court struck down the laws against racial intermarriage in 1967,[9] racial intermarriage increased steadily, but the odds of black-white intermarriage are still hundreds of times less than chance alone would predict. Barriers to interracial unions still exist. These barriers are not always as visible or as obvious as laws against racial intermarriage (the laws themselves were relatively invisible except to interracial couples considering marriage). Residential segregation by race is still widespread in the United States.[10] Whites have defended residential segregation passionately and violently in part because they wanted to control their children's social and romantic access to children of other races. As long as high school (embedded as it was in the segregated neighborhood) was the culmination of the educational experience, the segregated neighborhood was an effective system for preventing racial intermarriage.

As more and more young adults have left their parents' home to go away to college, the segregated neighborhood has lost some of its influence. The percentage of young U.S.-born adults who attended college was 12 percent in 1940, 23 percent in 1960, and 59 percent in 2000. Parents whose young adult children have left the nest have substantially less leverage over the kinds of unions their young adult children form. The independent life stage has decoupled children's behavior from parental attitudes. College-educated young adults have labor market skills that eventually make them more financially independent from their parents (even if the parents have paid for college). Nontraditional families emerge as a consequence of the decline of parental control.

From 1960 to 2000, the number of black-white married couples in the United States increased from 55,000 to 331,000. In the same forty years the number of Asian-white married couples has gone from 49,000 to 579,000. The number of marriages between Hispanics and non-Hispanic whites rose from 283,000 in 1970 to 1.5 million in 2000. In the decade of the 1990s,[11] the number of same-sex cohabiting couples recorded in the U.S. census increased from 145,000 to 593,000 couples, though a good part of the apparent increase in same-sex couples appears to be due to changes in Census Bureau procedures for handling data once assumed to be anomalous, that is, persons of the same sex who report that they are married to each other.[12] Despite the growth in numbers of interracial and same-sex unions, these nontraditional unions are still few in number compared with the 52.6 million heterosexual same-race married couples in the United States in 2000.

Given the small number of interracial and same-sex unions compared with the number of same-race married couples, one can hardly blame the general literature on marriage and the family for ignoring nontraditional unions. In the past few decades, interracial and same-sex unions have risen from invisibility and illegality to marginality and grudging societal acceptance. Though nontraditional unions are still very much in the minority, their rise offers intriguing clues about when, how, and why family patterns change. My objective in this book is to use the nontraditional and often marginalized interracial and same-sex unions to tell a story not only about nontraditional unions themselves, but also a more general story about family life in the United States.

What makes the rise of interracial and same-sex unions potentially interesting is the extent to which U.S. society (through laws, violence, segregation, and intimidation) worked to prevent these unions in the past. Emmett Till, a fourteen-year-old black boy from Chicago, was murdered for simply flirting with a white woman in Mississippi in 1955.[13] Interracial and same-sex couples were hounded relentlessly because any example of alternative family forms was seen (not unreasonably) as a radical challenge to the dominance and hegemony of heterosexual same-race marriage. The very foundation of the racial division in the United States depended on being able to reliably separate the "black" from the "white" population and thus demonstrate and reinforce the supposed inherent differences between the two populations. Given the depth and power of the racial division in U.S. society, even small numbers of interracial couples were viewed in the past as an unacceptable challenge to the hegemony of racial distinctions. Intermarriage blurs the lines of race by creating mixed families and interracial inheritance. Informal interracial sexual relations, however, such as between slave owners and slaves, were always present in some form in the United States and allowed white society to deny and disown the progeny of interracial couplings.[14]

The undeniable presence of interracial couples and their multiracial offspring led the U.S. Census Bureau to allow respondents to choose more than one racial category for the first time in the 2000 census. Seven million three hundred thousand Americans (2.6 percent of the U.S. population) identified themselves with more than one race on the 2000 census. The racial categories of the past are still with us, but their power and impermeability are diminishing.

yes — of Obama

Family Government

Since 1960, the rise of interracial unions and same-sex unions, along with the rise of divorce and heterosexual cohabitation, has made American families more diverse. In order to identify the source of new family diversity, one must first understand how diversity was suppressed in the past. In other words, how did U.S. society maintain same-race heterosexual marriage as the single accepted family form for so long? The dominance of heterosexual same-race marriage in the past was not accidental, but rather was due to the systematic application of what colonial leaders called "family government."[15]

Family government in the colonies meant that every individual had to be part of a family in order to ensure that the family could supervise, guide, and correct the individual's behavior. Colonial leaders understood that marriage is a system of social control and social as well as biological reproduction. In colonial New England towns, community leaders made it illegal for bachelors to live on their own, precisely because living outside of family government would put the bachelors outside of the most important system of social control. Bachelors were forced to either marry, move in with an existing family, go to jail, or leave the community.[16] Family supervision over individual behavior included guidance about who was, and who was not, an acceptable mate. Parental guidance and supervision were rarely ignored, because in the colonies parental permission and community acceptance were required before a legal marriage could be performed.[17]

The post-1960 diversification of families has taken place for a reason that colonial leaders intuitively understood: young adults are less subject to parental control when they live apart from their parents.

The Independent Life Stage from Different Perspectives

The independent life stage is the kind of demographic phenomenon that can be all around and still be invisible. The popular press has emphasized the phenomenon of young adults returning to the nest, the opposite of the independent life stage.[18] It is widely believed that young adults are more likely to live with their parents now than ever before. Contrary to popular belief, however, census data show that a much smaller percentage of single Americans in their twenties live with their parents today than at any time in the past. The reason we read more about children moving back home with their parents is that, paradoxically, such behavior is less common and therefore more noticeable than in the past.[19]

Virtually everyone has a family, and herein lies a great difficulty for scholars of the family: the subject is overly familiar. Everyone considers him, or herself an expert on the subject of his or her own families, yet we are too close to our own families to judge them dispassionately. Husbands and wives often have different views about the same marriage.[20] Without historically consistent data about the family, we can only understand the broad family system by extrapolation from our own personal family experiences. Given the haze of intimacy that covers our own family experiences, and given the certainty that family structure varies over time and space, personal experience can be a misleading guide to historical family change. And yet, until the census microdata for the nineteenth and early twentieth centuries became available in the 1990s, scholars had only individual observations, such as those by travelers like Tocqueville or the diaries of nineteenth-century women analyzed by Ellen Rothman, to rely upon.[21] Individual observations can provide a wealth of subjective information that the census cannot provide. The census data, however, because of their massive sample size, their national representativeness, and their historical consistency are the definitive source for issues that the census data do address, such as family structure changes over time.

Relying on subjective individual observations, historians have tended to believe that young Americans growing up during the industrial revolution of the late nineteenth century had a great degree of freedom from parental control.[22] Rothman's diarists, for instance, generally believed that they were free to choose mates without any interference from their parents. Tocqueville, who traveled in the United States during 1831 and 1832, wrote obsessively about the independent spirit of young Americans and their freedom from family government.

The census data have opened a new window into the past, which casts the late nineteenth-century American family in a new light. The census data show, for instance, that family government (in the form of intergenerational co-residence) was maintained throughout the industrial revolution. Young adults during this period nearly always lived with their parents or with parental surrogates. According to the census data, family government over young adults did not begin to decline until after World War II. A great deal of family life changed during the industrial revolution: infant mortality declined, fertility declined, household size declined, the divorce rate grew, and millions moved away from farming to work in the factories. The magnitude of the changes to family life during the industrial revolution has obscured the fact that some other (in my view crucial) aspects of family life remained stubbornly unchanged by the industrial revolution.

The fact that the decline in family government is a recent phenomenon and not a centuries-old phenomenon (as the prior historical consensus has held) helps explain the very interesting recent growth of nontraditional romantic unions. The census data demonstrate that nontraditional unions, to the extent that they can be measured in the nineteenth century using the census, were nearly nonexistent. Specifically, extramarital heterosexual cohabitation and interracial marriage were both practically unknown during the industrial revolution in the United States. The near absence of nontraditional unions during the industrial revolution is inconsistent with the prior historical consensus, which viewed nineteenth-century Americans as having unprecedented levels of personal independence. I discuss these matters in more detail in Chapters 3 and 4.

Family Change and Social Change

At the heart of this book is a fairly simple argument about how changing family structure, especially the rise of the independent life stage, is a force for social change. The reality of the independent life stage diminishes parental influence over children at the time in their lives when they are making decisions about romance, career, education, and where to live. The visibility of large numbers of interracial and same-sex couples reduces the moral authority of parental objections against such unions. As each successive cohort of young adults is more likely to form interracial or same-sex unions, the visibility of these nontraditional unions erodes the taboos against interraciality and homosexuality. Parents learn that objecting to their children's choice of partner is futile, and they make fewer objections. Eventually, as the number of interracial and same-sex unions rises and fewer objections are heard, the formerly taboo family forms become integrated into the social mainstream.[23]

The rise of the independent life stage and the rise of nontraditional unions are but two pieces of a much larger puzzle of social, familial, and political change in the United States since 1960. A few of the other notable changes include the rise of divorce and heterosexual cohabitation, the invention of the birth control pill, the sexual revolution, the civil rights movement, the rise of feminism and women's rights, the movement against the Vietnam War, the counterculture and youth movements of the 1960s, and the gay rights movement, to name just a few. The independent life stage is both a cause and an effect of these other changes. As a sociologist, I favor arguments about how social structures such as the independent life stage influence how we think, live, and see ourselves, but clearly the causal arrow works in the other direction as well: the social structures we create and inhabit are a product of the cultural values of our times.

Consider for a moment the timing of the civil rights movement. Why was the 1960s the decade of civil rights instead of some earlier decade? Black citizens' demands for greater rights and freedoms pre-dated 1960, to be sure. Historians of the civil rights movement have argued that the political system of the United States was more open to change in the 1960s.[24] The dominant role of the United States in the world after World War II focused new levels of international attention on the country's internal problems, and thereby raised the cost of continuing segregation and racial strife in the United States.[25] Though these explanations are sensible and persuasive, the demography of the 1960s suggests a different kind of explanation.

The 1960s movements, from civil rights to the antiwar movement, from Greensboro to the Student Nonviolent Coordinating Committee, from the Berkeley Free Speech Movement to the student upheavals at Kent State and Jackson State, from the Students for a Democratic Society (SDS) to the volunteers of Freedom Summer were all powered and led by college students, recent college graduates, college dropouts, and a broadly radical youth culture.[26] This kind of radical and activist youth culture had never existed quite this way before because the independent life stage gave young people not only greater freedom to object and dissent, but also the social and physical space to protest and disrupt. It is difficult to imagine an SDS or a Freedom Summer populated by high school students living at home or populated by young married adults with children. College students and young single people living on their own are more potentially rebellious because they are outside of what community leaders in the American colonies referred to as "family government." The "generation gap" was an idea invented in the 1960s, and it could not have easily described any previous generation.

Consider the first sentence of the Port Huron Statement of the SDS, one of the founding documents of the radical student movements of the 1960s: "We are people of this generation, bred in at least modest comfort, housed now in universities, looking uncomfortably to the world we inherit."[27] Being housed in the university rather than with their parents gave the students a detachment from the social controls of the family in a way that made possible the expression of a new and more strident critique of "the system."

It is also interesting to note the Port Huron Statement's reference to the economic prosperity of the society, that is, the upbringing "in at least modest comfort." One requirement for the independent life stage is a certain degree of economic prosperity. Not all families in the United States have the resources to send their children away to college, and not all young adults have the financial means to live on their own. We often assume that prosperity and higher education make people more liberal and tolerant, and there is a basis for these assumptions. However, nontraditional unions may be less common in poor families not because of stubborn social conservatism in general, but rather because young adults from those families have fewer resources and therefore less independence from their parents.

Age and life stage are key determinants of participation in social activism and radical politics.[28] Young adults who are not yet enmeshed in careers, who do not yet have mortgages and children to support, are the people most capable of radical activism, because they have the least to lose. For example, consider the now famous June 1969 police raid on the Stonewall bar in the Greenwich Village neighborhood of New York. The New York police routinely harassed gays and raided gay bars, so the raid on the Stonewall was nothing unusual. Ordinarily, the police had the upper hand in these raids because the threat of a phone call to employers or to landlords, with the suggestion that the person had been arrested at a gay bar, was enough to make anyone fearful of losing his job or apartment.[29] The young gay patrons of the Stonewall, however, were not so easily intimidated. They surprised the police and themselves by battling back. The young gay crowd quickly took control of the street and the police retreated into the bar to wait for reinforcements. When the gay patrons of the Stonewall uprooted parking meters to batter down the doors of the bar in order to get at the police who were cowering inside, it was clear that the usual power dynamic had been overturned. The police and the locals returned to the Stonewall to renew the battle for the next two nights. The riots at the Stonewall helped give birth to a militant gay rights movement in the United States, but older gay leaders were mortified at the time.[30] The New York branch of the Mattachine Society, a homophile organization made up mostly of older gay men who were still in the closet and afraid of losing their jobs or apartments if their sexual identity became known, pleaded for peace and calm.[31] The men of the Mattachine had a stake in peace and calm; the angry young patrons of the Stonewall did not.

We know a great deal about events like the Stonewall riots, the gay rights movement more generally, the civil rights movement, and the women's rights movement because historians and activists have written wonderful insider accounts.[32] The insider accounts of 1960s movements are so rich and informative, and the scholarship about those movements is so broad and varied, what could a new approach possibly offer? I suggest in this book that changes in family structure, changes that are generally invisible at the individual level, offer some potentially useful new ideas about why these movements took place when they did. I do not attempt to "explain" the civil rights movement and its many offshoots; the already existing literature does this better than I could ever hope to do. What I can add is merely a new perspective to what we already know about civil rights, women's rights, and gay rights.

No one could deny that the civil rights movement, feminism, and the gay rights movement have all had a profound effect on social and political life in the United States. The question is why these movements were able to galvanize so many young people into activism and why the activists were able to convince so many nonactivists of the basic rightness of their causes. Some of the answer lies, in my view, with the changing American family. I emphasize the underlying demographic structure of social change because I believe that demography has been neglected in our debates over social change. I also believe that great leaders matter, that organizational tactics matter, and that the efforts of a dedicated few can have an important effect on the lives of many. Since others have already written extensively about the leaders, the tactics, and the internal dynamics of the 1960s movements, I focus on the small part of the puzzle that I can add: the role of family change.

Data and Terminology

The main source of data I use in this book is the census microdata for the United States for 1850–2000, integrated and organized by the Integrated Public Use Microdata Series (IPUMS) project of the University of Minnesota.[33] The U.S. census provides an extraordinarily large sample size and unparalleled population coverage for many basic questions. Although the United States has had a national census every ten years since 1790, the individual records (which scholars refer to as "microdata") of the censuses prior to 1940 were never available to researchers until very recently when scholars (led by Steven Ruggles at the University of Minnesota) transformed the old census records into a modern publicly available database. The censuses themselves are old, but their availability to researchers is new. At the present time, the 1850 census data are the earliest census microdata that are available to researchers. As earlier census data become available, scholars will have to reexamine what we think we know about family life in the early American republic.

I use data from the General Social Survey (GSS) to study popular attitudes in the United States.[34] The GSS is a nationally representative survey of several thousand households performed approximately every two years since 1972.

To supplement the census data and the opinion survey data, I have interviewed twenty-eight couples (interracial couples and same-sex couples) in the San Francisco Bay Area. These interviews are few in number (especially when compared with the millions of individual records in the U.S. census), and the respondents are not representative even of couples in the Bay Area. Yet the interviews provide some things the census cannot: stories, perspective, emotions, and a retrospective view of the life histories of romantic and family relationships.

Throughout this book the terms "family" and "family structure" refer to the cross-generational family, specifically the children's relationships to parents, and more broadly to aunts, uncles, step-parents, grandparents, and so on.[35] "Independence from family" refers to cross-generational independence, that is, the independence of adult children from their parents. I use the term "unions" to refer to married or cohabiting couples and I use "heterosexual" as shorthand for couples who identify themselves as a man and a woman. Used in this way "heterosexual" is a measure of public sexual identity rather than private behavior.

In the currently available census data all married couples are heterosexual married couples by Census Bureau definition. Since the 2000 census, however, the state of Massachusetts and several localities have issued marriage licenses to same-sex couples, so I add the modifier "heterosexual" to married couples for clarity. I use the phrase "traditional" to describe heterosexual same-race marriages and "nontraditional" to describe all other kinds of unions. I recognize that the "tradition" of same-race heterosexual marriage is a socially and legally constructed tradition.[36] Since the word "miscegenation" was introduced into the American lexicon through a pro-slavery political hoax,[37] I avoid "miscegenation" where I can and use "intermarriage" instead. I use the phrases "homosexual couples," "gay couples," and "same-sex couples" interchangeably to describe cohabiting same-sex couples. Cohabiting same-sex couples are only a subset of the gay population, but the cohabiters are the part of the gay population that is easiest to study because same-sex cohabiters are identifiable in the U.S. census.[38]

This book describes changes in the American family over time. The "American family" is not a uniform category, of course. In addition to interracial couples, same-sex couples, married couples, and heterosexual cohabiters, there are important differences in American families across racial, ethnic, class, religious, regional, and national origin lines. The "black family" is usually treated by scholars as a subject unto itself.[39] In several places in the text I present separate analyses by race, and I sometimes divide urban, rural, and suburban families where it seems most appropriate to do so. Because this book is more concerned with broad changes over time than in the underlying racial and economic diversity between groups, most of the figures and tables in this book include all American families, regardless of race, class, or region. The general trends in family structure that I describe are most closely representative of non-Hispanic white families (since they compose the majority of all families). Although most of the trends I describe are applicable to most population subgroups as well as to the population as a whole, in this book I tend to neglect subgroup variation in favor of concentrating on the overall trends.

Relationship to the Literature

This book crosses several disciplinary boundaries. I draw together strands of literature from gay and lesbian studies, racial studies, social history, family studies, legal scholarship, child development, and social demography to build a synthetic picture of the role of parental control and social control over the children's mate selection process. The purpose of a comparative historical and theoretical analysis is not simply to sew disparate patches of literature together into one colorful quilt, but rather to use the insights and tools of one branch of literature to address unanswered questions in another branch.

Gay and lesbian studies has produced some of the most interesting, insightful, and innovative theoretical and historical work on the American family in recent years. Gay and lesbian studies in the academy has its main roots in history and literature departments. Until recently, scholars of gay studies have not been able to test their theories against nationally representative datasets because there were no such datasets with sufficiently large gay populations. The 1990 and 2000 U.S. censuses provided large nationally representative samples of same-sex cohabiting couples for the first time. I analyze the census data using the tools developed by social demography to test questions posed by the gay studies literature. The answers to these questions about family structure, nontraditional unions, and independence have, I believe, broad relevance for our understanding of family life in modern times.

I use quantitative analysis of 150 years of census data to describe changes in family structure, and I link changes in family structure to the rise of both interracial unions and same-sex unions. The literature on racial intermarriage and the literature on same-sex relationships in the United States have usually been quite separate, linked only tentatively and tangentially.[40] I hypothesize that interracial unions and same-sex unions are part of a continuum of nontraditional union forms that have been increasing over time for many of the same reasons.

If same-sex unions and interracial unions both have roots in the independent life stage (as I hypothesize), then one would expect to find that same-sex couples would be more likely to also be interracial compared with heterosexual married couples, and that is indeed what one finds. Among young heterosexual married couples in 1990, 5.7

percent were interracial, compared with 14.5 percent of young same-sex couples who were interracial.

The relatively high percentage of same-sex couples who are also interracial is not because of a mysterious compatibility between interracial and homosexual desires. Most of my gay interviewees felt that homosexuality was a fundamental part of their personal identity, whereas most of my interracial couples believed that finding a partner of another race was due to happenstance as much as to personal preference. Interraciality is associated with same-sex couples not because homosexuality and interraciality are inherently similar phenomena (they are not), but rather because the social control mechanisms that ordinarily prevent gay people from being "out" are similar to the mechanisms that prevent people from choosing mates of different races.

perhaps ot· reasons too— desire, migration

The gay rights movement in the United States took its cues from the civil rights movement, and gay activists have explicitly framed their legal and political claims as civil rights claims.[41] It is natural, therefore, to view the liberalization of popular U.S. attitudes about gays as part of a broad cultural and political change that began with the civil rights movement.[42] Both the majority opinion in the recent landmark Supreme Court decision of Lawrence v. Texas (the 2003 Supreme Court decision that struck down the state laws against private consensual homosexual sex), and the historians' amicus brief in the Lawrence v. Texas case make explicit reference to the precedent case of Loving v. Virginia, the landmark 1967 Supreme Court decision that struck down the state laws against racial intermarriage.[43] The court's argument in both cases was that consenting adults have rights to private intimate relationships regardless of whether those relationships offend local norms and values.

Outline of the Book

Given the different kinds of sources, the variety of analyses, and the eclectic perspective I offer in this book, some guidance to the reader is in order. In Chapter 2, I examine the history of the family in the United States beginning with colonial times, emphasizing the changing shape of parental control over the mate selection of young adults.

In Chapter 3, I describe the rise of the independent life stage with simple analyses of census data that cover the twentieth century and reach back (for some variables) well into the nineteenth century. In Chapter 4, I describe the rise of interracial and same-sex unions in the United States, and I show that the numbers of these transgressive unions have risen sharply in the post-1960 period. The timing of the rise of transgressive unions implicates the independent life stage as a potential cause.

In Chapter 5, I use recent census data to make the case that non-traditional unions are a direct consequence of the independent life stage. I show that individuals who settle far from where they were born, who live in cities, who have higher education, and who marry later are more likely to form nontraditional unions. The more non-traditional a couple is, the more likely the partners are to live far from where they were born.

Between 1990 and 2000, nontraditional couples have increased their presence and visibility in suburbs, in rural areas, in the South and the Midwest, in short, in the places where once they would have been shunned. The difference in geographic mobility between alternative couples and traditional couples is smaller than it used to be, which suggests that American families have become more accepting of nontraditional couples. Gay couples and interracial couples from the heartland are no longer universally compelled to flee the communities of their youth.

If the United States has become more tolerant of transgression against traditional family norms, it is natural to inquire into the source of this increased tolerance. In Chapter 6, I examine some of the historical changes in how parents have raised children in the United States. The new permissive and nonviolent child-rearing practices of the post-1960 era have undoubtedly shaped the life experiences of children.[44] It seems reasonable to suppose that adults who were raised under the new permissiveness, and who came of age in the age of independence, would be more tolerant than adults who were raised under the previous regime. Data from the General Social Survey, which I examine in Chapter 7, show that Americans who came of age after 1960 are substantially more tolerant of gay rights, even after taking other factors such as age, education, and urban residence into account.

Since the mid-1960s, the U.S. Supreme Court has repeatedly ex-

panded its definition of constitutionally protected privacy rights to
include the right to birth control, the right to abortion, the right for
heterosexuals to marry interracially, and, most recently, the right of
gay couples to engage in consensual sex, despite the fact that the
Constitution itself is silent on these subjects.[45] If the new privacy rights
do not originate in the Constitution, what is their origin? I attempt
to answer this question in Chapter 8.

In Chapter 9, I examine the question of same-sex marriage from
historical and demographic perspectives. One argument I make in
this book is that the post-1960 changes in the American family have
been even more dramatic than most observers have realized, given
the relative stasis of the family system (by some measures) in the past.
The dramatic changes in the post-1960 family system have energized
a conservative political backlash, but the dramatic post-1960 changes
have also created openings for further changes, such as legalized
same-sex marriage, which would have been considered simply out-
landish and fantastical a mere two generations ago.

TWO

◆ ◆ ◆

Family Government

IN ORDER TO UNDERSTAND the rapid change in the family over the past two generations, we must first endeavor to understand the stability of the past. How was the structure of the family preserved so effectively from generation to generation? If a new generation became adults and married every twenty-three years or so, how did U.S. society in the past ensure that young adults formed unions and families in such a way as to preserve what the elders considered the basic structure of the society?

Before we can explain social change, we must first grapple with the real historical prevalence of social stability and inertia. For social theorists, social stability is more problematic than social change. The seeds of revolution are always present, yet social upheaval is rare. One reason that societies are more inert than explosive is that each new generation of individuals is carefully socialized by the parents to fit in to the social norms that the parents have created. Parental socialization of children ensures a substantial degree of social stability across generations. Parental socialization of children is built around co-residence and the dependence of the children on the parents for affection and economic survival.

The symbol of generational transition in the past was the father walking down the aisle, giving his daughter's hand in marriage to an appropriate and approved-of young man. In the past, the daughter was "given away" to her husband, along with a dowry, in exchange for the new husband's agreement to support his wife economically. The

18

key idea of "giving away" was that the young woman was her father's possession in the first place; in other words, she was his to give away. American fathers still sometimes walk their daughters down the aisle on the wedding day, but any reference to "giving away" the daughter is now purely figurative.

The ordinary life course transition used to be from living with one's parents to living with one's spouse. One was almost always part of a family, either the family headed by the parents or the marital family and children. In the language of colonial times, individuals were nearly always subject to "family government."[1] Family government ensured that social norms were respected and renewed.

In at least several of the American colonies, bachelors could not legally live on their own without special permission.[2] Colonial leaders saw to it that family government was imposed on everyone because they understood the power of family government and they feared the absence of social control outside of the family. Not only did parents in the colonies have final legal authority over their children's marriage partners, but also custom, the physical density of individuals within colonial households, and the interdependence of households within communities gave parents and community members a high degree of supervision over the social lives of young adults.

In order to make the argument that intergenerational relationships are fundamentally different in the post-1960 era, I first need to describe intergenerational relationships of the past and explain how the family structures of the past impacted the mate selection of young adults. This is a focused historical review, not an exhaustive history of the American family over four centuries. My goal in this chapter is simply to discuss some of the ways in which U.S. parental society was historically organized to control and constrain the marital choices of children.

Parents and communities have always influenced the mate choices of young adults.[3] The belief that romantic love and individual preference have become the sole bases of mate selection[4] in the Western world has tended to obscure the many structural constraints (which were stronger in the past) of access to different kinds of potential partners. Structural constraints are so inherent in our lives that we do not appreciate the constraints unless we come up against them. The structural forces that constrain mate selection are the social, legal,

also polit v reld
ec frees

and demographic forces that create a narrow pool of dozens of potential mates from the vast pool of millions of people in the society.

Examples of social and demographic structural constraints to mate
selection include residential segregation, intergenerational co-
residence, closed labor markets, and early age at first marriage. Residential racial segregation is a structural constraint to interracial unions, because racial segregation greatly reduces interracial social
exposure. Young adults who live with their parents face increased parental surveillance and oversight of their courtship and mate selection
behavior, and therefore intergenerational co-residence tends to reduce nontraditional unions. Before World War II, when women did
not have substantial access to the formal labor market, women knew
that they needed the financial support of a man in order to survive.
The inability of women to support themselves forced women to
choose heterosexual marriage over other possible kinds of unions and
to marry earlier in the past than they do today. Early marriage in the
1950s meant that the mate was more likely to be a high school sweet-
heart, that is, someone from the (racially segregated) neighborhood
of their youth.

Historical parental controls over their children's marriages fall into
two categories. The first includes direct and explicit interventions to
prevent interracial unions, such as laws against racial intermarriage.
The second category includes the indirect but more pervasive social,
economic, and structural forces that have limited the pool of potential
mates available to young adults. One example of indirect parental
control is the suburbanization and residential segregation of the post–
World War II housing boom in the United States, which insulated
white adolescents from both racial diversity and from the sexual identity diversity of the central cities. Parental control, when applied,
nearly always promoted same-race heterosexual marriage.

Colonial America and the Early
Nineteenth-Century United States

In Puritan New England, as in most of the American colonies, parents
had final legal authority over the disposition of their children in marriage. The legal right of parents to choose the mates of their children
was sometimes overlooked, but parents and even community mem-

bers were expected to exercise a veto over marital choices perceived to be inappropriate.[5]

Before a young couple could be married, they needed not only parental approval but also they needed to post notices, known as banns, in the town square and in the local church to make their intentions known to their neighbors. Usually the notices needed to be posted on three separate occasions. Anyone who read the notices could potentially object to the union. Community members were not entitled to block marriages with personal or whimsical objections (after all, the colonists were few in number and marriage and fertility were community necessities), but the posting of the banns was intended to reduce bigamy, childhood weddings, and other unions that might trespass against law or custom.[6]

In the Delaware River valley, Quaker family government was less authoritarian and less patriarchal than Puritan family government in New England. Quaker women were allowed to be preachers, and Quaker families rarely bound out their children into servitude (as was the custom in other parts of the colonies) because the Quakers had a vision of domestic life that was different from their contemporaries.[7] Although the Quakers had an egalitarian view of family life in some regards, Quaker society exercised strict control (stricter even than the Puritans) over the mate selection of young adults. Marriages to non-Quakers were viewed as "mongrel marriages" and were absolutely prohibited.[8] In order to marry, a Quaker couple had to obtain the approval of both sets of parents and their congregations. The Quakers' tight communal control over marriage forced some young people to leave the Quakers, and it delayed marriage for many of the young people who remained within the community. Late marriage and out-migration caused the Quakers to have lower fertility and population growth rates than other colonial religious groups.[9]

The upper echelons of Anglican Virginia society took English law and custom with regard to marriage (including the posting of the banns and the necessity to formalize the marriage in church) very seriously.[10] For families with substantial plantations, the marriages of their children were serious matters for a simple economic reason: their sons and sons-in-law stood to inherit the estate, and one lazy or profligate young man among the group could easily dissipate a fortune that might have taken generations to acquire. Among the great majority of white Virginians who were not landed gentry, there was less oversight of children's choice of mate because the families had, economically speaking, less to lose. Virginia had laws that outlawed premarital and extramarital sex, similar to the laws in Massachusetts, but southern morality was reputed to be more flexible in practice than New England Puritan morality. As long as the transgressions remained informal and discreet, a Virginian gentleman's honor was assumed to be beyond reproach.[11]

Marriage in the colonies was subject to several different, sometimes conflicting authorities. Some of the more remote outposts of the colonies were beyond the reach of any formal authority. The Church of England only recognized marriages celebrated in the church, and the Church of England therefore viewed informal unions (unions not formalized in the church) as tantamount to extramarital fornication and adultery. However, English tradition, also known as "common law," was interpreted by American scholars as recognizing the equivalence of informal marriages to marriages sanctified by the church.[12] The colonies were a checkerboard of different religions and different national origins (the Anglicans, the Dutch Calvinists, the Puritans, the Quakers), each of which had its own traditions and ecclesiastical rules on marriage and the family. The lack of a single formal legal authority in the colonies made enforcement of any one set of rules difficult.

Some parts of the colonies were too remote to be influenced by any organized religious or civil authority. Some of the colonists who settled rural areas did so with the explicit intention of remaining beyond the reach of town and church officials. The rural colonial outposts were patrolled by itinerant preachers and ministers who were themselves exiles from established churches in Europe and America. The preachers and the independent-minded frontiersmen naturally came into conflict over basic family morality. The preachers condemned as mortal sins the informal marriage and informal divorce they found in rural areas. Rural communities, in response, became quite adept at resisting the imposition of religious authority. Some communities worked actively to discredit the itinerant preachers as hypocrites. The preachers, in turn, railed against the blasphemous immorality of the colonists.[13]

Lord Hardwicke's Marriage Act of 1753 in England decreed that marriages were valid only when celebrated in the church, with parental approval, and subsequent to the posting of banns.[14] Colonial American laws on marriage and family were directly influenced by English law, but the law was one thing and actual practice was something else. As one Anglican minister in Maryland lamented, "If the rule was established here that no marriage should be deemed valid that had not been registered in the Parish Book it would I am persuaded bastardize nine-tenths of the people in the country."[15]

Even when couples in the colonies married outside of the church and without posting banns, parental approval was usually necessary as a practical matter, because the parents controlled the land and therefore the parents controlled the colonial economy. Paternal control over the children was fundamental to colonial society. For young men who intended to learn their father's trade or inherit the family farm, and for young women who needed their parents to provide a dowry, marriage without parental approval was difficult if not impossible.[16] Most children lived with their parents until their own marriages, because it was difficult for young adults to support themselves away from the family farm or trade. Children and adolescents who moved away from home usually moved in with another family and worked as servants or apprentices; in most cases the earnings from this work were remitted to the parents.[17]

It was not uncommon for colonial families (except for the Quakers) to bind their own children into servitude with other families and to raise servants (that is, other families' children) in the place of their own biological children. Even wealthy families bound out their children as servants to other families, in order to ensure that their children received vocational training and to minimize the chance of childhood idleness and indulgence, which the Puritans of New England especially despised.[18] Servitude was a common life stage for children and young adults in the colonies.[19] The colonial family was a productive economic unit under strict paternal direction, to which everyone who was able contributed. The sentimental childhood idealized in modern times did not exist in the colonies.[20]

In the early days of the English colonies in New England and Virginia, the colonists were poor and colonial homes were little more than one large room with a central fireplace and chimney and perhaps a simple partition to divide the sleeping from the eating areas. Prosperity in the eighteenth century allowed some families to build

more elaborate homes, but fertility was so great that the living space
allotted to each person was small in the homes of all but the wealthiest
aristocrats. The close living quarters of persons within households and
of households within communities made mutual surveillance a fact of
colonial life.[21]

The colonial geography of widely dispersed towns, poor roads, and
harsh winters left young people to meet and socialize primarily in
their parents' homes, which gave the parents a great degree of supervision and control over their children's social lives. Consider the
colonial American ritual of bundling. Bundling was a courtship ritual
in which a male suitor visited a young woman at her parents' house.
After some time conversing with the young people, the young
woman's parents would retire to their bed, and the suitor and the
young woman would spend the night together in her bed, sometimes
with a wooden board between them. If the board came down and the
clothes came off, the young couple were engaged, though sometimes
the engagement was only enforced if the young woman became pregnant.[22] Premarital sex was illegal in the colonies, but was apparently
common nevertheless.[23] The very purpose of bundling was to allow
the young woman's parents to know the male suitor, so that in case
of pregnancy the parents could save their daughter's reputation by
forcing the suitor into marriage well before the birth of the baby.
Implicit in the bundling arrangement was that the young woman
would only have access to suitors that her parents deemed appropriate.

Bundling was common in New England, especially among the less-
prosperous farmers whose families shared one- or two-room homes
and who were, by necessity, used to sharing their beds with travelers
and visitors. In the late eighteenth century, preachers began to preach
against bundling as an invitation to sin, and ordinary families were
given to understand that bundling and any suggestion of premarital
fornication would stain the family reputation. Despite the religious
and moralistic arguments against bundling from religious leaders and
from the aristocracy, bundling continued as a matter of practical ex-
pediency wherever homes were small.[24]

The leaders of the Massachusetts colony recognized that family control, or what they referred to as "family government," was essential
for their desired social order. As a result, it was illegal for unmarried

adults in the colony to live independently. The fear that independent adults might undermine the social order was so great that bachelors (except for special exceptions) were forced either to marry, move in with an established family, be imprisoned, or leave the colony.[25] Hartford imposed a tax of twenty shillings a week on solitary men.[26] Married couples who lived apart from each other were prosecuted for the offense of desertion.[27]

Family government was of great importance in the colonies because state and local governments were too weak to take responsibility for feeding, clothing, and educating the young. Few colonial children went to formal schools; most were taught to read and write and instructed in the Bible and the catechism by their fathers. Parents were responsible for the practical and occupational instruction of their own children and of the servants, who were put to work beginning at the tender age of seven or eight.[28] The colonial family, in other words, was the central institution for education, economic production, and social control. No wonder that colonial society insisted that every individual be part of a family.

Family government in the colonies was too important to be left to the whimsy of individual families. The colony of Massachusetts in the late seventeenth century sent guardians of domestic virtue, called tithingmen, to police families and to assure that fathers in Massachusetts were teaching their children to read, were sufficiently rigorous in their application of discipline, were observing the Sabbath, and were not introducing any drunkenness or misbehavior into the community.[29] The tithingmen were chosen by town councils, and each supervised about a dozen families.

Involuntary servitude was a common remedy for social transgression in the colonies. If a family could not keep their children sufficiently clothed or fed, the children were taken away and placed with another family. If a young woman became pregnant and the father could not be found, the young woman might be fined or whipped and then bound out as a servant to another family where her conduct could be better supervised. The purpose of involuntary servitude was to reestablish family government by uprooting young people from families whose government was suspect and replanting them in families whose government and oversight over the young was known to be more strict.[30]

Divorce was discouraged or prohibited in the colonies in part because colonial authorities wanted to maintain the family government that would be broken if families split apart. Men with wives still in Europe were ordered to send for them, lest the lonely men be given over to temptation and sin. In the case of the death of either spouse, rapid remarriage was the norm because it restored family government to two unmarried adults. Some second marriages followed so quickly after the funeral that the leftover food from the funeral was served again at the wedding party, and even this kind of haste was not seen as improper.[31]

The Young Republic and the Victorian Age

The independence of the United States from England opened up western territory (specifically Native American lands) that the English had previously prevented the colonists from exploiting.[32] The westward expansion of the United States gave young adults the option of marrying young and moving west, rather than waiting for their parents to provide a dowry or an inheritance. The opening of the west undermined parental control over their adult children. The independence of young adults in the early nineteenth-century United States alarmed American religious leaders and amazed observers of American life such as Alexis de Tocqueville. The independence of young adults during this time is reported to have led to a diversification of forms of unions with high rates of cohabitation and common-law marriage, though the evidence is fragmentary.[33]

Alexis de Tocqueville, who traveled in the United States for nine months in 1831 and 1832, was highly impressed with the independent and self-governing spirit of American democracy.[34] One of the reasons Tocqueville's view of American life resonates so well with modern American readers is that life in the United States in the 1830s, the age of Andrew Jackson, makes an interesting analogy to the post-1960 United States.[35] The American city of the 1830s was typified by riots, unrest, disorder, and volunteer fire companies that set as many fires as they put out. The volunteer fire companies set fires because they were, in fact, organized street gangs as well as public servants.[36] Then, as now, there was a flowering and diversification of family forms, much to the consternation of religious leaders and guardians of con-

servative or traditional values. Premarital sexual relations (as evi-
denced by the percentage of first-born children born within six
months of the wedding) rose during the eighteenth century, peaked
around the time of the American Revolution, declined in the nineteenth century, and remained low before rising again in the twentieth
century.[37] In the early nineteenth century as in the 1960s, college
campuses in the United States were marked by riots and disorder.[38]
At Brown University in the 1820s, the students "took to stoning the
president's house virtually every night."[39]

According to one view of the social tumult of the early nineteenth-
century United States, the "spirit of republicanism" and specifically
the overthrow of the authority of the unyielding paternalism of the
king of England undermined the power of family government in the
young United States.[40] Since colonial family government depended
on the unquestioned patriarchal authority (one might even say the
monarchical authority) of white fathers over children and servants
and of husbands over wives,[41] and since the rhetoric of the American
Revolution was fervently anti-monarchical, the revolution could not
help but undermine the legitimacy of parental control over their adult
children.[42]

To the extent that the historical lessons of the early nineteenth
century are applicable today, the lessons are sobering. The independent spirit of the early American republic was relatively short lived.
Parents and civic leaders, fearing their own loss of communal authority over the younger generations, created state and local government institutions to step into the social void and regulate family behavior. City leaders replaced the volunteer fire companies with more
orderly and reliable professional firefighters. Universities became
more bureaucratic and more organized, and student disorder died
down. Over the course of the nineteenth century, religious leaders
and family reformers enlisted the growing power of the state to marginalize informal marriages and force couples to come to the county
courthouse for a marriage license. Those who failed to formalize their
marriages at the county courthouse could not ensure that the law
would recognize their union; spouses and children could find they
had no rights (such as the right of inheritance) if the marriage was
not formalized.[43]

In the middle to late nineteenth century, parents, social reformers, and church leaders mobilized against prostitution, homosexuality, birth control, and "indecency."[44] The temperance movements, the Young Women's and Young Men's Christian Associations, and other religiously oriented civic institutions worked tirelessly to enlist the lost souls of the city and to castigate and marginalize those who could not be enlisted. The American Medical Association worked with religious groups to make abortion illegal in the United States for the first time in the late nineteenth century.[45]

In the early 1870s, a young dry goods dealer named Anthony Comstock was working with the Young Men's Christian Association of New York to fight against sexually explicit pamphlets, newspaper advertisements, and books. Frustrated by the law's apparent inability to curb what he saw as rampant indecency, Comstock went to Washington and lobbied Congress for stronger legislation. In 1873 Congress passed the Comstock Act, and Anthony Comstock was appointed as a postal inspector to enforce the new law. In the next four decades and with the support of the YMCA and leading New York industrialists like J. Pierpont Morgan, Comstock led a religious crusade against newspapers, publishers, gambling houses, nightclubs, artists (including, in one famous case, the New York Art Students League, for advertising a nude painting), avant-garde theater, prostitutes, advocates of birth control, feminists, and freethinkers of all types. After receiving information about the publication of supposedly indecent materials, Comstock typically would order the materials under a false name. After receipt of the materials, Comstock used his authority as a postal inspector to declare the materials indecent, and then he would escort the local police to the source of the publication to arrest the publishers and destroy the stock of offending materials. Often, Comstock was the only prosecuting witness in the indecency cases, but judges sympathetic to Comstock and a strong federal law meant that many of the accused were convicted, spent years in jail, and saw their careers and livelihoods ruined. Comstock bragged that no fewer than fifteen of his accused subjects committed suicide rather than face the humiliation and financial ruin of trial and conviction.[46] New York's powerful financial elites supported Comstock's crusade against vice and indecency because they saw Comstock acting to suppress the restive classes of workers and immigrants whose numbers were rapidly growing.[47]

Women in the Nineteenth Century

The new American republic of the early nineteenth century provided sharply increased geographic and social freedom, but these new freedoms were limited to the white men whose votes counted and whose legal liberties were enshrined in the new Constitution. White women, who would not universally gain the vote until the passage of the Nineteenth Amendment in 1920, were still without basic property or personal rights. At marriage, a woman's property was transferred to her husband, who was legally responsible for her as he would be for their children; the English common law name for this gender subordination was coverture.[48] Women were raised and educated to be obedient domestic servants, workers, helpmates, and mothers to what was expected to be a substantial brood of children. Within the domestic sphere of the household, white women had substantial moral and persuasive authority, which they attempted to expand into political and social rights over the course of the nineteenth century.[49]

Mount Holyoke, the first true college for women in the United States was founded in 1837. In subsequent decades Vassar (1861), Smith (1871), Wellesley (1870), Radcliffe (1879), Bryn Mawr (1885), and Barnard (1889) opened their doors to young women.[50] Oberlin College began in 1833 as the first coeducational college in the United States, and it remained the only one until the first class entered Antioch college in 1852. Cornell and the University of Michigan allowed a few women to join their previously all-male student bodies after the Civil War. The women's colleges, and the increasing coeducational status of previously all-male universities, gave a small number of white women access to higher education for the first time. Traditional conservatives were uncomfortable with the idea of women's higher education, arguing that "the effect of sustained brain activity is to drain away energy that should go to maternity."[51]

College-educated women became the backbone of a new women's movement, which took issue with the limited opportunities for women in the nineteenth-century United States. While living at college (and away from their parents), women met each other and developed passionate romantic friendships. Historians have had a difficult time determining the extent to which these romantic friendships were sexual, in part because nineteenth-century Americans had a different understanding of sexuality and romance than we do today.[52] A few women wrote to each other about erotic passion in such specific terms that little is left to doubt, but most American women who had romantic friendships with other women and who did write to each other were coy or indirect in their language. Americans (in the era before Freud and before the European sexologists) did not yet use or understand words such as "homosexual" or "lesbian."[53] Women had previously been assumed to be only passively sexual beings, so few American men or women in the Victorian age worried about sexual interaction between women. Women's sexuality in the nineteenth century was hidden behind what Lillian Faderman has called "the veil of sexual innocence."[54] In the late nineteenth century, as human sexuality came under more careful study, Americans became more aware and more afraid of homosexuals.[55]

Nineteenth-century American women were actively discouraged from working outside of the home, and when they did find paid work, the pay was substantially lower than a man would receive for the same job. Nineteenth-century employers treated women workers like children; instead of paying the woman worker directly, employers paid her wages to her husband. The inability of women to support themselves meant that unless they were widowed by successful husbands or had received a substantial inheritance, heterosexual marriage was the only way they had to ensure their economic survival. Some women circumvented the problem of labor market access by moving to a new town, cutting their hair, dressing in pants, and passing as men in order to work, but this pathway left women vulnerable to exposure and unemployment.[56]

Historian Carroll Smith-Rosenberg relates the story of Helena and Molly, two women who met in 1868 when they were students at the Cooper Union Institute for Design in New York.[57] Helena's and Molly's letters show they were passionate friends and probably lovers as well. After graduating from Cooper Union, Molly and Helena had planned to live together, but Molly's parents objected, and Molly was not in a position to disobey her parents, so Molly and Helena lived apart.[58] Within two years of their college graduation, and to their great chagrin, both Molly and Helena were married to men. Heterosexual marriage satisfied Molly's and Helena's parents and was a nearly unavoidable outcome for young women of that era. Some women attended college with the intention of finding an alternative to marriage and child rearing, but there were in fact few practical alternatives to heterosexual marriage.

Few nineteenth-century women had the economic independence to live without the support of parents or husbands. The small number of women of independent means who lived with other women were said to have "Boston marriages," a reference to Henry James's novel *The Bostonians.*[59] Women in Boston marriages were able to be discreet about the exact nature of their relationships because U.S. society was not yet aware of or vigilant about homosexuality.

The Black Family and Interracial Relationships in the Nineteenth Century

Prior to the Civil War, the vast majority of blacks in the United States lived as chattel slaves, groaning under the burdens of hard work in the fields without social or civil rights. Marriages between slaves were not legally recognized because slaves were legally the property of their respective masters, and legal marriage between slaves would have created a set of legal obligations among the slaves that would have conflicted with the master's authority over all the slaves. Furthermore, slaves had no legal standing to enter into contracts, and slaves generally had no property of their own to pass on to their children. On some southern plantations, the master's record books recorded marriages or unions between slaves, but it is difficult to know what the practical significance of informal slave marriages really was.[60]

To emphasize the master's sole dominion over the slaves and to reinforce the legal irrelevancy of unions between slaves, masters sometimes separated slave couples by sending one or both slaves to auction. Slave sales that divided slave couples were at times controversial, but such sales took place nonetheless.[61]

Slaves could do little to protect their children from the physical and sexual abuse of the white masters, from the privations of poverty, or from the familial separation that would follow a trip to the auction block. Slave children were sometimes forced to watch as their parents were beaten, whipped, or humiliated.[62] The birth of a child, therefore, brought both joy and sorrow to slave parents.[63] Because slave parents could not protect their own children, slave husbands did not have the legal authority or the means to protect their own wives, slave couples could not promise to always be together, and slave parents had nothing to bequeath to their children beyond the bitterness of slavery itself, the slave family was a fragile shell. This is not to say that the slaves did not love each other and make their own informal families: they certainly did. But slavery itself prevented the slaves from fulfilling the kinds of long-term commitments to each other that family life properly entails.

Blacks have had lower rates of marriage and higher rates of marriage dissolution than whites throughout the twentieth century in the United States. Some scholars have argued that black marriage rates continue to be low because the black family never fully recovered from the disastrous effects of slavery.[64] Because historical cause and effect are difficult to prove, scholars continue to debate the long-term effects of slavery on the black family in the twentieth century, though there can be little doubt that the oppressive and pervasive experience of slavery had repercussions for blacks for generations after slavery's disappearance.[65]

One open secret of the slavery system was sexual relations, both exploitative and consensual, between slave masters and female slaves.[66] Many slave women bore their master's children, and in almost all cases the slave masters, even such prominent men as Thomas Jefferson, denied parentage and therefore freedom to their own mixed-race children, who then followed their mothers into slavery.[67] Thomas Jefferson was accused by political opponents of fathering children with Sally Hemings, one of his several hundred slaves. Jefferson denied the charges. Because Jefferson was the primary author of the Declaration of Independence, the country's third president, and one of the young nation's leading statesmen and philosophers, Jefferson's moral credibility easily withstood the charges against him. For 170 years after Jefferson's death, historians generally discounted the rumors of his relationship with Sally Hemings.[68]

In 1998, DNA tests demonstrated something that biographers and hagiographers of Jefferson had long dismissed: that Thomas Jefferson was the father of Sally Hemings's children.[69] The case of Thomas Jefferson and Sally Hemings is especially interesting because Jefferson kept elaborate records of every detail of his plantation business (which included hundreds of slaves) and saved a mountain of personal correspondence for posterity. The vast collection of personal papers in the Jefferson archive gave no hint of Jefferson's three-decade-long intimate relationship and seven children with Sally Hemings. The official records of slave holders were scrupulously silent about the realities of slave life. Before the fateful DNA tests, biographers of Jefferson almost always favored the official sources (which showed no evidence of an intimate relationship between Jefferson and Hemings) over the oral tradition of the Hemings family, which claimed Jefferson as their ancestor. The case of Sally Hemings has reminded scholars of the fundamental difficulty of understanding the slave experience.[70] The slave owners and their supporters imposed a life of fear and intimidation upon the slaves, which, in combination with the forced illiteracy of the slaves, prevented all but a few slaves from writing their own stories to challenge the slave owners' sunny vision of their "peculiar institution."[71] Even seventy years after the end of slavery, when surviving ex-slaves were interviewed by the federal government's Works Progress Administration, many former slaves were too bitter, too untrusting, or too used to lying to white people to tell their stories accurately.[72]

Although Jefferson's massive archive of personal correspondence has nothing to say about Sally Hemings, Jefferson's letters do have quite a bit to say about African people in general. Jefferson wrote that African people were inherently mentally inferior and physically unattractive and, further, that racial mixing would have disastrous consequences for the United States, and few of his white contemporaries would have disagreed with him.[73] Jefferson claimed to believe that the beauty of white women was so great and the unattractiveness of black women was so obvious that slave rebellions to capture white women were inevitable. Clearly, Jefferson was a man whose private behavior was inconsistent with his expressed beliefs about African people, to say nothing of his inconsistency (which had always been apparent) in piously endorsing individual freedom while holding hundreds of slaves.

Racial mores of the antebellum South tolerated interracial sexual relations as long as whites could maintain plausible deniability, that is, as long as the interracial liaisons were kept in what modern gay studies literature calls "the closet." In the North prior to emancipation, the number of free blacks were few, and those few were continually subjected to the dangers of riot, violence, and kidnapping with the intention of reintroducing them as slaves in the South.[74] Prior to emancipation, there were few openly interracial black-white marriages in the North or the South. Black-white marriages were so few, and the social control over blacks, black bodies, and black sexuality was so great in the pre–Civil War United States, that interracial couples were sometimes tolerated as strange and unthreatening anomalies.[75] After the Civil War, emancipation, and the passage of the Thirteenth, Fourteenth and Fifteenth Amendments to the U.S. Constitution, the main legal bulwark of social control of blacks disappeared. During Reconstruction, southern states moved to pass laws prohibiting interracial marriage, known as "antimiscegenation" laws, but these efforts were hampered by Republican state judges who interpreted the antimiscegenation laws as inconsistent with the equal protection clause of the Fourteenth Amendment. After Reconstruction, when southern white Democrats regained control of the South, all the states of the old Confederacy (and many border states and western states) enacted antimiscegenation laws, and these remained in effect in most of those states until 1967 when the Supreme Court's ruling in Loving v. Virginia finally made the antimiscegenation statutes unconstitutional.[76]

In the aftermath of the Civil War, the industrial revolution spread west and south from New York and Philadelphia. Millions of American families gave up farming and moved to the rapidly growing cities to work in the factories. Late nineteenth-century observers (both politically liberal and conservative) predicted that urbanization and the new industrial economy would completely overturn the traditional family system of marriage and procreation.[77] For the first few decades of the twentieth century, in the absence of hard data, American and European scholars believed that the industrial revolution *had* completely reshaped the family.[78] The creation or rediscovery of historical data on the family (along with the tools to analyze the data) has overturned some of the theories of how historical change affected families.[79] I return to this subject in the next chapter.

The Early Twentieth Century

At the beginning of the twentieth century in the United States, courtship rituals in white America had more in common with bundling (from colonial times) than with the ritual now known as dating. The term "dating" was not part of American English until after 1900.[80] The early twentieth-century courtship ritual for middle-class families was "calling." The young woman would invite a male suitor to call on her, in her parents' home. The young man would "call" on her at the appointed time and, if it was a first meeting, the mother of the young woman would usually stay in the common room and talk with the young people. Calling was a more chaste activity than bundling, because bundling entailed the male suitor spending the night, whereas calling was expected to end with the young man graciously exiting well before nightfall.[81]

Calling was a courtship ritual that gave parents a good deal of oversight. Young people naturally chafed under this blanket of parental supervision. Economic and technological change in the early twentieth century began to give young people other options. Dating was created as cars, roads, and telephones began to lower the cost of travel and communication. Young women began to expect men to take them out, rather than to entertain them in the parlor of their parents' house. Beth Bailey's history of the rise of dating in the United States describes the popular literature of the 1920s, when young women were advised to meet gentlemen callers at the door "with their hat on," in order to indicate that they expected to be taken out of the house on a date.[82]

Anthony Comstock, the Connecticut merchant who spent his life pursuing the Victorian dream of purging the American mind of indecent thoughts, died in 1915. It was the Comstock Act that threatened Margaret Sanger with prosecution for promoting the idea of birth control in the *Socialist Call* and in her own magazine *The Woman Rebel*. Sanger fled to England to avoid a trial in the United States, but she returned in 1915 and demanded a trial. In her absence, her husband was tried and convicted of indecency, and served thirty days in jail.[83] The indecency charges against Margaret Sanger were eventually dropped, but she was later prosecuted and jailed for opening a birth control clinic. The death of Anthony Comstock and the celebrity status of Margaret Sanger helped usher in the swinging 1920s.[84]

In 1920, with the ratification of the nineteenth Amendment to the Constitution, women in the United States finally won the right to vote. Over the next decade and a half, women voters and activists dismantled most of the state apparatus of coverture and legalized gender subordination.[85]

The Great Depression and World War II

In the 1930s, two related forces combined to diminish the bonds of parental control over young adult children. During the Great Depression, so many men were unemployed or underemployed that women and children had to take up the slack. This communal struggle to provide for the family diminished the father's patriarchal authority over his wife and children.[86] The Great Depression led to the passage of the Social Security Act of 1935, which for the first time provided national retirement insurance and therefore reduced the parental need to ensure that their children would support them in their dotage.[87]

The Social Security program and public welfare programs more generally represent one part of the steady encroachment of the state into roles once played only by the family. Education of the young and care for the old and infirm were once upon a time family roles that, for better or worse, bound the generations together. In the twentieth century, the government (and to a lesser extent big business with their pensions and training programs) took the core of these functions away from the family.

Great social dislocations, like the Great Depression and World War II, inevitably undermine the established order in unpredictable ways. Scholars of gay history have emphasized the importance of World War II in the establishment of the seeds of a national gay consciousness in the United States.[88] World War II removed a whole generation of young men (and many women) from the homes of their parents and placed them in a new institutional environment far from parental supervision. The U.S. military went to great lengths to suppress homosexual activity during the war, but the absence of parental supervision and the gender segregation of the armed forces created a fertile ground for the seeds of a communal gay consciousness to grow, despite the best efforts of the military bureaucracy.[89] On the home front, the displacement of a generation of young men into the war left women to work and socialize independently from men, which allowed women to trespass against sexual and sex-role norms more easily.[90] The great irony is that those who believe that the U.S. military should continue to discriminate against homosexuals deny not only the history of gay service in the military, but also the special role that the wartime military has played in promoting self-awareness for gays in the United States.[91]

Beth Bailey's study of quiet and socially modest Lawrence, Kansas, exemplifies some of the changes that World War II brought to the American heartland.[92] The first effect was the arrival of a munitions factory that employed several thousand workers. Town elders were fully aware of the potential social disruption that several thousand unattached men (and later women) could cause. The elders debated the wisdom of allowing the plant to be located in Lawrence, but in the end patriotism and the desire for economic development won out. The infusion into Lawrence of so many outsiders undermined the ability of Lawrence's parents and civic leaders to impose their own rules and norms over the social and sexual behavior of the town's young people, since the plant workers were not subject to the "family government" of Lawrence's adults. The second effect of World War II was the rising influence of national media (radio and subsequently television) and the mass consumer culture that the media promoted.[93] The national media broadcast messages from far away and more cosmopolitan places directly to the young people of Lawrence. Mass media messages tended to undermine the more provincial parental attitudes that had previously prevailed without question or opposition in places like Lawrence.[94]

Post–World War II Residential Segregation and Suburbanization

The history of residential segregation in the United States is, among other things, a history of white parents' attempts to shield their children from social and intimate exposure to members of other racial groups.[95] In his monumental mid-century analysis of segregation and discrimination in the United States, Gunnar Myrdal argued that the fundamental motivating force behind systems of residential segregation was the prevention of social mixing between the races, interracial dating, and especially interracial marriage.[96] In Emory Bogardus's mid-twentieth-century work on social distance, intermarriage was the ultimate taboo.[97]

White ethnic and immigrant families in Chicago in the 1940s and

1950s were willing to work with blacks, but they were not willing to live with them. Workplaces were generally more segregated by gender than by race; white men were usually willing to tolerate the presence of black men on the factory floor. The mere sight of a black family moving into the white neighborhood, however, was a crisis. White working-class neighborhoods like Trumbull Park, Cicero, Englewood, and Park Manor exploded in riots against blacks who had the temerity to try to move into one of the white neighborhoods. What were the white residents of these neighborhoods so afraid of? Black neighbors meant black children in the local school, which meant that the white children might befriend the black children which in turn raised the specter of dating, sex, and marriage. According to Arnold Hirsch's description, the Eastern European immigrants in these neighborhoods of Chicago were desperately striving to achieve acceptance as whites in the United States.[98] Their claim to "whiteness" was tenuous, and they feared that the presence of blacks in their neighborhoods, or even a small number of intermarriages with blacks, might relegate their groups to a minority racial status rather than the white racial status to which they aspired. As a result of the perceived danger of social mixing with blacks, white ethnic residents of Chicago neighborhoods fought, with bricks and bats and whatever weapons they had, against the black families that tried to integrate their neighborhoods.

Local violence in support of residential segregation was important, but the local rioters were not nearly powerful enough or ubiquitous enough to preserve residential segregation by themselves. The preservation and reinforcement of the ghetto walls in American cities required a substantial public policy investment. The U.S. federal government's Home Owner's Loan Corporation in the 1930s invented the policy of what later came to be called "redlining," that is, refusing to underwrite loans to black or racially mixed neighborhoods. White violence and collusion among real estate professionals kept blacks out of the new suburbs. After World War II, the policy of redlining was adopted by the Federal Housing Authority during the greatest expansion of home ownership in U.S. history. Federal Housing Authority policy favored new construction over renovation, so new, prosperous, and exclusively white suburbs grew up around decaying central cities with their large populations of racial minorities. Federally subsidized highways eased the flow of traffic and capital away from the cities to the suburbs.[99]

Racially segregated neighborhoods ensured that young adults had minimal exposure to potential mates from other racial groups. The constraint on the pool of potential mates would have been invisible to the young people as long as they remained within the racially segregated neighborhood. As long as young adults married soon after high school (the normative behaviors of the 1950s baby boom),[100] the residentially segregated neighborhood was an effective system for promoting same-race heterosexual marriage and preventing other kinds of unions.

One of the central research interests of sociologists who studied marriage and the family in the 1940s and 1950s was the way that mate selection in American cities was shaped and constrained by residential propinquity. Study after study in the leading sociology journals showed that the chance of marriage between people declined sharply with the distance between their addresses.[101] The typical finding was that 30 percent of marriage licenses were granted to couples who lived within roughly five blocks of each other, despite the low frequency of premarital cohabitation. As Bossard wrote in 1932, "Cupid may have wings, but apparently they are not adapted for long flights."[102] Most of these sociological writers cheered their findings as evidence that communities and neighborhoods still mattered, despite the urbanization of American society and the imagined decline of the socially insular farming communities of prior times. Sociologist Ruby Jo Reeves Kennedy noted, however, that the premarital residential propinquity of couples applying for marriage licenses was also a function of the sharp lines of racial segregation, which kept whites and blacks from socializing with each other.[103]

The great housing boom of the 1950s was fundamentally a suburban housing boom, as whites withdrew from the urban core.[104] As suburbanites retreated from cities, they left behind not only the racial heterogeneity of the city, but also the diversity of sexual identities that was flourishing in cities, albeit quietly and despite the efforts of the local police.[105] The political antecedents of the gay liberation movement were in a formative stage in the United States in the 1950s.[106] Organizing around gay political and gender issues was then and has always been a fundamentally urban phenomenon.[107] Suburbanization had the effect of uprooting families away from the culturally boisterous urban core, where a diversity of sexual identities were practiced with some degree of openness, and replanting families in an environment in which the hegemony of the dominant sexual and gender roles was easier for parents to enforce.[108]

The independent life stage has slowly begun to loosen the grip that residential segregation has had on the marital choices of young adults. Young people who left the neighborhood to go to college encountered a potentially new social context within which new kinds of racial socialization and sexual experimentation could take place. Naturally, racial segregation and antigay norms also exist in college, in the workplace, and in the cities, but the independent life stage does give young adults more control over their own social environments.

Conclusion

In this book, I propose a simple theory of social change based on family structure and the independent life stage. Although my quantitative approach to the theory is new, the theory itself is not new. Historians of the family and especially historians who study gay life, culture, and politics have proposed similar explanations for the modern rise of nontraditional unions and the previous invisibility of such unions.[109]

Consider Allan Bérubé's marvelous history of gays in the U.S. military in World War II.[110] Although the U.S. military officially excluded gays from service in World War II and dishonorably discharged soldiers who were discovered to be gay, Bérubé makes the case that military service was nonetheless a watershed for gay rights and self-awareness for several reasons. First, there was no simple, practical, and efficient way to identify and therefore to exclude gays. Second, the need for soldiers was so great that the identification and persecution of gays (though enthusiastic at times) was relegated to a secondary priority. Third, and most important, the war took young men and women away from their homes and families and, therefore, away from parental supervision. "Once they left the constraints of family life and watchful neighbors, many recruits were surprised to find that military service gave them opportunities to begin a 'coming-out' process. . . . The massive mobilization for World War II relaxed the social constraints of peacetime that had kept gay men and women unaware of themselves and each other."[111]

According to Renee Romano, World War II had a similar effect on black-white intermarriage, but on a smaller scale. Black men in the U.S. Army who served in Europe had some access to European women and were able to form relationships that would have been impossible within the social system of the United States. The interracial social groups in U.S. cities were called *Club Internationale* after the war, in reference to the effect of foreign service on intermarriage.[112] The U.S. military worked hard to discourage such interracial unions, of course. One does not usually think of the military as the kind of socially open institution that allows new and transgressive relationships to flourish. One key insight from the literature on gay culture in World War II is that parental control is mediated through co-residence and through the young adult's physical proximity to the community of origin. No matter how much the U.S. military tried to repress homosexuality, the large and anonymous military bureaucracy was never able to be as successful in surveillance and social control as the parents and the communities the young men had left behind.

The post–World War II domestic society began to offer young adults more and more of the kind of independence and geographic mobility that the war had temporarily provided to a few. According to William J. Goode's 1963 study of family change:

> Of course the greater independence of the young has been reported for all Western countries. One consequence of this greater freedom is that the young people who marry are more likely than before to have met outside the circle of the family. Even when they meet at a dance, the circumstances are different from what they used to be. Two generations ago the young couple might well have met at a dance, but their parents had brought them there and their parents remained to take them home afterwards.[113]

◆ ◆ ◆

THREE

The Independent Life Stage

CHANGE IS THE GREAT CONSTANT of post-1960 scholarship on the American family. The rise of divorce, the increasing postponement (or complete avoidance) of first marriage, and the rise of extramarital cohabitation are but three of the changes that have replaced a supposedly unitary nuclear family system with a more plural and diverse range of family structures.[1] Interracial unions and same-sex unions were nearly invisible two generations ago; now they are common enough to be part of the social circles of a substantial proportion of Americans.

American scholars certainly appreciate the magnitude of changes to the family that have taken place in the last forty years. Scholars and the general public, however, always seem to see a family revolution taking place before them. From the individual perspective, the family always seems to be changing. Moving backward in time, before 1960 there was the baby boom of the 1950s, the great dislocations of World War II, the Great Depression of the 1930s, and the swinging 1920s. Moving further back in time we find World War I, the enormous immigration wave of the early twentieth century, urbanization and industrialization in the late nineteenth century, and the Civil War before that. All of these periods (and other intervening ones I have neglected here) were described in their own times, not without reason, as fundamentally reshaping the family.

Arthur Calhoun, for instance, at the end of his innovative and otherwise sober treatise on the history of the American family (last volume published in 1919), claimed that the industrial revolution had completely overturned American family life. Calhoun was so impressed by the changes of industrialism and urbanization in the late nineteenth and early twentieth centuries that he predicted that marriage, capitalism, and prostitution were all soon to be extinct in the United States.[2] Subsequent history has not been kind to Calhoun's predictions.

Calhoun did not have any demographic data about the American family at his disposal. Instead of original data analysis, Calhoun's exaggerated sense of the effect of industrialization on the family simply reflected the common and scholarly wisdom of his day. Calhoun's misreading of the effect of the industrial revolution on the American family is an example of the difficulty inherent in assessing family change over time without the benefit of historically consistent demographic data.

The industrial revolution is a useful starting point in any discussion of historical change and the family. For scholars of the pre-1960 period, the industrial revolution was the period that divided historical time into before and after. Karl Marx and Friedrich Engel's sweeping analysis of history made the rise of industrialism and the bourgeois class the crucial fulcrum of historical change.[3] The founders of sociology (Marx, Emile Durkheim, Max Weber, Frédéric Le Play, W. I. Thomas) lived and worked in the late nineteenth century and early twentieth century, and their intellectual agendas were inevitably driven by the social effects of the industrialization and urbanization taking place around them.[4] It is not too much of an exaggeration to say that urbanization and the industrial revolution gave birth to sociology. Marxists and non-Marxists alike assumed that the industrial revolution must have turned family life and customs completely on their head.

In this chapter, I compare the record of family change in the post-1960 period with the family changes that took place during the industrial revolution in the United States (roughly 1850–1920). Despite the industrial revolution's powerful grip on the imaginations of the early generation of sociologists, the pace of change in family life was less during the industrial revolution than many observers supposed. One reason the family system was more stable during the industrial revolution than it appeared to be at the time was that the independent life stage did not exist.

The first wave of revisionist scholarship about the influence of the industrial revolution appeared in the 1960s. Peter Laslett's 1965 book *The World We Have Lost,* with reconstructed family data from parish records, showed that in Europe the age at first marriage had been in the twenties, as back as far as the sixteenth century, and an influential article by John Hajnal in the same year echoed Laslett's findings.[5] Laslett's subsequent work argued that the preindustrial family had always been a nuclear family (albeit a larger one) and that preindustrial European extended families (or what Le Play had called the "stem family") hardly ever lived together under one roof.[6] In addition, Laslett found that preindustrial populations in England migrated surprisingly often.[7] By showing that the industrial revolution had less effect on family structure in Europe than had previously been assumed, Laslett's research deflated prior assumptions (which dated back to the founding of modern sociology) about the way industrialization had affected the structure of the family.[8]

Despite Laslett and his colleagues' skeptical view of family change under industrialization, we now know that the industrial revolution in the late nineteenth and early twentieth centuries United States had a strong effect on many important aspects of family life.[9] Mortality (especially infant mortality) declined. Fertility of U.S.-born women had been declining steadily for more than 100 years, and this decline continued through the industrial revolution. As a result of the decline in fertility, household size declined. The divorce rate rose in the United States during the industrial revolution, and it continued to rise through most of the twentieth century.[10] The introduction of compulsory public schooling in the late nineteenth century was revolutionary.[11] The percentage of Americans engaged in subsistence farming dropped dramatically, and millions of Americans migrated to the cities to find factory work. I describe a few of these changes in more detail later in this chapter, and I quantify all these changes in Appendix Tables A.1 and A.2. Given the important changes that industrialization imposed on American families, it is not surprising that early twentieth-century American scholars such as Arthur Calhoun would have imagined that the industrial revolution changed everything about the American family.

Despite the very real changes of industrialization, some crucial aspects of the American family structure remained stubbornly unchanged in the late nineteenth century. Interracial marriage remained rare, even in states where it was legal. Same-sex unions were unknown, or invisible. Age at first marriage did not change during the industrial revolution in the United States. Single young adults continued to live with their parents, or to live as servants with surrogate parents. Family government over young adults, in short, was maintained during the industrial revolution. Although many aspects of family life (household size, mortality, fertility, formal education, urbanization) did change during the industrial revolution, the family system remained intact enough to promote heterosexual same-race marriage and exclude all other family forms.

In the midst of the sweeping economic and social changes of industrialization, the family system managed to continue to exclude transgressive unions because family government over young adults was maintained. The size of American families changed, where they lived and how they worked changed, but the *kind* of romantic unions they formed did not change during the industrial revolution. Although the conservative social critic Anthony Comstock and the liberal academic Arthur Calhoun both imagined that the industrial revolution was overturning the entire structure of American family life,[12] they both failed to understand that the continuity of family government ensured the reproduction of the traditional social order.

People living through the industrial revolution in the United States seem to have *felt* that new freedoms and social options were available to them. Ellen Rothman's study of courtship and marriage, based on the nineteenth-century diaries of American women, reflects these women's sense that their choices of mates were completely uninhibited and unimpeded by parental intervention.[13] Yet the census data I present in the next chapter show that nontraditional unions such as interracial unions and extramarital cohabitation were practically nonexistent during the industrial revolution. Young adults in the industrial revolution may have perceived that their mate selection choices were made without any external constraints, yet the actual mating pattern revealed in the census demonstrates that powerful social constraints must have been in place to exclude nontraditional unions. Family government limited the mate selection choices of young adults in subtle, rather than overt ways. Living with one's parents (or with parental surrogates) necessarily shaped and constrained the social groups that the young adults would have had access to. Within the

social world shaped by intergenerational co-residence, young adults
in the late nineteenth century (especially the well-to-do white women
whose diaries Rothman studied) may have had something like free
rein to choose their mate. Individuals are always most conscious of
the immediate choices before them. Individuals tend to be less aware
of their inability to form romantic unions with people they have never
met. One reason the social effects of family government (or its absence, the independent life stage) are sometimes overlooked is that
individuals do not feel them directly. To properly assess the impact of
changes in family structure, one needs historically consistent demographic data at the individual and household level.

The fact that the United States industrialized a century later than
England presents researchers with a felicitous opportunity. The industrial revolution in the United States was recent enough to have
taken place within the time of nationally representative census surveys. Individual-level U.S. census data from the nineteenth century
have only become accessible to researchers in the past few years.
Whereas Laslett's work on family structure during industrialization in
England and Europe had to rely on many different and inconsistent
local sources of varying quality, the U.S. family under industrialization
can be studied using historical census data that are nationally representative and reasonably consistent with modern census data. And
whereas Laslett's data often did not explicitly specify family relationships within the household,[14] the U.S. census data is a household
survey that does explicitly describe relationships between members of
each household. The national representativeness and historical consistency of the U.S. census allow for family structure comparisons of
unprecedented detail and reliability from the industrial revolution to
the present.

The Census Data

In order to quantify the rise of the independent life stage in this
chapter, and the effects of the independent life stage in the next two
chapters, I rely on U.S. census microdata files from the Integrated
Public Use Microdata Series, or IPUMS.[15] The census data have both
strengths and weaknesses. Before continuing to the next sections,

which are full of census data analyses, I review some features of the U.S. census so that readers may gain an idea of how my choice of data sources might influence the analyses.

The census files available through IPUMS cover all decennial censuses from 1850 to 2000, except for 1890 and 1930.[16] Some of the questions of interest here were not asked in the earlier censuses, so the time range of the data I present will depend on the question. Most of the census files are 1-in-100 files, which means that individual records are available for 1 percent of the U.S. population. For 1980, 1990, and 2000 I use the weighted 5 percent samples. Five percent samples mean that the data contain individual records for 5 percent of the U.S. population, or one out of every twenty persons.[17]

The public use records of the U.S. census have a number of wonderful advantages, including massive sample sizes. The 1850–1910 samples have between one hundred thousand and 1 million individual records each. The 1920–1960 samples have between 1 million and 2 million records each. The 1970 sample has about 2 million records. The 1980–2000 census microdata samples each have more than 10 million individual records. Summing across all the available census data, the number of individual records is more than 40 million.

Along with massive sample sizes, the U.S. census microdata is nationally representative. That is, the U.S. census files are supposed to contain the same proportion of men and women, young and old people, doctors and janitors, whites and free blacks (but not slaves), married people, divorced people, and cohabiting people as the entire society. A truly representative sample of households is difficult to obtain, of course, and some populations (the poor, undocumented migrants, the homeless) are always harder to reach.

The U.S. census data are not perfect. There are inconsistencies between censuses in how variables are measured and coded. Metropolitan area designations change from census to census. The basic census methodology shifted from surveyor interview to self-report in 1960, though this is thought to have had little effect on the quality of the data.[18] The data on same-sex cohabitation is not fully comparable between 1990 and 2000, and this issue will occupy some attention in the next two chapters.[19] The race and ethnicity variables have undergone changes over the years. Despite the limitations and inconsistencies, the U.S. census comes as close to an accurate representation of the basic demography of a diverse country over time as any survey effort ever has.[20]

The Industrial Revolution

The United States industrialized a century after England, and even then the process of industrialization in the United States was far from uniform. New York and Philadelphia were great industrial centers by the mid-nineteenth century, whereas the western territories and the southern states did not see heavy industry until decades later.[21] The Civil War was a stimulus for industrialization in both the North and the South. The North had to use and increase its industrial might to win the war, whereas in the South the result of the war shattered the main obstacles to industrialization—the planter aristocracy and the slave system.

The industrial economy of the nineteenth century was organized around the population centers of the cities because the cities had access to the shipping lanes and the cities had the necessary population density to supply wage laborers to the factories. The story of industrialization is therefore a story of the rise of the cities and the concomitant decline of subsistence farming. In the mid-nineteenth century, the United States was still mainly a preindustrial agricultural country. Figure 3.1 shows that in 1850, only 8 percent of Americans lived in cities, and another 6 percent lived on the outskirts of cities (the term suburb was not yet known). In 1850 few Americans lived in or around cities, but 58 percent of Americans were part of a farming family, meaning they had at least one full-time farmer in their household. From 1850 to 1920, the central cities swelled with immigration from abroad and from rural America. Over the course of 150 years from 1850 to 2000, the percentage of Americans who lived in farming families dropped from 58 percent to 1 percent, whereas the percentage who lived either in the cities or in the suburbs grew from 14 percent to 70 percent of the population.[22]

The crowded American cities of the late nineteenth and early twentieth centuries were disorderly and unhygienic.[23] Some young people in the cities, unable to find the kind of jobs they wanted and unable to afford housing, turned to crime and prostitution in order to sur-

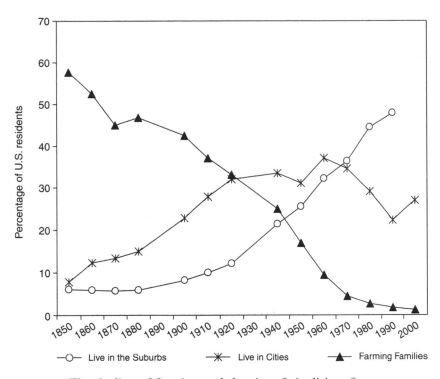

Figure 3.1. The decline of farming and the rise of city living. Source: Weighted census microdata from IPUMS, 1% files. Suburban percentage not shown for 2000 because of too much data is missing. 1850 and 1860 data exclude slaves.

vive.[24] To guardians of the public morals (such as Anthony Comstock), the American city at the dawn of the twentieth century was a breeding ground for venereal disease, a corrupter of the youth, a venal and callous and anonymous place where traditional family values were trampled and destroyed.[25]

Both progressive and conservative social critics declared the traditional family dead at the beginning of the twentieth century.[26] Curiously, despite the hand-wringing of experts and the outrage of moral crusaders, the industrial revolution in the United States had (at least by some measures discussed below and in the next chapter) only a modest effect on the family. Age at first marriage remained constant. Most unmarried young adults continued to live with their parents.

Interracial marriage remained rare. Most gays remained firmly in the closet.

Family Life in an Industrial Town

The Amoskeag textile mill of Manchester, New Hampshire (the largest textile mill in the world in the late nineteenth century), had a relationship not only with workers but also with their families, which helps explain how family government was maintained during the industrial revolution. According to Tamara Hareven, the Amoskeag selectively recruited entire families to move together to Manchester.[27] Family recruitment had several benefits for the company. First, by recruiting whole families, the company ensured their future work force because in each family the children were socialized to work at the mill by their elders. Sometimes the children worked as assistants to their parents and were apprenticed to them directly. More often, the children learned indirectly from their elders about the different specialized kinds of textile work (and how to avoid their inherent dangers) and about which particular factory foremen were the best to work for. Since industrial work was a fundamentally different kind of work from the subsistence farming most families had known before, the familial socialization to factory work was crucial to the successful recruitment of new workers.

The Amoskeag Company especially recruited French Canadian families to the mills in part because French Canadian families had higher fertility and therefore brought more children (that is, more future mill workers) to Manchester when they migrated. Hareven notes that there were also "mill girls," single women who worked at the mill and who lived in company dormitories. The company subjected these women to the kinds of social constraints that the times demanded—no alcohol was permitted and all women had to be in their rooms alone by 10 P.M. The company was very explicit in its recruitment advertisements that the company treated workers in the paternalistic way that families treated their own children. Rather than undermining the family, Hareven's analysis of Manchester's textile industry shows how industrialism relied on and reinforced family government.

The industrial revolution certainly presented new challenges to late nineteenth-century families. Industrialism changed the rhythms and obligations of the workday quite dramatically.[28] Industrialism separated work from the home.[29] In the later stages of industrialism, when factories were larger and as children were prevented from working by child labor laws and compulsory schooling, work kept family members apart.[30] But although factory work kept family members apart during the workday, after work family members all returned to eat and sleep under the same roof. Household survey data such as the U.S. census tend to show that the internal social structure of the family remained remarkably unchanged through the industrial revolution.

The Demographic Roots of the Independent Life Stage

In the post-1960 era, young men and women have spent an increasing amount of time living on their own before getting married. Figure 3.2 shows the percentage of U.S.-born[31] single men and women who lived with at least one parent from 1880 to 2000. Between 1880 and 1940, the tail end of the industrial revolution in the United States, the percentage of single young adults who lived with their parents increased. This increase was due in part to the increasing life span of older Americans. Young adults who were in their twenties in 1900 would have been born around 1875. Their parents would have been born around 1850. A person born in 1850 in the United States who lived to be old enough to have children would have been expected to live to age sixty, or until about 1910. A substantial number of people born in 1850 who had children around 1875 would have been deceased by 1900.[32]

In the early part of the twentieth century, as life expectancy increased, more and more unmarried young adults lived with their parents because there were more parents available to live with, living with parents was the normative behavior, and there were few other practical options. Prior to 1950, parental mortality was the most important limit to the ability of adult children to live with their parents.[33]

Although 68 percent of young single women and 59 percent of young single men lived with their parents in 1880, the percentage of young adults who were subject to family government was actually much higher. The vast majority of unmarried young adults who lived apart from their parents either lived with relatives, were servants in

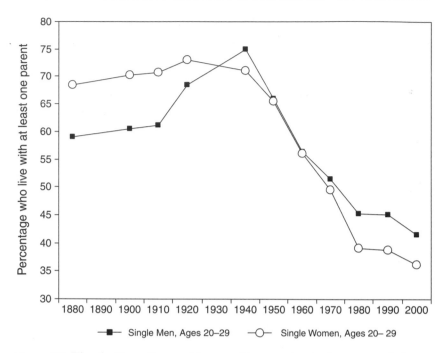

Figure 3.2. The decline of co-residence with parents: single young adults, 1880–2000. Source: Weighted IPUMS census microdata for U.S.-born individuals, 1% samples 1880, 1900–1920, and 1940–1970, and 5% samples 1980–2000.

other families' households, or lived with another family as boarders or lodgers.[34] Families who took in boarders or lodgers were surrogate families who were expected to supervise the young adults in their charge. Adult supervision over servants was usually expected to be at least as strict and as vigilant as adult supervision over their own children.[35]

Household arrangements such as servitude, boarding, and lodging were prevalent in the past but went into steep decline toward the end of the industrial revolution.[36] Because family government over young adults was maintained in so many different ways in the past, the declining percentage of single young adults who lived with their parents does not convey the full measure of the decline in family government over time. A better and more consistent measure is the percentage of single young adults who headed their own households; this, after all, was the kind of independent living arrangement that colonial leaders had worked so hard to prevent.[37]

Figure 3.3 shows that the percentage of single young adults who headed their own households was less than 5 percent in 1880, and actually declined somewhat between 1880 and 1920. The percentage of single young adults who were truly independent began to rise after 1950, reaching 36 percent for women and 28 percent for men in 2000.

In other words, the industrial revolution of the late nineteenth century did not break the bonds of family government. City life presented new challenges to late nineteenth-century families, to be sure, but the continued co-residence and mutual surveillance of the family (or family surrogates) meant that young adults continued to find spouses the way they always had—under the watchful eyes of their parents (or parental surrogates).

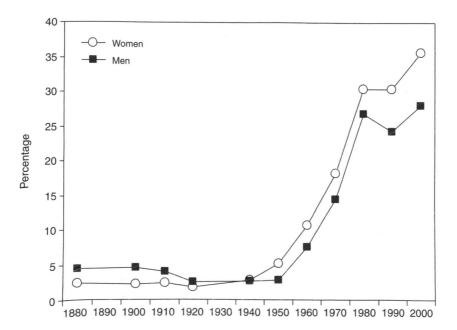

Figure 3.3. Percentage of young unmarried men and women who head their own household, 1880–2000. Source: Weighted census microdata from 1880, 1900–1920, and 1940–2000 via IPUMS. Individuals are U.S. born, ages 20–29, never married.

Around the middle of the twentieth century, the long-established norm of intergenerational co-residence began to change. After 1950, even as parents were living longer and longer (so that more and more adult children had living parents), the percentage of children living with their parents began to decline. From 1880 to 1940, fewer than 5 percent of single young adults were living on their own, heading their own households. By the end of the twentieth century, a third of single young adults were heads of their own households. The modern residential independence of single young adults represents a decisive reversal of the old system of family government, which was based on surveillance and co-residence.[38]

Like all census analyses, the data in these figures represent a series of snapshots in time. For individuals, separation from parents is a reversible process. In fact, individual young adults may return to the parental home several times before moving out on their own for good. One can not deduce individual life course paths from census records of reversible events.[39] One does not know, for instance, how many years any individual spent living on his or her own before marriage. The census data do, however, provide insight into the typical family structure at the time of census. Because the data on family structure are highly consistent over time, and because the U.S. census is a nationally representative household survey, changes in family structure from census to census do reveal fundamental changes in American family structure over time.

Between 1880 and 1940, despite the dramatic changes of industrialization and urbanization in the United States, the demographic structure of young adults' lives remained surprisingly constant. Table 3.1 shows that between 1880 and 1940, the proportion of young U.S.-born women who were either living with their parents (the second category) or married (the third category) remained fairly constant, and these two categories summed to around 90 percent of the total.

The proportion of women who were single and living apart from their parents was 12.6 percent in 1880 and remained at this level or slightly below until the middle of the twentieth century. The industrial revolution did nothing to make young adults more residentially independent from their parents. The percentage of young women who lived on their own hit a low of 8.5 percent in 1950 and then began to rise. By 2000, 39 percent of all U.S.-born women in their twenties

Table 3.1 The rise of the independent life stage: family structure for
U.S.-born women ages 20–29

	Single, live apart from parents (Pct)	Single, live with parents (Pct)	Married (Pct)	Total
1880	12.6	27.3	60.1	100
1890				
1900	12.8	30.0	57.3	100
1910	12.0	29.1	59.0	100
1920	10.4	28.1	61.5	100
1930				
1940	10.7	26.5	62.8	100
1950	8.5	16.1	75.3	100
1960	9.7	12.4	77.9	100
1970	15.0	14.7	70.3	100
1980	26.8	17.2	56.1	100
1990	32.6	20.7	46.7	100
2000	39.3	21.1	39.6	100

Sources: Weighted census microdata 1880, 1900–1920, 1940–2000 via IPUMS.

were single living on their own. The picture for young men is similar.
The rise of residential and geographic independence among young
adults in the United States is a result of the decreasing tendency of
single adults to live with parents (Figure 3.2), and the well known
post–baby boom trends of increasing age at marriage and increasing
rates of divorce.[40]

Figures 3.2 and 3.3 and Table 3.1 demonstrate that the independent
life stage is a fundamentally new force in American family life. There
have always been some young adults who lived on their own before
marrying, but since 1960 the independent life stage has become increasingly routine for young adults in the United States. The independent life stage began to be more influential in the 1960s. The
period of growing influence of the independent life stage corresponds
to the timing of so many social upheavals and transformations in the
United States in which young adults played a critical role: civil rights,
women's rights, gay rights, the counterculture, the antiwar movement
of the 1960s, the sexual revolution, and the broad diversification of
families and unions.

how does census count students in residential colleges?

The independent life stage has received attention from scholars, especially recently, but the social impact of the independent life stage is still underappreciated, for several reasons.[41] First, the phenomenon of the independent life stage is itself relatively new. Second, the historical census data that is necessary for long-term comparisons of family structure were only recently computerized and made generally available. Third, the independent life stage is an in-between life stage. Unlike childbirth, high school graduation, marriage, divorce, and death, the independent life stage leaves no official record behind.

Ironically, the rise of the independent life stage has been accompanied by public and cultural perceptions that young adults are *more* likely to live with their parents than in the past. Despite the fact that the probability of living on one's own has increased steadily for young adults since 1950, the popular press is full of reports of children moving back in with their parents.[42] If one includes both married and single young adults in the denominator (as Table 3.1 does), then it appears that the percentage of young adults who live with their parents went up between 1960 and 2000.[43] The problem with this view is that it confounds two very different populations, the married and the unmarried. Married young adults in the United States hardly ever live with their parents; unmarried young adults often do. Since the age at first marriage has been increasing (see Figure 3.6 below), the percentage of young adults in any given age group who are married has been declining over time.

What the popular press has misleadingly called the "boomerang effect," that is, the apparent trend of young adults returning to the parental nest, is actually due to the postponement of marriage and the ever-increasing span of years that young adults spend being romantically unattached.[44] Since young married people in the United States almost never live with their parents, postponement of marriage increases the percentage of young adults who live with their parents. If, however, one examines only the unmarried young adults (see Figure 3.2, above), it is clear that the percentage who are living with their parents has been declining steadily, and it was at an all-time low in the 2000 census.

Consider the case of an imaginary but typical young woman who leaves home to attend college at age eighteen, returns to the live in the parental nest after college at age twenty-two, moves out of the parental nest again at age twenty-four, and settles down (perhaps far from the parental nest) to start her own family at age twenty-seven. The two years the young woman spends living with her parents after college might be the most conspicuous stage for the young woman and her parents, but the years spent living on her own (in college and in her late twenties) would be the parts of her young adulthood that would most differentiate her from her pre-1960 ancestors. Goldscheider and Goldscheider explain the disjuncture between popular perceptions and demographic reality by pointing out that living with one's parents used to be normative, so no one noticed it.[45] The independent life stage has overturned old norms, so now both parents and children expect children to eventually achieve some measure of independence. The paradox is that we notice single young adult children moving back in with their parents more because living with one's parents is less common behavior than it once was.

Living on their own, single men and women in the late twentieth century have had the freedom to meet, date, and experiment beyond the watchful eyes of parents, in ways that would have been mostly unknown in 1900. Some young adults who live on their own are financially dependent on their parents. In most cases it is the parents of college students, rather than the students themselves, who pay for college.[46] Even if the parents pay the bills for higher education (as most do) and even if the college students live with their parents (as some still do) while going to college, college nevertheless paves the way for financial and social independence after graduation. College education gives young adults labor market skills, and the labor market skills enable them to work outside of the family business or trade. As recently as 1940, just over 12 percent of U.S.-born men and women in their twenties had been to college. In 1960, 27 percent of young men and 20 percent of young women had been to college. In 2000, 54 percent of young men and 63 percent of young women had been to college (Figure 3.4).[47]

The college experience itself has changed over time. In the university or college, the teachers and staff of the institution fill the role of the parents; the legal term for this is *in loco parentis*. College policies for the treatment of students are interesting not only because they reflect societal norms about how much freedom and leeway young adults have while attending college, but also because the written rules

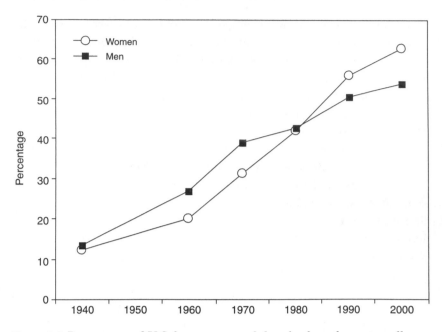

Figure 3.4. Percentage of U.S.-born young adults who have been to college, 1940–2000. Source: Weighted IPUMS census microdata, 1940, and 1960–2000. All individuals are U.S.-born, ages 20–29.

of the colleges were designed to reflect the unwritten rules and customs of the upper-middle-class families that sent their children to college.

In the early nineteenth century, colleges in the United States had a patriarchal and authoritarian view of student behavior. College manuals were marked by extensive and exquisitely detailed injunctions about such things as the appropriate conduct during attendance at mandatory daily religious services. Students had to transcribe the detailed book of rules before they were allowed to enroll.[48] Strict limits were placed on the ability of the (all-male) students to leave the campus.[49]

In the early twentieth century, the authoritarian higher education system, with its emphasis on obedience, was being replaced by a form of moral education that relied more on persuasion and less on intimidation. Colleges and universities had begun admitting women as well as men, but the colleges kept the women and the men strictly separate. An elaborate set of rules, including curfews, sign-ins, and chaperones, was deployed to manage relationships between the sexes.[50] In attempting to control the access of college students to potential mates, colleges were simply applying the norms and standards of the contemporary white upper-middle-class society.

Over the course of the twentieth century, the collegiate reliance on curfews and chaperones faded, just as they faded outside the university. By the 1970s, coeducational college dorms were common, curfews were a thing of the past, and the college campus had become an important site of social and sexual experimentation.[51] Just as the college education became more of a necessity, young adults became more independent from their parents and life on the college campus became more and more independent from parental and societal control.

It is not surprising that the college curriculum and university standards of behavior have been a key battle ground in the U.S. culture wars.[52] Despite the conservative condemnation of feminism, multiculturalism, academic Marxism, and insufficient patriotism in the Ivy League, the elites of the conservative movement continue to send their children to those very same Ivy League universities.[53] A college education (and preferably a high-quality college education) is a requirement for entry into the best jobs and careers in the post-industrial U.S. economy. The college experience is too important to be forsaken, so elite conservative families cannot avoid sending their children to college, nor can they send their children to small conservative Christian colleges (colleges whose educational priorities might be more consistent with the social and cultural beliefs of politically conservative parents) instead of the Ivy League without hampering their children's ability to advance in society. The elite universities offer something of value that conservative and liberal parents all seem to want for their children. Without being able to retreat from the university and the educational credentials it offers, liberals and conservatives are left to battle over the structure of the curriculum and the rules of campus behavior.

In the early 1960s, students were organizing at the University of California–Berkeley campus to fight racial segregation in San Francisco, Oakland, and Berkeley. Several hundred Berkeley students were arrested in a series of sit-ins at San Francisco hotels that eventually forced the hotels to agree to hire blacks at all levels. Local business leaders, politicians, and conservative citizens were alarmed by how well organized the students were and by how little control university officials seemed to have over the students.[54]

Local elites responded to student demonstrations by pressuring the university administration to exclude "off-campus issues" from the political dialogue of students at Berkeley. The business leaders complained that the university had become "a base of operations for attacks on the community."[55] When the distinction between academic and "off-campus" issues proved untenable, the university administration attempted to discourage all kinds of political activism on campus. The students mobilized to oppose the new restrictions and gave birth to Berkeley's "Free Speech Movement." The faculty at Berkeley eventually backed the students, who won back their right to distribute literature on campus.

In the late 1960s, the students at Berkeley fought increasingly bitter battles against local police as the students demonstrated against the Vietnam War, and then they battled the police to shut down a military draft induction center in Oakland. Community leaders and political conservatives were outraged by the apparent freedom and willingness of the students to be disruptive. Ronald Reagan spoke to and fanned the community's fears of college students run amok, and he was elected governor of California in part by running against "the mess up at Berkeley."[56] When the Berkeley students seized a university parking lot, tore up the pavement, planted grass, and renamed the land "Peoples' Park," Governor Reagan held a public meeting with Berkeley faculty to berate them for allowing the students to appropriate university property to their own uses. The Berkeley faculty and Governor Reagan simply had divergent views about the appropriate degree of intergenerational social control. As one faculty member explained to an exasperated Governor Reagan, "The time has past when the university can just ride roughshod over the desires of the majority of its student body."[57]

The polarizing cultural debates of the post-1960 United States have many of their roots in the radical politics of college student life and the conservative reaction against the perceived excesses of student radicalism. Student radicalism, in turn, was catalyzed by the independent life stage. The University of California administration was unsure about how much control it could or should exert over its students. The university's uncertainty reflected a broader social transformation in the relationships between parents and children.[58]

Despite the industrial revolution, few married women in the late nineteenth-century and early twentieth-century United States were in the formal labor force. According to legend, every member of the late nineteenth-century family was toiling in the factories, but the data show a different pattern. Husbands, fathers, and employers were successful until the mid-twentieth century in their efforts to keep married women home with their children. In 1880, only 6 percent of married women were wage laborers. The percentage of married women in the labor market rose slowly so that in 1940, only 13 percent of married women were in the labor force. After 1940, the percentage of married women who worked rose sharply and steadily. In 2000, 66 percent of married women were in the labor force (Figure 3.5).

Unmarried young women of the industrial revolution (who would have nearly always lived with their parents or parental surrogates) did sometimes work in the factories. For these women, several years of working in the factories before they married gave them a taste of independence. On several occasions, such as the great 1909 shirtwaist strike in New York City, women workers flexed their political and organizational muscles in ways that flummoxed the men who owned the factories and bewildered the men who ran the unions.[59]

The ability of women to find long-term employment in industries that once employed only men has increased the financial stability and independence of heterosexual and lesbian couples (that is, couples with at least one woman partner). Women in the past knew about work, of course. Young women in colonial times and in the nineteenth century were often servants in other families' homes.[60] In the nineteenth and early twentieth centuries, adult women could work as teachers or nurses, but women who were married were discouraged from working by their husbands and by their employers. In the late nineteenth century, in some states married women's wages could only be paid to their husbands.[61] Because women in the past had limited career options of their own, there was little practical alternative to marriage. The sense of being trapped into marriage, rather than

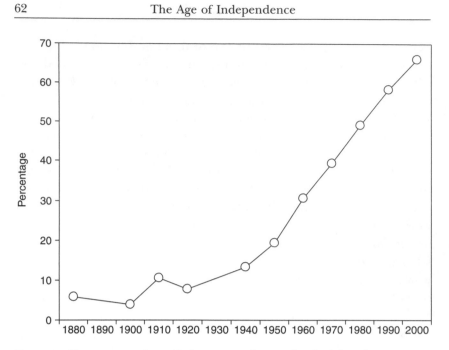

Figure 3.5. Percentage of married women who are in the labor force.
Source: Weighted IPUMS census microdata 1880, 1900–1920, and 1940–
2000. Includes all married women regardless of age or nativity.

choosing it freely, was a key complaint of the first wave of feminist
writers.[62]

Figure 3.6 shows the median age at first marriage for U.S.-born
persons from 1880 to 2000. The median age of first marriage is the
age at which exactly half of the age cohort remains unmarried. Age
at first marriage is closely related to the independent life stage because it is the first marriage (rather than a second marriage later in
life) that historically defined the succession of generations and that
now defines the end of the independent life stage for young adults
who marry. The transition from never married to first marriage is an
irreversible transition because, whereas one can become divorced or
separated or widowed after a first marriage, one cannot return to
"never married" status.[63]

Median age at first marriage for U.S.-born women was about 22
years of age from 1880 to 1940, reflecting little change during the
last part of the industrial revolution, before dropping to 20 during

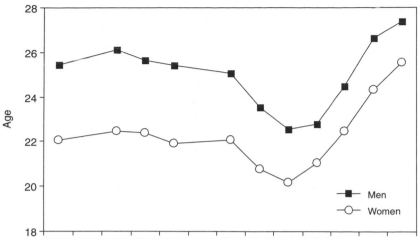

Figure 3.6. Median age at first marriage, U.S.-born men and women, 1880–2000. Source: Weighted IPUMS census microdata 1880, 1900–1920, and 1940–2000. Includes U.S.-born men and women only.

the great baby boom that followed World War II. From 1960 to 2000 the age at first marriage for women climbed sharply, by more than one year per decade, to 25.5 years in 2000. The pattern for men is similar: a slow decline in the median age at first marriage from 26.1 years in 1900 to 25 years in 1940, a dramatic decline in age at first marriage during the postwar baby boom, and then rising age at first marriage after 1960.[64]

The causes and effects of the great post–World War II baby boom have been intensively studied.[65] For men, the age at first marriage of 27 years in 2000 is higher than the historical precedent, but not dramatically so. It is possible to view the post-1960 pattern of age at first marriage for men as simply a return to the prewar status quo. In this view, the baby boom is the only anomaly that requires explanation.

For American women, however, the age at first marriage of 25.5 in 2000 represents a dramatic delay in marriage compared with previous generations. Fragmentary local records suggest that women in the American colonies and in preindustrial England may have had a median age of first marriage of roughly 22 years.[66] Since World War II, the age at first marriage for women in the United States underwent a rapid decline during the baby boom and then a rapid increase in the post-1960 period. The changes in the age at first marriage for women in the last fifty years are especially impressive given the stability in age at first marriage between 1880 and 1940.

In the past when unmarried children lived with their parents, late marriages were a sign of the dependence of children on their parents. Couples could not marry without financial assets in the American colonies even if both sets of parents endorsed the match. The main asset of value was land, and the problem in colonial towns like Amherst, Massachusetts, was that parents were already farming all of the available land. In order for young couples to gain title to the land, their parents had to give it to them and that meant the parents had to give up control over their own livelihoods, which many parents were unwilling or unable to do. Late marriage in the colonies reflected patriarchal control of fathers over the destinies of their children.[67]

In the post-1960 society, late age at first marriage is a result of increased independence. Because single young adults no longer live with their parents, late age at first marriage prolongs the independent life stage. In modern times, young men and women with some education and even modest labor market skills can support themselves and do not need to marry in order to survive. Late marriages in the post-1960 period mean exactly the opposite of what they used to mean, because the fundamental relationship between the generations has changed.

In the Quaker settlements of the Delaware Valley, well-to-do colonial young adults married early because their parents could afford to give them land at an early age. Quaker children whose parents did not have surplus land had to wait for marriage until they had amassed some savings of their own, and, as a result, they married six or seven years later than their more wealthy neighbors.[68] In the post-1960 world, the relationship between social class and age at marriage has been reversed. The poor (especially poor whites) marry earlier whereas the well-to-do postpone marriage for post-secondary education and for promising careers. For U.S.-born white women in the 2000 census, the median age at first marriage was 22.7 years for those with less than a high school degree, as compared with 26.5 years for those with a college degree.[69]

   Higher education has diversified the kinds of careers young people can aspire to, but the diversification has meant that the eventual success of young people in their chosen field is harder to predict. Whereas once young people from small towns married others from the same town whose key attributes (work ethic, ownership of land) were already well known, now the mating game is more complicated. Information about potential mates is harder to gather because young people meet in places like universities and cities whose geographical draw is diverse. Along with an intentional extension of the independent life stage by young adults who are not ready to settle down, the delay in marriage in the post-1960 period is also due to the more lengthy search required in a modern world where more potential mates are available but less is known about each of them.[70]

Scholars who wrote during the industrial revolution in the United States and more recent scholars who have relied on first-person accounts from the industrial revolution have generally argued that the industrial revolution was the time in American family life when all the old patriarchal family customs first began to change.[71] From this perspective, the post-1960 changes in family life are nothing more than a continuation of more than a century of family change. The census data demonstrate, however, that many of the post-1960 family changes, such as the decline of family government, cannot be traced back to the late nineteenth century, but rather they are fundamentally new phenomena. My analysis of historical census data suggests that despite changes in mortality, fertility, and urbanization, family government over single young adults was maintained during the industrial revolution of the late nineteenth century. If we examine intergenerational co-residence, the percent of single young adults who headed their own households, age at first marriage, or the labor force participation of married women, it is difficult to detect any effect of the industrial revolution. Given that the industrial revolution, the primary historical transition of modern times had (by some measures) only a modest effect on family structure, the rapid post-1960 changes in the family, including the rise of the independent life stage, must be considered all the more astonishing.

FOUR

◆ ◆ ◆

The Rise of Alternative Unions

DEBRA, ONE OF MY INTERVIEWEES (all interviewee names have been changed and identifying characteristics have been obscured to preserve confidentiality[1]), grew up in a suburban, white, Catholic family in the 1970s. As a child Debra knew that she was attracted more to women than to men, but she was not sure that this made her different from her peers until she went to college: "My sisters through school were just the good students, the ones who followed all the rules; they didn't go outside the boundaries, but I always made a point of going outside the boundaries. I shaved my head, I smoked, I went to the city every weekend secretly. . . . My mother was my teacher in Sunday school. I hated it. I questioned a lot of things about religion from the time I was very little." While Debra was in college, two of her best friends came out to her. Debra began to realize that she, too, was gay, and the fact that her friends were not only gay but open about it made it possible for Debra to imagine a gay life for herself for the first time. After college, Debra traveled to Korea to teach English.

If Debra had married soon after high school (without going to college), as women in the 1950s did, she might never have identified herself as a lesbian. The late age of marriage and college attendance of the post-1960 era has given young adults, especially young women, years of social experience before they are expected to settle down. Before 1960, it was unusual for a young unmarried woman to have the independent means and the social freedom to travel on her own. In Debra's generation, travel abroad was nothing unusual, and her parents never questioned her decision to work in Korea.

The substantial geographical and social distance between Korea and Debra's family of origin also made it easier for Debra to confirm her own homosexuality, far from any potentially countervailing familial pressure. In Korea Debra was happy, and she decided that in order to feel comfortable with her own sexuality, she needed to tell her parents. So she came back to the United States.

I made a trip home, to tell them. But I couldn't. I waited; I think I had maybe a ten-day vacation and I waited until day nine, and I struggled with it for nine days until finally I came out to my dad only. I never came out to my mom because my dad thought it would be better if he came out to her for me. Yeah and apparently she was hysterical and screaming "Why, what did we do so wrong?" And I'm glad I wasn't there to witness that.

But two years after, my mom and I had talked a lot on the phone. Things were OK on the surface; she just never wants to talk about it. And still now, she's never going to say, "Oh, so how do you feel about being a lesbian?," You know, she never brings it up but she's just accepted that this is my life now. But I never talk about it with her.

Soojin was a woman in Debra's English class for Korean adults, who shared Debra's interest in world travel. They found themselves talking for hours after class, and they started meeting away from school to do platonic cultural things, like go to museums. One day Debra cancelled a museum visit and Soojin was angry, angrier than Debra had expected her to be. Soojin's anger made Debra realize that there might be more to the relationship than a common appreciation of culture. Debra had been attracted to Soojin from the beginning, but she suppressed the feelings as unrealistic. The next time they were together, Debra came out to Soojin, and Soojin was surprised and a little bit alarmed. There was an awkward period of several weeks when they did not talk at all. The next time they met, Debra tried to backtrack—they could still be friends, she was sorry for putting Soojin on the spot, things could go back to being how they were. But Soojin did not want that; she wanted a relationship.

Soojin had a responsible job in the public health system in Korea. She was rising up the ranks, challenging herself professionally, and being rewarded for her initiative. Debra was living and teaching in Korea, and Debra and Soojin were having a very quiet and discreet affair. Eventually Debra got tired of teaching English in Korea and wanted to return to California. She wanted Soojin to come with her. Soojin wanted to be with Debra, but her parents were hysterical about her leaving such a good job, and leaving them. Despite parental opposition, Soojin left the family and the responsible job to move with Debra to California and start all over again as a student. Soojin believes that her parents have no idea that she is gay. Soojin keeps her relationship with Debra a secret from her parents because she believes that if they did know, "it would kill them both with a heart attack."

Because Soojin was trained to be a nurse, and because she was the younger child, her parents expected her to stay in Korea and tend to them in their old age. And Soojin herself wants to take care of her parents. She thinks that the Korean tradition of honoring the older generation is a worthy tradition. Soojin's sense that she is obligated to care for her parents in their old age is a sense that was not shared by any of my interviewees who were born in the United States. Soojin would consider moving back to Korea and taking care of her parents, and Debra would go with her, but Debra is not sure she is willing to put her homosexuality back into the closet. Soojin remembers that there is at least one gay nightclub near her small town in Korea, but the club is ostentatious and showy and, in Soojin's view, "weird." So if they go back to Korea, Debra would probably live in Seoul, and Soojin would live with her parents.

Debra and Soojin could not have met if Debra had not moved to Korea to work. Soojin would not have lived with Debra in Korea, whereas in California Soojin lives with Debra without having to disclose the relationship to her parents. Living independently, working, and delaying marriage has enabled Debra and Soojin to meet and to form a relationship that would have been quite improbable several generations ago.

The Rise of Interracial and Same-Sex Unions

Figure 4.1 shows the number of various types of nontraditional couples in the United States over time. The key finding in Figure 4.1 is that the number of nontraditional couples has risen dramatically since 1960. Same-sex and interracial unions have increased in numbers at the same time as the independent life stage has given young adults greater freedom. The time trend for same-sex unions only covers two

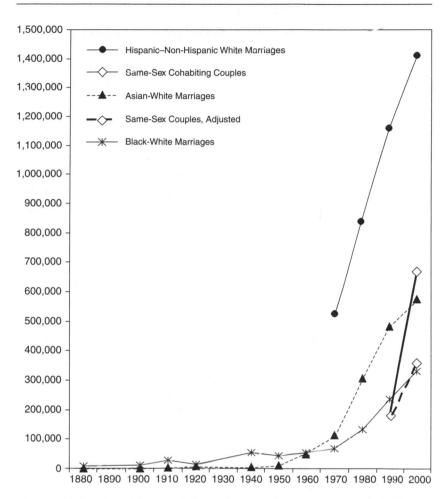

Figure 4.1. The rise of interracial marriages and same-sex unions, 1880–2000. Source: Weighted census microdata via IPUMS, 1880, 1900–1920, and 1940–2000. Includes married persons of all ages and all nativities. Hispanic ethnicity was first identified in the 1970 census. Adjusted same-sex couple total for 2000 excludes dual marital status recodes.

censuses, but the black-white and Asian-white marriage trends extend back to the nineteenth century. The trends for black-white and Asian-white intermarriage show no significant increases during the industrial revolution of the late nineteenth century, because, despite protestations to the contrary, the urbanization and industrialization of that period did not fundamentally diminish parental control over children.

The number of heterosexual cohabiting couples, 3.1 million in 1990 and 4.6 million in 2000, is not shown in Figure 4.1 because the large numbers of heterosexual cohabiters would dwarf the scale of the other alternative unions. The growth of heterosexual cohabitation from 1990 to 2000, however, is consistent with the rapid growth of other types of nontraditional unions shown in Figure 4.1.

The number of marriages between Hispanics and non-Hispanic whites rose from 527,000 in 1970 to 1.4 million in 2000. Part of this increase is due to the growth of the Hispanic population in the United States in the aftermath of the immigration reforms of 1965, but a substantial part of the increase is also due to an increasing tendency for Hispanics to assimilate with and marry whites.[2]

For most of the twentieth century, the number of black-white intermarriages was less than 50,000. The number of black-white intermarriages began to rise in the 1970s and reached 345,000 in 2000. Because the vast majority of whites still marry whites, and the vast majority of blacks still marry blacks, the trend of increasing black-white intermarriage has not been obvious.[3] The rising number of Asian-white intermarriages has garnered a good deal of attention because the Asian population in the United States is still relatively small, and nearly half of recent marriages among U.S.-born Asian Americans have been to non-Asian white Americans. There were 579,000 Asian-white married couples in the United States in 2000, up from negligible numbers prior to 1960. As with marriages between Hispanics and non-Hispanic whites, most of the growth in Asian-white intermarriage can be attributed the growth of the Asian community in the United States, which postdated the 1965 changes in immigration law.[4] However, Asian-white and Hispanic–non-Hispanic white intermarriage have both grown faster than minority population growth alone would explain.[5] Appendix Tables A.3–A.5, provide further perspectives on racial intermarriage with percentages (controlling for the population size of one group) and odds ratios (controlling for the population size of two groups).

Cohabiting couples, or what the census questionnaire refers to as "unmarried partners," were distinguished from ordinary roommates for the first time in the 1990 census.[6] The population of cohabiting same-sex couples captured in the census is somewhat different from the population of gay couples described in the classic histories of gay life because the histories of urban gay life include many persons who did not live with their same-sex partners, but rather encountered them casually in bars, parks, and bathhouses.[7] The same-sex cohabiting population captured in the census is representative only of the "out" gay population who lived with their partners.

Weighted census microdata show a sharp rise in reported same-sex cohabitation, from 174,000 couples in 1990 to 670,000 in 2000.[8] The nearly fourfold increase in same-sex cohabitation in ten years is misleading because the Census Bureau expanded its definition of same-sex cohabitation between 1990 and 2000.[9] If we attempt to adjust for the changes in Census Bureau procedures, same-sex cohabitation would appear to have roughly doubled (rather than quadrupled) between 1990 and 2000.

The Census Bureau has always changed individual census answers that it considered impossible or inconsistent. Since same-sex marriage was impossible in the United States in the past, the Census Bureau assumed that same-sex "married" couples had made a typographical mistake when filling out their form. To correct what they perceived to be mistaken answers, the Census Bureau prior to 2000 changed the gender of one partner, or the relationship between partners, for *all* same-sex couples who reported their relationship as "married."

In the 1990 census, 174,000 same-sex couples chose the new "partner" status, but those same-sex couples who identified themselves as "married" were still reclassified, mostly as heterosexual married couples. In the 2000 census, the Census Bureau followed their own tradition by refusing to accept "married" as a legitimate relationship between two persons of the same sex (in part because of the Defense of Marriage Act of 1996), but they broke with prior tradition by changing all same-sex "married" couples to "unmarried partner" status instead of transforming them into different-sex couples, or siblings. In other words, the Census Bureau decided that same-sex couples who reported themselves as "married" on the census form were no longer making a typographical error (as their previous policy had assumed) but rather were attempting to describe the true nature of their relationship. The inclusion of both self-reported "married" and self-reported "partner" couples led to a more realistic (and larger) count of same-sex couples in 2000 compared with the 1990 counts.[10] Although it is not possible to make the census counts of same-sex couples perfectly consistent between the 1990 and 2000 censuses, it is possible to mitigate the inconsistency. In all of the census tables and figures that follow, I report two values for same-sex couples in 2000: the unadjusted value (which is the more accurate measure of same-sex couples) and an adjusted value (which includes only the self-reported "partners" but not the self reported same-sex "married" couples and which is therefore more consistent with the 1990 data).[11]

Gay and lesbian studies in the United States have always been hampered by a lack of nationally representative data with sufficient samples of gays and lesbians. The 1990 and 2000 censuses go a long way toward solving this glaring data deficiency. The unweighted individual level data from the one-in-twenty files of the U.S. censuses of 1990 and 2000 include 8,000 and 32,000 same-sex couples (and twice as many individuals), respectively, two orders of magnitude more than any other nationally representative data source.

Even leaving aside inconsistencies in Census Bureau procedures, which cannot be precisely accounted for, the evidence strongly suggests that the number of same-sex couples in the United States is growing. The increase in respondents who identify themselves as part of a same-sex couple could be due to two factors: an actual increase in the number of same-sex couples and an increasing willingness of gay couples to be "out" and to report their status as a couple accurately. The increase in the willingness of same-sex couples to report their status accurately on the census (factor two) and an actual increase in same-sex cohabitation (factor one) are complementary forces that need not be disentangled. The data suggest a remarkable increase in the "out" gay population of the United States from 1990 to 2000.[12]

The visible size of transgressive or nontraditional populations is crucially important for several reasons. Successful suppression of sexual or social transgression relies in part on a hegemonic ideology that the transgression in question is "unnatural."[13] The hegemonic view that transgressive unions (in this case interracial or same-sex unions) are "unnatural" loses credibility when the size of the transgressive populations increases. People who feel themselves drawn to

interracial or same-sex partners are more likely to follow their desires
if they know of others who have followed the same path and suc-
ceeded or survived. The size of the gay or homosexual population is
especially controversial because reliable data have been so difficult to
come by. The lack of reliable data on the size of the homosexual
population is not accidental—it is a byproduct of a repressive social
system that keeps gays closeted and decreases the visibility of gays and
same-sex couples to each other and to the wider population.[14]

Many of the same-sex couples I have interviewed reported that they
had cousins or aunts or uncles whom they never heard about growing
up. In several cases, they heard erroneously that a known relative had
died. Later on in life, when my interviewees were adults living on
their own, they encountered the long-lost relatives and found them to
be in good health, living reasonably happy lives with same-sex partners. Every family has its own informal history. Often, these informal
family histories celebrate the individuals whose lives and successes are
most normative and erase or hide the others, just as the U.S. census
erased any sign of same-sex couples before 1990.

The Complexities of Counting Gays in the United States

One of the reasons Alfred Kinsey is such a revered figure among
scholars of gay studies is that Kinsey's estimate of the gay population
(especially the gay male population) was far larger than prior estimates.[15] Kinsey estimated that in the late 1940s 10 percent of adult
white males in the United States were predominantly homosexual for
at least three years of their adult lives, and 4 percent of adult white
men were exclusively homosexual throughout their lives. The percentage of men who had any sexual experience with other men over
their lifetimes was far higher—37 percent according to Kinsey.[16]
These estimates, along with Kinsey's nonjudgmental language, forced
public opinion to come to grips with the notion that homosexual
activity was far more common than people had thought, and this inevitably undermined the formerly dominant idea that homosexuality
was completely "unnatural."

Kinsey's findings were then and continue to be controversial.[17]
Kinsey's sample was not a random sample but something more like a
convenience sample of interested and cooperative subjects. Laumann

and his colleagues suggest that Kinsey's research method systematically overestimated the gay population because Kinsey's network of acquaintances were themselves disproportionately urban and disproportionately gay.[18] When Laumann and his colleagues fielded their own sexual history survey to a nationally random sample of subjects in the United States in 1992, they found that the prevalence of same-sex sexual contact was much lower than Kinsey had found. Laumann found that only 1.3 percent of sexually active women and 2.7 percent of sexually active men had had same-sex partners in the previous year, and the lifetime incidence of same-sex sexual contact was less than 10 percent for men and less than 5 percent for women.[19]

Laumann and his colleagues found much lower rates of adult homosexuality than Kinsey had found forty-five years earlier. Laumann's data-gathering procedure, using a small army of professionally trained interviewers, was more modern and scientific, whereas Kinsey's method was more personal and unscientific. It seems unlikely that adult homosexuality would have declined from the late 1940s to the early 1990s in the United States; all the data and the knowledgeable historians suggest an increase over time in the number of gay couples.[20] The question, then, is whether it is possible to adjudicate between the divergent findings of Laumann and Kinsey.

Although Laumann's study had the advantage of a nationally representative random sample, the impersonal nature of the study along with the professional status of the interviewers undoubtedly led to an underreporting of socially stigmatized behaviors such as homosexuality. In fact, socially stigmatized behaviors are almost always underreported. The very nature of social stigma ensures underreporting. The women in Laumann's sample reported substantially fewer heterosexual partners in the years prior to the survey than the men did. If the sample of persons was truly nationally representative, the men and women should have reported nearly the same total number of heterosexual partners, because every coupling would add exactly one to each gender's total.[21] The discrepancy in the number of reported heterosexual partners is almost entirely due to the very basic problem of self-report bias. Laumann and his coauthors, as well as their most vocal critics, agree that women underreport the number of heterosexual partners and men overreport because social norms view male sexuality (and male promiscuity) more favorably.[22]

If the sexual double standard continues to skew self-reported data on the number of heterosexual partners, one can well imagine the difficulty of obtaining reliable data on homosexual activity, which faces even stronger social sanctions. Social science data that rely on self-report, whether it be U.S. census data on same-sex couples or survey data on the details of sexual behavior, are always vulnerable to self-report bias if the issue in question is socially taboo. Despite the limitations of self-reporting, in many cases self-report is the only source of data that we have. The task of the social scientist is to gather and use the best available data to try to answer questions without diminishing or underestimating the true difficulty of arriving at reliable answers.

Many of the gay couples I have interviewed made an effort not to reveal their sexual identity or the gender of their partner to those who are outside of their inner social circle. Most of my other gay interviewees were careful to keep landlords, coworkers, neighbors, or acquaintances in the dark about their sexual orientation. All of my U.S.-born gay interviewees were more forthright with their parents than Soojin was with her parents, but a few had merely led their parents to believe that they might be gay without saying so explicitly. Even though gays in the United States are no longer as isolated and invisible as they were in the past, "the closet" still exists as a selective barrier between gays and the wider society.[23] Given that my interviewees are likely to be more open and forthright than average (my gay interviewees cohabit with long-term same-sex partners, they live in the San Francisco Bay Area where homosexuality is relatively well accepted, and they volunteered to tell their stories to a complete stranger), their selective use of nondisclosure implies that the closet is still influential. Straight society is still allowed to see (or wants to see) only a fraction of gay society. Debra is a woman who describes herself as always challenging social boundaries; she is openly gay with her friends, family, and coworkers, but with strangers she is actively committed to nondisclosure.[24]

There's still a part of me that doesn't want to tell people, and I say Soojin's my roommate. . . . But I don't want to say that. But I feel like at times . . . like when we were looking for apartments, just a few weeks ago in San Francisco, and even in San Francisco I feel like saying she's my roommate. But I don't want to be saying that, so maybe I'm not yet 100 percent open about it. One woman renting apartments said, "But there's only one bedroom." Yeah. We understand that. I'm a teacher. I can do the math.

The continued existence of the closet helps explain the sharp rise from 1990 to 2000 in the number of same-sex couples who were willing to identify themselves as such on the U.S. census. The closet contains a reservoir of gay couples, which, as it empties out, increases the visible number of gay couples quite rapidly. Because the interview data suggest that the reservoir of closeted gay couples is far from empty, it is reasonable to presume that the number of "out" gay couples may continue to grow rapidly in the future.[25]

In 2000 in the United States there were 56,220,000 married couples and 5,240,000 cohabiting couples of whom 670,000 were same-sex couples, according to weighted census microdata. In the 2000 census, same-sex couples constituted 1.1 percent of the 61 million co-resident couples in the United States. Since many homosexuals were not cohabiting with partners at the time of the census in 2000, and some same-sex couples were naturally hesitant about declaring themselves accurately to an unsympathetic federal government, the figure of 1.1 percent probably underrepresents the real population of same-sex couples and is only a fraction of the population that has regular or occasional sexual contact with same-gender persons.

Heterosexual Cohabitation

Along with same-sex cohabitation, the rise of heterosexual cohabitation is another measure of the greater flexibility in mate formation in the post-1960 era. In the nineteenth century, religious leaders and social reformers in the United States led a long and ultimately successful battle to limit the legal rights of heterosexual cohabiting couples (also known as common law unions).[26] The official state sanction of formal marriage in combination with laws against sexual relations outside of marriage (that is, laws against adultery and fornication) amounted to a legal exclusion of heterosexual cohabitation.

Prior to 1990, the U.S. Census Bureau did not distinguish between unmarried partners and roommates. "Partner" and "roommate" carry different meanings, of course. The vast majority of roommates have always been same-sex roommates. Different-sex roommates or boarders were frowned upon in the past because of the appearance of impropriety. Extramarital heterosexual co-residence raised the possibility of sexual access, which in turn would have challenged the exclusive place of heterosexual marriage. Same-sex roommates did not raise a specter of impropriety in the nineteenth century in part because nineteenth- and early twentieth-century Americans were naive about homosexuality.[27]

To make a historically consistent comparison of heterosexual co-residence and cohabitation using census data from before 1990, it is necessary to include both "partners" and "roommates," which is not so problematic since U.S. society in the past was suspicious enough about men and women living together outside of marriage to make both heterosexual "partners" and "roommates" rather rare.[28]

Between 1880 and 1960, the fraction of U.S.-born male heads of household ages 20–39 who were cohabiting with young women remained steady at 0.1 percent, or one per thousand. In the post-1960 era, however, a new pattern emerged. The percentage of young men cohabiting with women outside of marriage rose steadily, reaching 7.9 percent in 2000 (Figure 4.2). Note that the historical trend in heterosexual cohabitation consists of two periods. During the first period, 1880–1970, the rate of heterosexual cohabitation was consistently low. After 1970, an entirely different regime emerged as the heterosexual cohabitation rate increased in a rapid and linear fashion.

Alternative Unions and Their Circles of Influence

"Demography is destiny" is one of the favorite phrases of demographers. The phrase means, in part, that population size and distribution determines much of social life. Social systems of strict control and exclusion of transgressive unions mutually reinforce the small numbers and invisibility of such unions. Social stigmas, parental pressure, and the law kept the number of visibly transgressive unions very low before 1960, and the low numbers reinforced the stigma against actual or would-be transgressors by isolating them. In the post-1960 period, rapid social change, growing numbers of alternative unions, and sexual liberalization have been mutually reinforcing. As social atti-

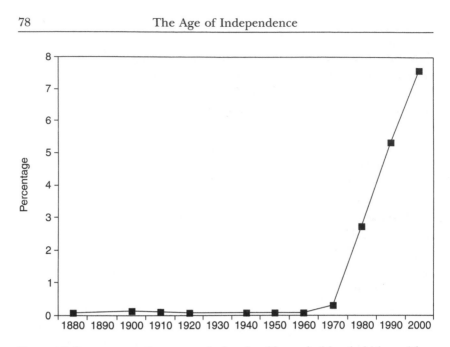

Figure 4.2. Percentage of young male heads of household cohabiting with a young woman, 1880–2000. Source: Weighted census microdata from 1880, 1900–1920, and 1940–2000 via IPUMS. Male heads of household (the denominator population) were ages 20–39, U.S.-born, not living in group quarters. In order to be counted as heterosexual cohabiters, the male householders must have been living with a woman (not related by family) in the same age range, both unmarried, neither living with their parents. Census categories include friends, lodgers, boarders, roommates, and partners.

tudes have liberalized, U.S. society has taken a more permissive view of same-sex and interracial unions, and the number of transgressive unions has increased as a result. The growing numbers of same-sex and interracial unions means more visibility for interracial and same-sex couples, and the increased visibility further erodes the social barriers against transgressive unions.

Simple interpersonal exposure is a necessary, but not a sufficient ingredient for becoming a friend, confidant, or lover. Not all kinds of interpersonal contact facilitate trust and friendship. In *Streetwise*, Elijah Anderson describes the tension that exists between the residents of an economically up-and-coming, mostly white neighborhood and their neighbors from a poor black neighborhood.[29] The initial mistrust and unease that characterizes the daily interactions of blacks and whites on the streets and in the public spaces leads to overly cautious or overly aggressive behaviors that reinforce and reify the initial mistrust between racial groups.

Interpersonal contact can produce friction and disharmony as well as friendship and romance. Forced school integration, by itself, does not break down racial barriers. Central High School in Little Rock, Arkansas, was integrated by nine black students in 1957 over the objections of the governor and thousands of white protestors. The integration of Central High raised white popular opposition to an angry boil, and the photographs of the famous moments when the black students ascended the schoolhouse steps show the black students clearly terrified by the hostile crowd.[30]

In order to make students form allegiances across the usually impermeable boundaries of race, education scholars have employed classroom learning strategies that force students from the different racial groups to work together as a team with equally distributed responsibilities.[31] The idea behind this research is that interpersonal exposure alone is not enough, but that interpersonal exposure in the context of cooperation and trust can begin to break down the barriers of race. The context of cooperation and trust is more easily created and imposed in the laboratory of a classroom than in the broader society.

Mark Twain's *Huckleberry Finn*, one of the best-loved and most widely read American novels of the nineteenth century, offers an interesting perspective on interracial friendship and social exposure.[32] In the novel two young men, Huck and Jim, have known each other all their lives, but they have never been friends until circumstances force them to flee their homes and escape down the Mississippi River together on a raft. Jim is a black slave, and Huck is a white boy. The friendship they build while on the raft is possible only because they are completely cut off from their families and from adult society in general. Huck struggles with the moral dilemma of choosing between his friendship for Jim and his allegiance to a white society that seeks to recapture Jim and return him to slavery. In the end, Huck decides to protect his friend Jim and reject the racial order that his family accepts. Huck is able to befriend Jim only because Huck and Jim are physically beyond the reach of their families and therefore beyond "family government," and because the trials and dangers of the river force Huck and Jim to cooperate and trust each other in order to survive.

Alternative unions are most influential upon close friends and relatives, that is, the people who are personally close enough to know the couple well, whose relationship to the couple might force them to reassess prior prejudices. Given that alternative unions compose a relatively small percentage of all unions, what percentage of Americans have at least one same-sex couple or interracial couple among their circle of closest friends and relatives? The answer to this question depends on the prevalence of the type of couple in question and how large the social circle of closest friends and relatives is. The higher the prevalence of specific type of couple, and the larger the social circle one considers, the higher the chance that any American will have at least one couple of that type within his or her inner social circle.

Table 4.1 shows the population size of various types of couples from the 2000 census. Out of 61.4 million couples, 5.2 million were unmarried cohabiting couples (that is, co-resident couples who identified themselves as "partners") and 56.2 million were married couples. There were 4.35 million interracial couples in the United States in 2000, which includes black-white, Hispanic–non-Hispanic, Asian-white, Native American-white, multiracial-white, and a variety of other combinations. There were 484,000 black-white interracial couples, including 345,000 black-white married couples.

The last two columns of Table 4.1 estimate the probability of finding at least one couple of the specified type in a random group of five or ten couples.[33] The calculation of theoretical exposure makes one important assumption, that the probability of any couple being nontraditional (same-sex, interracial, or heterosexual cohabiting couples) is independent of the couples already in the social circle, which is not a very good assumption for friends (because, for instance, a gay person might have mostly gay friends), but may be a more reasonable assumption for a social circle of blood relations.[34]

This method allows me to estimate the percentage of Americans who had at least one same-sex union, interracial union, or hetero-

Table 4.1 Prevalence of nontraditional couples and probability of exposure, 2000

Type of couple	Number of couples	Prevalence (percent of total)	Probability of finding at least one couple of this type in group of five couples	Probability of finding at least one couple of this type in group of ten couples
Total couples	61,457,141	100.0%		
Cohabiting couples	5,235,799	8.5	36%	59%
Married couples	56,221,342	91.5	100	100
Total interracial couples	4,352,771	7.1	31	52
Interracial cohabiting couples	711,884	1.2	6	11
Interracial married couples	3,640,887	5.9	26	46
Total black-white couples	484,832	0.8	4	8
Black-white cohabiting couples	139,180	0.2	1	2
Black-white married couples	345,652	0.6	3	5
Same-sex cohabiting couples	669,984	1.1	5	10
Heterosexual cohabiting couples	4,565,815	7.4	32	54

Source: 2000 5 weighted microdata, via IPUMS. Includes individuals of all races, all ages, and all places of birth. Interracial couples include all couples that have different racial groups among these four categories: (1) non-Hispanic white; (2) non-Hispanic black; (3) Hispanic; (4) Asians, Native Americans, multiracial persons, and others.

Probability of finding at least one couple of each type in group of N couples is $p = 1 - (1 - r)^N$ where N is the number of couples in the group and r is the prevalence.

sexual cohabiting union in their inner social circle at the time of the census in 2000. If we take ten couples as the arbitrary size of a person's inner circle, then 10 percent of Americans had a same-sex couple in their inner circle, 54 percent knew a heterosexual cohabiting couple, 52 percent knew an interracial couple of any type, and 8 percent had a black-white couple in their inner circle.

Even though heterosexual cohabitation accounted for only 7.4 percent of all couples, more than half of all Americans had a close tie to someone in a heterosexual cohabiting relationship (if we assume people had close ties to ten other people in relationships). The high probability of exposure to cohabitation at close range helps explain why heterosexual cohabitation has lost so much of the stigma it used to have. Interracial couples touch a substantial minority of Americans, in part because the interracial category includes the very numerous Hispanic–non-Hispanic white couples. Black-white interracial couples, the type of interracial couples that have been most stigmatized and persecuted in the United States, are much less numerous and touch a correspondingly smaller percentage of Americans (approximately 8 percent). Same-sex cohabiting couples touch approximately 10 percent of Americans at any one time. Assuming that social networks change over time, the lifetime close personal exposure to same-sex cohabiting couples would be substantially higher than 10 percent. The dense web of social connections (some chosen, some biological) that we inhabit magnifies the effect of even small minority groups.

The simple model of social ties I have been using in this section has some interesting implications for how quickly firsthand familiarity with nontraditional couples spreads through a society. If the prevalence of nontraditional couples is zero, then of course the percentage of people who have close social ties to nontraditional couples is also zero. But if the prevalence of nontraditional couples is a mere 1 percent of all couples (for example same-sex couples in 2000), then 10 percent of the population might be expected to have a nontraditional couple within their circle of ten closest partnered friends and relatives. In other words, as the prevalence of nontraditional unions grows from zero to 1 percent, the rate of firsthand familiarity with nontraditional unions grows from zero to 10 percent. The reason the popu-

[handwritten marginalia: what trends in gender age gap? i.e. older 2083 ♀ ♂ ?]

lation of friends and family of nontraditional couples grows so quickly *[handwritten: ← comp]* when the prevalence of nontraditional couples is low is that the circles of close friends and relatives of the nontraditional couples overlap very little. At low prevalence rates, every new nontraditional union contributes a full set of friends and relations who have never known someone in this kind of nontraditional union before. As the preva-lence of nontraditional unions grows, it is more and more likely that some of the people in anyone's close social circle already know some-one else in a nontraditional union. At the high end of the prevalence spectrum, in contrast, increases in prevalence do not increase first-hand exposure at all. Heterosexual same-race married couples com-posed 91.5 percent of all couples in 2000, implying that 100 percent of people in the United States had at least one such couple in their social circles. An increase in heterosexual same-race marriage would have no effect on the exposure of Americans to heterosexual same-race marriage because nearly everyone has already been exposed to heterosexual same-race married couples.

The lesson is that the steepest change in social exposure to new or transgressive family forms occurs when the new family form is first beginning to emerge in the society. This is perhaps why the first signs of social change are always fought with the most bitterness. Once new family forms gain a visible foothold, the firsthand social exposure to (and therefore potential acceptance of) the new forms grows rapidly.

Alternative unions have grown rapidly in the post-1960 era. We cannot say for certain what the number of openly gay cohabiting cou-ples was before 1990 because reliable nationally representative data are unavailable, but historical scholarship allows us to infer that there were relatively few openly gay cohabiting couples in the United States prior to 1960.[35] Since the census record for heterosexual cohabitation and black-white and Asian-white marriages reaches back to the nine-teenth century, those time trends are our best guide to the presence of transgressive unions in the United States over the past century. The number of interracial marriages and the rate of heterosexual cohab-itation have grown since 1960 in a historically unprecedented way. I suggest that the unprecedented rise of transgressive unions since 1960 is due in part to the equally unprecedented shifts in family structure, especially the rise of the independent life stage. The timing of the rise of alternative unions, contemporaneous as it is with the rise of the independent life stage, is suggestive but not conclusive evidence for a causal connection between the two. In the next chapter, I examine that connection in more detail.

◆ ◆ ◆

FIVE

Alternative Unions and the
Independent Life Stage

VERONICA IS A WHITE WOMAN, born in the 1950s, and raised in an all-white staunchly conservative town fifty miles outside of New York City. Veronica had so little exposure to blacks that she can remember very distinctly the black nurse who came to take care of her mother.

I think I was probably about seven, and I remember distinctly, in fact we laugh about it now, being in the bathroom, sitting on the toilet, and my dad was shaving. And I looked up at him and I asked him if the nurse had a black bottom [laughs]. He almost fainted; he couldn't believe it. And then he explained to me, yes that's the race and everything. And then we had to drive her [the nurse] to a nearby town, which had more blacks in it than our town did. And she wouldn't apparently let us take her to her house, so we had to have a meeting place. So we went to stop at this one meeting place, and Dad was driving, and this man was coming down the hill. And I said to the nurse, "Oh, is that your daddy?" And my father was embarrassed yet again. And luckily it was her brother; it wasn't just another black person. So that was when I was initially introduced to a mixed culture, to a black culture. But where I grew up was all white, so I wasn't introduced to any other kind of races.

Karl is a black man, born in the early 1950s and raised in inner-city Detroit. Karl's father was a janitor, and Karl's mother was a housekeeper, occupations that were dominated by blacks in those days. Karl's parents found an integrated public school for Karl and his siblings to attend—the school started out as mostly white, but ended up being mostly black. After high school Karl joined the Air Force, and the Air Force helped pay for his college education. After his time in the armed forces was over, in the late 1970s Karl became a restaurant manager for a restaurant in a big East Coast city. Karl remembers:

> The elementary school was great; I remember very vividly, it was a wonderful time of my life. I remember the teachers to this day and they had great influences on me. My parents always pushed education. My sister graduated from the state university, and all my siblings are educated, had college degrees. Um . . . I remember high school as being kind of tense because it was during that time period, junior high, high school, semi-tense, because that was during the civil rights riots and those kinds of things.
>
> [When asked about the riots that shook Detroit in the late 1960s] Well that was downtown, it was pretty far removed, and they . . . I don't remember ever discussing it. My brother was a big influence on me. He was kind of a radical kind of guy, you know. I sort of formed my own opinions as a result of some of the images. And um . . . my biggest response to racism was I never understood it; it was not logical to me. So that was my impression of the entire issue of racism. I never understood; it just wasn't logical.

Three generations ago, Karl and Veronica might never have met. Karl's parents had sought integrated schools for their children, but Veronica's family had chosen the most segregated community and therefore the most segregated school system they could find. In the post–civil rights era, blacks in the United States have generally had a preference for racial integration, whereas whites have generally resisted integration.[1] In the 1940s, few young adults went to college. By the 1970s, however, even socially conservative families sent their daughters to college. Veronica's family sent her to a private Catholic college, in a nearby East Coast city, to study nursing. The college was carefully selected to be socially conservative and nearly all white. In order to pay the bills, Veronica looked for a part-time job. Karl's restaurant happened to be hiring. Veronica started working for Karl, and she turned out to be the most reliable worker in the restaurant. Karl and Veronica were often at the restaurant together, closing up after everyone else had gone home. They fell in love. Karl asked Veronica to marry him.

Veronica said, "No." She knew her family would not approve. Karl moved to California and said that he would wait for her. Veronica dated other men, but did not find anyone she liked as much as Karl. Finally she moved to California to be with him. Veronica says:

When I came to California, Karl and I lived together [laughs] and we had two phones. So when the one phone rang we knew that it was my mother. And Karl put up with it for a long time until finally he's like, "Enough is enough. If you love me you need to tell your parents; you need to come forward." And I kept promising him I would and I never did, I don't think, until I got pregnant. . . . And he told me, you need to go. . . . And then I knew that if I could just give my parents time they would come around. Because I wasn't prejudiced and I knew in my heart I wasn't prejudiced, and I knew my parents couldn't have been prejudiced because then I probably would have been prejudiced. I mean that was my rationale over the whole thing . . .

So Karl put me on a plane to send me to tell them that I was pregnant and we were getting married. . . . And my mother said, "Oh great, I hope you choose not to have children; that wouldn't be fair for the children." So then I clammed completely and didn't say anything. And then she looked at my little brother and said, "How do you feel about having a black brother-in-law?" My poor twelve-year-old brother just sat there and got these big, watery eyes, and he didn't know what to say; I felt so bad for him.

And then I guess we didn't really discuss it any more. But when I came back my parents were calling me, telling me that I was making a mistake, telling me that my mother was having a nervous breakdown and that it was gonna be all my fault. And then my father would call and say he's coming out with a gun and he's gonna shoot Karl and he's gonna shoot me. My father said he'd end up in jail and everybody would be happy then. He was so upset that my mother was upset. My mother was worse I guess. . . . But in the meantime Karl and I went ahead with the wedding. And we went to Tahoe and got married, and they refused to come. My sister came, however, she was kind of wishy, washy about the whole thing. But we had a wonderful wedding. . . . There were probably about twenty-five people there I guess.

Over the years, Karl and Veronica had three children. As the years passed, Veronica's mother, and then father, came to visit the family in California. Everyone is cordial. Karl and Veronica have visited Veronica's parents, but after twenty years of marriage Karl has still never set foot in Veronica's parents' house.

Karl and Veronica's story is an essentially modern story that could not have happened the same way fifty years earlier. In an earlier time, Veronica would have been meeting and dating men while living with her parents. If Veronica had been living with her parents when she met Karl, she would probably have known that the relationship was impossible. If she had gotten involved with Karl anyway, her parents would have found out fairly early in the relationship, and they would have been in a much stronger position to prevent the marriage. Prior to World War II, few American women attended college, and most who did lived at home.

Veronica's nursing degree gave her confidence that she could find work and support herself anywhere in the United States. Karl also had a college degree, and he had experience in the armed forces. Education and valuable labor market skills gave Karl and Veronica confidence that they could support themselves if they had to. But even with good education and labor market skills, Karl knew that Veronica would never marry him if her parents were anywhere nearby. So Karl moved to California without knowing a single person west of the Mississippi. Once Veronica and Karl were living together in California, thousands of miles from either one's family of origin, the power dynamic was different. The physical reality of distance mediates and moderates the power and consequences of interpersonal relationships. Even when Veronica's father threatened to kill them, the psychological impact of the threat, though still strong, was tempered by the practical reality of physical distance.

Geographic Mobility

Geographic mobility is crucial to people in nontraditional unions. Nontraditional and transgressive unions are nontraditional and transgressive precisely because many parents and extended families will not accept them. In the era of the independent life stage, not only do young people meet potential mates far beyond the watchful eyes of their parents, but young people with some education or labor market skills also have the option of moving far from home if the home environment becomes hostile.

Table 5.1 shows the geographic mobility of different types of young U.S.-born couples. Geographically mobile couples live in a different state from the birth states of one or both partners. Non-mobile couples live in the birth state of both partners. In 1990, 48.1 percent of young same-race married couples were mobile, meaning that slightly more than half (100 percent − 48.1 percent = 51.9 percent) lived in the birth state of both spouses. In 2000, only 46.6 percent of the young same-race married couples were geographically mobile, a slight decline from 1990, indicating that despite the increasing opportunity for young Americans to move, there is some slight evidence for an "increasing rootedness" of Americans to the places they grew up.[2]

I use the state where a person was born as a proxy for where the family roots are, and where the extended family lives. Lifetime interstate mobility is a crude (but the best available in the census) measure of distance from family and community of origin. Many kinds of ge-

Table 5.1 Geographic mobility for young couples by type of couple, 1990–2000

	1990		2000	
Type of couple	Percent movers	Odds ratio compared with (1)	Percent movers	Odds ratio compared with (1)
(1) Heterosexual, same-race, married	48.1		46.6	
(2) Heterosexual, same-race, cohabit	50.7	1.11***	46.9	1.01
(3) Heterosexual, interracial, married and cohabit	59.1	1.56***	58.4	1.61***
(4) Same-sex, cohabit	67.5	2.24***	51.7	1.23***
(5) Same-sex, interracial, cohabit	74.4	3.13***	64.1	2.05***

* $p < .05$ ** $p < .01$ *** $p < .001$, two-tailed test.

Source: Weighted 1990 and 2000 5% microdata via IPUMS.

Note: All couples are U.S.-born and ages 20–29. Geographically mobile couples live in a different U.S. state than the birth state of one or both partners. Adjusted estimate for same sex couples in 2000 (discarding dual marital status recodes): geographic mobility is 55.9% for all same sex couples, 71.7% for interracial same-sex couples.

ographic mobility may intervene between birth and union formation; families can and do make interstate moves together. Furthermore, interstate geographic mobility fails to capture mobility within states, such as mobility from suburbs or rural areas to the urban centers in the same state, a kind of mobility that nontraditional couples are especially likely to make.

Because the census is a cross-sectional (rather than longitudinal) survey, it is impossible to determine which individuals lived with their parents prior to mate selection. Once the young adults are married or cohabiting, nearly all couples live in a different household from their parents (roughly 99 percent do so) so that "living with parents" cannot be used to differentiate between union types. Couples who are embedded in the social world of their parents tend to live near the parents, whereas couples whose union transgresses against the values of their parents tend to live farther away.

If geographic mobility is an important catalyst for nontraditional unions, then we would expect to find that nontraditional unions are more geographically mobile than traditional same-race married couples. Furthermore, the more transgressive and nontraditional the couple is, the more geographically mobile the couple should be. Table 5.1 provides strong evidence to support the hypothesis of a correlation between geographic mobility and nontraditional unions.

Heterosexual same-race cohabiting couples were more geographically mobile than same-race heterosexual married couples in 1990 (50.7 percent compared with 48.1 percent), but in 2000 the heterosexual same-race cohabiting couples were only very slightly more mobile (46.9 percent compared with 46.6 percent). The narrowing gap in geographic mobility between same-race heterosexual couples who cohabit and who marry is evidence that cohabitation has lost most of the social stigma that it used to have.[3] Cohabitation is not a particularly visible form of nontraditional union because strangers cannot tell whether a couple is married or not.

When I compare percentages, I use the odds ratio to make comparisons.[4] The odds ratio compares each group's mobility percentage with the mobility percentage of the traditional heterosexual same-race married couples. If the odds ratio is not significantly different from 1 that means the geographic mobility of the group cannot be distinguished from the geographic mobility of traditional couples with statistical certainty. An odds ratio of significantly greater than 1 indicates that the geographic mobility of the nontraditional couples is significantly greater than the geographic mobility of traditional couples in the same census year. According Table 5.1, in 1990 and 2000 every type of nontraditional couple had significantly greater geographic mobility than heterosexual same-race married couples (that is, odds ratios significantly greater than 1) except for heterosexual same-race cohabiting couples in 2000 (odds ratio of 1.01).

The census allows for a dizzying number of different racial, ethnic, and ancestry categories. For practical purposes, I collapse the Census Bureau's racial and Hispanic categories into four: (1) non Hispanic white; (2) non-Hispanic black; (3) Hispanic; and (4) Asians and all others. Couples whose races are different (according to the four broad categories) are interracial.[5] I use "race" in a broad sense to encompass both traditional racial categories (black, white, Asian) and the ethnic category "Hispanic." Hispanic–non-Hispanic white couples are the largest group among the interracial (as I have defined the category) couples, followed by Asian-white and black-white couples. Heterosexual interracial couples in 1990 had 1.56 times higher odds of geographic mobility than same-race married couples.[6]

Same-sex cohabiting couples (67.5 percent mobility) were more geographically mobile than interracial couples in 1990 (but less mobile in 2000), whereas couples that were interracial and same-sex were the most geographically mobile in 1990 and 2000 (74.4 percent and 64.1 percent mobility, respectively).[7] The more couples transgress against traditional family norms, the more likely it is that their families of origin will be hostile or reject them completely, and the more likely the couples are to want to relocate to someplace far away.

In 1990, same-sex couples had an average geographic mobility of 67.5 percent, implying an odds of mobility more than twice as high as same-race married couples. Between 1990 and 2000, the geographical mobility of same-sex couples declined sharply (whether one uses the full sample or the adjusted sample for 2000). Young gay couples in 2000 were only slightly more geographically mobile than the comparison category of young heterosexual same-race married couples. To the extent that comparisons can be made between the 1990 and 2000 samples of same-sex couples, the pattern of sharply declining relative geographic mobility is consistent with rapidly increasing acceptance of gay couples by their parents and extended families.

The different union types in 1990 and 2000 can be ranked by geographic independence and, therefore, by implied nonconformity to prevailing norms of union formation, race, and heterosexuality. According to Table 5.1, heterosexual same-race cohabitation was slightly nonconformist in 1990, but it became conformist in terms of geographic mobility by 2000. Interracial unions were moderately nonconformist in 1990 and 2000. Same-sex couples were the most geographically independent in 1990, but only moderately more geographically independent than traditional married couples in 2000. Interracial same-sex couples, facing both the stigma of interraciality and the stigma of homosexuality, were by far the most geographically mobile couples in 1990 and in 2000.

Union formation can occur before or after geographic mobility. Either order of events can be consistent with the rise of the independent life stage, and both patterns emerge from my in-depth interviews with interracial and same-sex couples. Karl and Veronica (the couple I described at the beginning of the chapter) met when Veronica was living on her own, but not far geographically from her parents. Karl moved to California in order to induce Veronica to move and separate herself from the influence of her parents.

Sometimes the geographic movers moved first and then met their future partners. This order of events is consistent with the idea that geographic mobility is inherent in the independent life stage and, furthermore, that travel away from home exposes young adults to new kinds of social situations and new kinds of potential partners. Young adults living away from home are able to nurture a relationship before they have to disclose the relationship to their parents.

Alternatively, some respondents met their future partners in their home states before moving. In this second order of events, the independent life stage is a potential outlet, a possibility that couples may turn to if their choice of partners results in parental or familial disapproval or sanction. Even when young adults meet their partners close to home, the ability to move far away and to start a new life far from home is an important option that was previously less available. Parental authority and control is diminished because young adults know they can move away. In premodern times, parental authority was heightened by the lack of external options; banishment from one's family and community of origin was tantamount to banishment from organized society.[8]

Union formation is not an event, but a process. It may be possible to define the exact moment when two people first meet (though often couples disagree about this). The date of a marriage or the date two people first moved in together is usually easy to define. It is much more difficult to define the exact moment when two people become a couple. Love affairs sometimes break up only to be reignited years later. Similarly, moving away from home is a reversible process. A young person may move away to college, then come back home to live with his or her parents for a few years, then move away again.

Reversible or amorphous processes (such as geographic mobility and union formation) are difficult to put in sensible logical order.[9] Cross-sectional data such as the U.S. census are especially ill-suited for distinguishing the order of reversible events. The census contains no information about when or how couples first met. My theory implicates the independent life stage in the rise of nontraditional unions, but the theory is not specific (and the census data do not allow specificity) about the precise order of events.

Geographic Mobility for Different Kinds of Intermarriage

Table 5.1 shows that geographic mobility is higher the more transgressive the type of couple, and it also shows that the relative geographic mobility of nontraditional couples has declined over time as the taboos against interraciality and homosexuality have softened in the United States. Figure 5.1 extends this analysis in several ways. Table 5.1 grouped all the interracial couples together. This is somewhat problematic. In U.S. society, the black-white unions have always been the most controversial, whereas other types of interracial unions such as unions between Hispanics and non-Hispanic whites have been much less stigmatized.[10] If geographic mobility were indeed a sign of and a response to societal taboo, we would expect black-white intermarried couples to be the most geographically mobile of the interracial couples.

Figure 5.1 shows the percentage of geographic mobility for black-white, Hispanic–non-Hispanic, and three types of same-race married couples for 1970–2000. The interracial couples were more geographically mobile than the same-race couples across all four censuses.[11] Among the same-race couples, blacks and whites had similar levels of

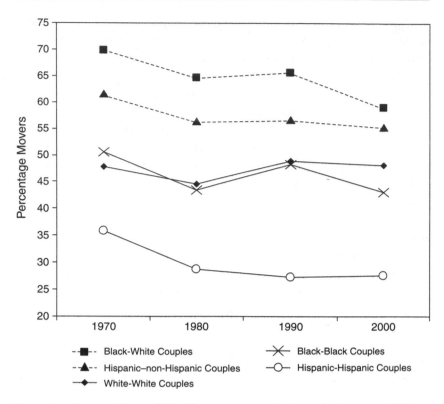

Figure 5.1. Geographic mobility for young married couples by race, 1970–2000. Source: 1970 1% census microdata, 1980–2000 weighted 5% census microdata via IPUMS. Blacks and whites exclude Hispanics. All individuals are ages 20–29 and U.S.-born.

geographic mobility, whereas Hispanic couples were by far the least geographically mobile type of couple. Hispanics are highly concentrated in just a few U.S. states (California, Texas, Florida, Illinois, New York), so it is not surprising that Hispanic couples should be more likely to settle in the birth state of both spouses. In 2000, only 27.5 percent of young Hispanic-Hispanic couples were geographically mobile, whereas 55.2 percent of the young Hispanic–non-Hispanic couples were geographically mobile.

Black-white married couples were the most geographically mobile type of couple across all four censuses (58.9 percent of young black-white couples were geographically mobile in 2000). The high level of geographic mobility of black-white couples is consistent with the hypothesized correlation between geographic mobility and the strength of the social taboo that couples transgress. In other words, black-white couples may be more geographically mobile than Hispanic–non-Hispanic couples because black-white couples are a more transgressive kind of racial pairing.

Nontraditional Unions and the City

American sociology has always recognized the importance of the city as a place where social, racial, ethnic, and sexual subcultures flourish.[12] The suburban dream of the 1950s was created as a retreat from everything the city had come to stand for: racial diversity, the presence of artists, bohemians, homosexuals, voyeurs, immigrants, the red-light districts, disorder, political corruption, crime, and a general lack of social control.

The modern city, with its anonymity and transient populations, is quite the opposite of the premodern rural community whose powerful systems of social control were based on intimate knowledge of one's neighbors' affairs and a communal web of interdependence and mutuality.[13] Of course, the modern city is not as diverse and disorderly as critics have described it, and the premodern community was not as consensual and communal as the historical myths made it out to be, but the differences are too great to be brushed aside.

Even scholars, such as Peter Laslett, who have been critical of the myths and assumptions about premodern life have recognized the vast difference in scale and lifestyle between the premodern community and the modern city.[14] In the late nineteenth century, when urbanization was taking place in the United States at a rapid pace, religious leaders and social reformers recognized urbanization as a threat to the sexual morals of the young. The reformers worked feverishly and successfully to build a new system of laws and reform organizations, from the Comstock Act of 1873 to the temperance movement, which attempted to re-impose social control on the behavior of urban young adults.[15]

Table 5.2 shows urbanization across the different types of unions for young U.S.-born couples. Among the young heterosexual same-race married couples (the "traditional" form), only 17.9 percent lived

Table 5.2 Urban residence for young couples by type of couple, 1990–2000

Type of couple	1990		2000	
	Percent living in city	Odds ratio of urban residence compared with (1)	Percent living in city	Odds ratio of urban residence compared with (1)
(1) Heterosexual, same-race, married	17.9		19.0	
(2) Heterosexual, same-race, cohabit	30.7	2.03***	29.8	1.81***
(3) Heterosexual, interracial, married and cohabit	30.7	2.03***	26.8	1.56***
(4) Same-sex, cohabit	56.6	5.97***	37.3	2.54***
(5) Same-sex, interracial, cohabit	#	#	54.0	5.01***

*** $p < .001$, two-tailed test.

Sources: 1% Metro Sample 1990, 5% sample 2000 census via IPUMS.

Note: All couples are composed of U.S.-born individuals, ages 20–29. Households whose urban status is unknown (a larger group in 2000 than in 1990) are excluded from the sample. Adjusted estimate for same-sex couples in 2000: urban residence = 43.7%.

Insufficient data.

in the urban areas in 1990. The rate of urbanization is even lower for heterosexual white married couples, but the relationship between nontraditional unions (heterosexual and same-sex cohabiting couples) and urban residence is the same for whites (see Appendix Table A.6). For heterosexual same-race cohabiting couples the rate of urban residence was 30.7 percent in 1990. For heterosexual interracial couples the rate of urban residence was also 30.7 percent in 1990. Same-sex couples were by far the most likely to live in the cities in 1990 (56.6 percent did so). Interracial same-sex couples, facing the dual stigmas of homosexuality and interraciality, were the type of couple most likely to live in the cities in 2000.[16] The urbanization of same-sex couples has been often suggested in the historical and ethnographic literature, but prior to the U.S. censuses of 1990 and 2000, little hard evidence was available.[17]

Same-race married couples seem to be repeating the residential patterns of their parents by retreating from or remaining away from urban areas. For young people in same-sex and interracial unions, the cities are the source of diversity, commonality, and mutual support. The need for commonality and mutual support is greatest among same-sex couples, whose families are most likely to reject them.[18]

Between 1990 and 2000, the relative urbanization of interracial and same-sex couples declined. For interracial couples, the decline was modest, from an odds ratio of 2.03 in 1990 to an odds ratio of 1.56 in 2000. For same-sex couples, the decline in relative urban concentration from 1990 to 2000 appears to be more dramatic whether one considers the full sample for 2000 or the adjusted sample, though comparisons of the 1990 and the 2000 same-sex data from the U.S. census must be made with caution.

The geography of gay life in the United States is an urban geography, but it is more than that—it is an urban geography with a strong concentration in a few major cities. The most well-known cultural meccas of gay life in the United States, especially gay male life, are Greenwich Village in New York, the Castro in San Francisco, West Hollywood in Los Angeles, and Boys Town in Chicago. In the 1950s, long before Stonewall and the modern gay rights movement, gay rights advocacy was undertaken furtively and cautiously in the major cities by the early homophile organizations. Harry Hay founded the Mattachine Society in Los Angeles in 1951. The Daughters of Bilitis was founded by a group of women in San Francisco in 1955.[19]

The local police harassed gays regularly and relentlessly, even in New York and San Francisco, well into the 1970s.[20] People who were arrested for dancing in gay bars or for soliciting sex in the park were rarely prosecuted but were often threatened with exposure and humiliation. In both New York and San Francisco, it was illegal for bars to serve alcohol to homosexuals until the late 1970s, but gay bars (especially Mafia-run gay bars that could pay bribes to the police) thrived anyway.[21] The Mattachine and the Daughters of Bilitis had a hard time finding members even in the major cities where there were established gay communities. Outside of the major cities gays were isolated, which is why gay-curious young people did whatever they could to find their way to the cities.

Harvey Milk (who would later go on to be the first openly gay elected official in San Francisco, and one of the first in the United States) was raised in suburban Long Island in the 1950s. Before he knew exactly why he was different, Milk knew that he *was* different, and he found himself getting away to New York City every chance he could. He explored the Metropolitan Opera, he met older gay men and younger gay hustlers, and he was initiated to sex in Central Park. As a young adult living in New York City, Harvey Milk was beyond the reach and social control of his parents. While working for a financial securities firm and keeping his sexual identity hidden from employers and coworkers, he was also able to build a social life for himself, complete with gay lovers and gay friends.[22]

Table 5.3 shows the leading metropolitan areas (including cities and surrounding suburbs) for same-sex cohabiting couples in the 2000 census, regardless of age or nativity. I have included all ages and all national origins of same-sex couples here because otherwise the unweighted counts (which are roughly 1/20 as large as the weighted counts) in each metropolitan area would be too small to make the rankings reliable. The list of metropolitan areas is unremarkable in several regards. New York, Los Angeles, and Chicago are the three largest metropolitan areas in the United States, and they are also at the top of the list for married couples, heterosexual cohabiting couples, and other union types. The San Francisco Bay Area is the metropolitan area with the highest concentration of same-sex cohabiting couples compared with heterosexual cohabiting couples.

Table 5.4 compares the metropolitan concentration of different

Table 5.3 Top 10 metropolitan areas in the United States by number of same-sex couples, 2000

Rank	Metropolitan area	Number of same-sex cohabiting couples
1	New York	47,603
2	Los Angeles	34,829
3	San Francisco	23,185
4	Chicago	20,293
5	Washington, D.C.	13,363
6	Atlanta	13,356
7	Dallas	12,912
8	Boston	12,475
9	Philadelphia	12,052
10	Houston	11,210
	(a) Total number of same-sex couples in top 10 metros	201,278
	(b) Total number of same-sex Couples in the United States	669,984
	(a/b) Proportion of same-sex couples who live in the top 10 metros for same-sex couples	30.0%

Source: Weighted 2000 5% microdata via IPUMS.

Note: Includes same-sex cohabiting couples of all ages and national origins. Metropolitan areas include cities and surrounding suburbs.

kinds of couples (regardless of age or country of birth) for 1990 and 2000. The metropolitan concentration of same-sex couples in 2000 was 30.0 percent, just as in Table 5.3. The metropolitan concentration of same-race married couples is lower; 23.1 percent of the traditional married couples lived in the ten largest metropolitan areas in 2000 (22.9 percent in 1990). The lists of ten largest metropolitan areas are similar between the groups; the main difference is that the nontraditional couples are more highly concentrated in those metropolitan areas. In 1990, 42.2 percent of the same-sex couples lived in the ten largest metropolitan areas. Between 1990 and 2000, the metropolitan concentration of same-sex couples declined sharply (the adjusted data for 2000 also show a decline from 1990). The decline in metropolitan concentration for same-sex couples (along with a small decline for interracial couples) is consistent with the findings of geographic mobility and urban concentration. Nontraditional couples, and especially

Table 5.4 Metropolitan concentration by type of couple, 1990–2000

	1990		2000	
Type of couple	Percent living in the top 10 metro areas for that group	Odds ratio of metropolitan concentration compared with (1)	Percent living in the top 10 metro areas for that group	Odds ratio of metropolitan concentration compared with (1)
(1) Heterosexual, same-race, married	22.9		23.1	
(2) Heterosexual, same-race, cohabit	25.4	1.14***	22.7	0.98***
(3) Heterosexual, interracial, married and cohabit	33.6	1.70***	30.1	1.44***
(4) Same-sex, cohabit	42.2	2.45***	30.0	1.43***
(5) Same-sex, interracial, cohabit	60.4	5.11***	40.3	2.25***

*** $p < .001$, two-tailed test.

Sources: Weighted 1% Metro Sample 1990, 5% sample 2000 census via IPUMS.

Note: Couples include individuals of all ages and all national origins. The list of top ten most populous metropolitan areas is different for each group and for each year, but the lists are similar. Metropolitan area definitions vary between censuses. Metropolitan areas include cities and surrounding suburbs. Adjusted estimate of metropolitan concentration for same sex couples in 2000: 33.9%, for same-sex interracial couples: 44.1%.

same-sex couples, are rapidly reintegrating themselves into smaller cities, small towns, suburbs, and rural areas. Whereas gay couples who live in the cosmopolitan cities have been out of the closet for decades, gays in the suburbs and in the rural hinterland are only now beginning to emerge from the closet. Same-sex couples are still over-represented in the urban areas and in the largest metropolitan areas, but the geographic and residential differences between same-sex couples and traditional heterosexual married couples are quietly and quickly disappearing.

A Multivariate Test of Geographic Mobility and Alternative Unions

I have hypothesized that geographic mobility of nontraditional couples reflects the effect of social taboos and social distance from family. The high degree of urbanization of same-sex and interracial couples suggests an alternative hypothesis: the apparent geographic mobility of nontraditional unions observed in Table 5.1 could be due to the pull of the great urban centers (New York, Los Angeles, Chicago, San Francisco) rather than the push of disapproving families. It could be the case, in other words, that interracial and same-sex couples are only more geographically mobile than traditional couples because of the attraction of and the diversity of the largest and most cosmopolitan American cities.

Alternatively, the theory of geographic mobility for nontraditional couples could apply generally. A general theory of geographic mobility implies that regardless of where they live, interracial and same-sex couples should be more geographically mobile than traditional same-race married couples. If distance from the family of origin is by itself important to nontraditional couples, then nontraditional couples should be especially mobile regardless of their destination.

There are several ways to test the relative influence of the push factors of family disapproval and the pull factors of the city on geographic mobility. One way is to compare the relative geographic mobility of traditional and nontraditional couples separately for urban, rural, and suburban destinations. I show in Appendix Table A.7 that interracial couples and same-sex couples are more geographically mobile than traditional same-race heterosexual married couples regardless of whether they live in the cities, in the suburbs, or in rural areas. This result bolsters the hypothesis that the elevated levels of geographic mobility for nontraditional couples are due to both the pull of the cities and the push of disapproving families.

Although analyzing geographic mobility separately for different destinations is useful, modern social science prefers to test key interactions (such as the interaction between geographic mobility and nontraditional unions) using multivariate regression, which allows for many potential confounders (urban residence, education, age) to be controlled simultaneously. Table 5.5 presents results of four such multivariate regressions.

The dependent variable in these regressions is geographic mobility for partnered men from the 2000 census. The key interaction is the odds ratio of geographic mobility for same-sex couples compared with heterosexual couples. When this odds ratio is significantly greater than one (as it is in all four models), it indicates that the men in

Table 5.5 Individual geographic mobility and same-sex unions for partnered men, from logistic regressions

	Model 1	Model 2	Model 3	Model 4
Odds ratio of geographic mobility × same-sex union	1.32***	1.37***	1.27***	1.28***
Additional controls:				
Education	yes	yes	yes	yes
Age	no	yes	yes	yes
Pct gay in current metro area	no	no	yes	yes
Urban residence	no	no	no	yes
df	8	15	16	17
Change in model chi-square (Δ −2LL)		2,512	4,220	3,820

$* p < .05$ $** p < .01$ $*** p < .001$, two-tailed test.

Source: Weighted 5% census 2000 microdata, via IPUMS. Unweighted N is 2,706,642. Geographically mobile men live in a different state from the state of their birth.

Note: Adjusted odds ratios (dual marital status recodes excluded) for geographic mobility's influence on same-sex cohabitation 1.59 (Model 1), 1.71 (Model 2), 1.58 (Model 3), 1.60 (Model 4); all statistically significant. Age and education are categorical variables, nine categories each. "Pct gay" is the percentage of adults in the respondent's metropolitan area who were in a same-sex union.

same-sex unions were significantly more geographically mobile than the men in heterosexual unions.

Model one controls for only the education of the men in the sample. Model two adds men's age as a control. Models three and four add controls for the presence of same-sex couples in each respondent's local metropolitan area and urban residence, respectively. Nontraditional couples have a special affinity for the cities, and the sexual identity diversity of the cities is one reason that gay couples are especially geographically mobile. Controlling for the exposure to potential gay partners and urban residence reduces the key odds ratio from 1.37 (model two) to 1.28 (model four). The similarity of the key odds ratio across models indicates that the association between geographic mobility and same-sex unions is largely independent of the powerful effects of education, age, exposure to other gays, and urban residence. In simple terms, individual characteristics (such as age and education) and the characteristics of the destination community explain some, but by no means all, of the association between same-sex unions and geographic mobility.[23]

Table 5.5 demonstrates the robustness of the association between geographic mobility and same-sex unions. Appendix Table A.8 presents these models in more detail, and Appendix Table A.9 presents a variety of different multivariate tests of this type, for different types of nontraditional unions, all with the same result. Even when education, age, metropolitan composition, and urban residence are taken into account, the association between geographic mobility and alternative unions remains strong and statistically significant. The basic result of Table 5.5 (that the association between alternative unions and geographic mobility is robust) is the same for other subpopulations, including white women, black men and women, and same-sex couples.[24]

Immigration and Nontraditional Unions

Tables 5.1, 5.2, and 5.5 included only U.S.-born persons because U.S. natives can be geographically either movers or stayers, whereas immigrants are all movers by definition. Although the U.S. census tells us nothing about the social contexts in which immigrants were raised, their international geographic mobility makes them an important test case. International immigrants are the ultimate geographic movers, leaving their families and the entire social networks of their youth behind to start new lives in a country whose social and sexual rules, not to speak of language, are likely to be different.

Epidemiologists have shown that human migration routes are the prime transmission routes for sexually transmitted diseases. International migration is a factor in diseases such as HIV because migrants tend to be poor and vulnerable, and also because migrants have left their families behind and are free to experiment sexually and socially in ways they would not or could not have had they remained in the community of their birth.[25] International migration, which is a strong form of geographic mobility, blunts the power of communal and familial social control and therefore leads to an increase in transgressive sexual encounters and nontraditional unions.

Although U.S. society has been hostile to gays in the past and U.S. immigration law has sought to exclude gay immigrants in the past on the grounds that homosexuality was a mental illness (a policy that remained in place until 1990),[26] most immigrants to the United States come from Latin America and Asia, where homosexuality may be even less well accepted than it is in the United States.[27] Many, though by no means all, gay immigrants have safer and more comfortable lives in the United States than they could have had in their communities of origin. In the Philippines, gay men are not persecuted as much as hidden from view. In New York City, the same Filipino gay men have more options in how they can express themselves, how they can be gay, and what kinds of partners they can find.[28] As Martin Manalansan writes, "Many Filipino gay men are able to do things [in New York] that they would never have done under the surveillance of family living nearby."[29] Just as gay Americans move from small towns to cities like San Francisco, New York, and Los Angeles to escape from disapproving families and antigay prejudice, so too might young gays in Asia or Latin America find immigration to the United States (and escape from oppressive conditions at home) especially attractive.[30]

International migration changes the economic relationship between young migrants and their families who remain in the sending country. Young gays and lesbians know that their choice of partners and companions might make it difficult for them to survive economically in their communities of origin, and it might make them an economic or social burden on their parents. In the United States, even immigrants with menial jobs earn enough money to remit something of value back to their families in Asia or Latin America. Parents become economically dependent on their children in the United States, and this economic dependence (along with the powerful social intermediary of geographic distance) diminishes familial disapproval and traditional social sanctions.[31]

Table 5.6 shows the percentage of cohabiting couples who are same-sex couples by nativity for 1990 and 2000. In both 1990 and 2000, the U.S., born couples were the least likely to be gay, the immigrant couples were most likely to be gay, and the mixed immigrant-native couples were intermediate in their probability of being gay. Immigration is correlated with homosexuality, as the theory of geographic mobility and social control predicts, because the sexuality of homosexuals from Asia and Latin America gives them an additional reason for immigrating to the United States.[32]

International migration and international geographic mobility both tend to increase the number of nontraditional unions. There is, however, one interesting difference. The association between interstate mobility and nontraditional couples *declined* sharply from 1990 to 2000 (see Table 5.1). The preferential migration of homosexuals to

Table 5.6 Rates of homosexuality by nativity for young cohabiters, 1990–2000

	1990		2000	
Type of couple	Percent gay	Odds ratio of homosexuality compared with (1)	Percent gay	Odds ratio of homosexuality compared with (1)
(1) Both U.S.-born	2.73		4.82	
(2) One partner U.S.-born, one partner immigrant	3.29	1.21***	6.32	1.33***
(3) Both partners immigrants	3.93	1.46***	8.48	1.83***

* $p < .05$ ** $p < .01$ *** $p < .001$, two-tailed test.

Sources: Weighted 1990 and 2000 5% microdata via IPUMS, cohabiting couples ages 20–29.

Note: Alternative estimate of percent gay for 2000 (dual marital status recodes excluded): U.S.-born couples, 3.02%; mixed immigrant-native couples, 3.82%; dual immigrant couples, 3.64%.

the United States seems to have *increased* at the same time, or held roughly steady if one relies on the alternative values for 2000. According to Table 5.6, in 1990 the odds of being gay for immigrant cohabiters was 1.46 times as high as that for U.S.-born couples, but by 2000 this had increased to 1.83 times as high.

The difference reveals something interesting about the relative acceptance of gays in different places. In the United States, same-sex couples are becoming less geographically mobile, a change that is consistent with the outward spread of tolerance toward homosexuals from the largest cities to the suburbs and the rural areas. The hypothesized increase in tolerance of homosexuality in the United States (a subject I return to in Chapter 7) has had the opposite effect for international migrants. The tolerance gap (that is, the difference in social tolerance toward gays) between the United States and Latin America and Asia may now be greater than it has ever been, and the preferential migration of homosexuals might be expected to increase as a result, though the evidence is mixed on this point.

When it comes to interracial unions and immigration, the picture is completely different. Gender is a category that is reasonably consistent from society to society; race is not. In the United States, we have a racial categorization system that treats Mexicans or Chinese each as one race, whereas within those societies there are internal racial differences that are obvious within that society but invisible to the U.S. audience.[33] In addition, the gender balance between men and women is roughly even in most societies, whereas the racial distribution (however one defines race) fluctuates wildly between nations.

Because most of the post-1965 immigration to the United States has come from Latin America and Asia,[34] and because current practice in the United States defines Hispanics and Asians as separate races (or in the case of Hispanics, a separate ethnic group) from the numerically dominant non-Hispanic white native population of the United States, it follows by how race is defined that unions between natives and immigrants to the United States should have a high rate of what I define as interraciality. Table 5.7 shows that among young couples in the United States in 1990, 28.2 percent of the mixed immigrant-native couples were interracial, and this rose slightly to 30.3 percent in 2000. Interraciality for U.S.-born couples was much lower, 6.3 percent in 1990 and 10.3 percent in 2000.

Table 5.7 Rates of interraciality by nativity for young couples, 1990–2000

Type of couple	1990		2000	
	Percent interracial	Odds ratio of interraciality compared with (1)	Percent interracial	Odds ratio of interraciality compared with (1)
(1) Both U.S. born	6.3		10.3	
(2) One partner U.S. born, One partner immigrant	28.2	5.86***	30.3	3.80***
(3) Both partners immigrants	2.9	0.44***	3.1	0.28***

* $p < .05$ ** $p < .01$ *** $p < .001$, two-tailed test.

Sources: 1990 and 2000 5% weighted microdata via IPUMS, cohabiting and married couples ages 20–29.

Note: Interracial couples have partners with different races, where race is defined by the four categories, non-Hispanic white, non-Hispanic black, Hispanic, non-Hispanic Asian and all others (including those who identify as multiracial in 2000).

When U.S.-born young adults in the independent life stage travel to or work in Asia, Africa, or Latin America, they are exposed to populations whose racial profile differs from the U.S. population. In the past, Americans who traveled abroad were likely to be men in the military, whose experiences of foreign countries were mediated by a military hierarchy that discouraged marriage to local women. Despite the official disapproval of the military, many American soldiers stationed abroad returned to the United States with wives, and many of these marriages were interracial.[35] Now, in an age of global tourism, young American men and women are more likely to travel abroad without the powerful constraints of the U.S. military, and these travels abroad often result in interracial unions, which are captured in the U.S. census when the couple moves to the United States.

Our socially constructed racial classification system does not recognize the internal racial divisions of other peoples. Ignorance in the United States about the differences between the Asian national cultures (China, Japan, Korea, the Philippines), which have different languages, different religious systems, and a mutual history of war and colonization, forces those divergent national identities into an amalgamated pan-ethnic "Asian" identity in the United States.[36] As a result of the inevitable national myopia in our system of racial classification (myopia that misclassifies all Chinese, for instance, as one race), immigrant couples (couples composed of two immigrants) have the lowest rates of interraciality.

Because the traditional patriarchal family system retains more influence in most of Latin America and Asia (compared with the United States), immigration to the United States from these immigrant-sending areas can take on a character of social emancipation.[37] Female immigrants who migrate to the United States with their husbands may use the different social climate in the United States to renegotiate gender roles within the family.[38] Immigration increases the chances that the migrants will form interracial or same-sex unions, or flout other standards of family behavior that are traditional in their places of origin. This does not mean that immigration to the United States is necessarily a pathway to social liberation; thousands of women and children are trafficked to the United States for prostitution every year, and millions of other immigrants experience a grinding poverty that severely limits their social options.[39] Some women who migrate with their husbands find that their linguistic and social isolation makes them even more dependent on their husbands than they were in their country of origin.[40] Despite the dangers of migration, especially for economically disadvantaged migrants, immigration is associated with nontraditional unions because immigration, like geographic mobility in general, frees migrants from the social control of their parents and extended families.

Education and Nontraditional Unions

There are a variety of theoretical reasons for assuming that nontraditional unions should be more common among persons with higher levels of education. First, Milton Gordon argued that intellectuals were much less closely tied to their (historical and provincial) racial identities, and therefore they would more easily marry across racial lines.[41] Second, research on attitudes has consistently found that for whites, higher social class is associated with lower levels of anti-black opinions and affect.[42] Third, college education provides skills that provide students with access to jobs that give them greater independence from their parents. Fourth, college attendance itself usually implies residential independence from parents and, therefore, reduced parental surveillance. Fifth, higher education can promote a humanistic and universalistic ethos that undermines provincial divisions between groups. Sixth, the presence of gay studies on some college campuses could increase the likelihood of gay students coming "out."

There are, however, also reasons why college education might suppress nontraditional unions. First, some scholars have argued that higher education promotes conformity and a sense of entitlement rather than truly liberal beliefs.[43] In this view the apparent liberalism of the college-educated is just a mirage; college-educated persons simply have a more sophisticated sense of how sensitive questions about subjects such as race are supposed to be answered. Second, ethnic and racial studies on college campuses could increase nationalism for minority groups, which might discourage interracial dating. Third, blacks and Hispanics have lower rates of college attendance than whites and Asians, so higher education reduces some types of interracial exposure and therefore also reduces the opportunity for certain kinds of interracial unions.

Table 5.8 shows the percentage of different types of young couples who had at least one spouse or partner with some college education in 1990 and 2000. Among young heterosexual same-race married couples, 61.7 percent had at least one spouse with some college education in 1990, and due to the general increase in access to higher education, 66.2 percent had at least one spouse with some college education in 2000.

Young heterosexual same-race cohabiting couples had slightly lower educational attainment than traditional same-race married couples (57.3 percent in 1990, 64.3 percent in 2000, odds ratios significantly less than one). Heterosexual same-race cohabiting couples are less likely to have been to college because cohabitation is a precursor for marriage and therefore might predate college attendance for some couples, and because cohabitation is a substitute for marriage for some couples who are not financially secure enough to marry.

Young interracial couples had slightly elevated levels of college attendance compared with traditional same-race married couples.[44] Same-sex couples were substantially more likely to have at least one partner with a college education in 1990, though by 2000 the education gap between heterosexual couples and gay couples had narrowed considerably. Interracial same-sex couples, the most transgres-

Table 5.8 College attendance for young couples by type of couple, 1990–2000

	1990		2000	
Type of couple	Percent at least one partner has been to college	Odds ratio of college attendance compared with (1)	Percent at least one partner has been to college	Odds ratio of college attendance compared with (1)
(1) Heterosexual, same-race, married	61.7		66.2	
(2) Heterosexual, same-race, cohabit	57.3	0.84***	64.3	0.92***
(3) Heterosexual, interracial, married and cohabit	64.3	1.12***	71.8	1.30***
(4) Same-sex, cohabit	78.3	2.25***	69.0	1.14***
(5) Same-sex, interracial, cohabit	88.7	4.88***	81.6	2.26***

* $p < .05$ ** $p < .01$ *** $p < .001$, two-tailed tests.

Sources: 1990 and 2000 5% census microdata, via IPUMS.

Note: Couples have husband or head of householder ages 20–29, wife or partner any age, partners and spouses of all native origins and races are included. Alternative estimate of college attendance (dual marital status recodes excluded) for same-sex couples in 2000: 73.8% for all same sex couples, 82.8% for interracial same-sex couples.

sive kind of couples, were also by far the most educated kind of couples in 1990 and in 2000.[45]

Consider the story of Brett, one of my interviewees. Brett is a gay white man who was raised in rural Georgia in the late 1970s and early 1980s. His grandfather had been in the Ku Klux Klan. Brett knew at the beginning of adolescence that he was attracted to other boys, but he also knew that it would be impossible to be gay in his small town. As Brett says, "There were plenty of clues in the common culture of where I grew up to tell me that being gay was really wrong." Brett's mother was a housewife who had always wanted to get a college education but had never been allowed to. When Brett was a young teenager, his parents divorced and Brett's mother began saving money to send Brett to college. When Brett was eighteen, he moved to Atlanta and began attending college, and his life changed.

> I was so ready to get away from home. For me it was just liberty. It was a revolution. I had the good fortune that my mom wanted to help me go to college. She made a lot of sacrifices to send me to college. And I worked part time summers and through some of the course work but mostly I didn't have to. My mother made college happen for me. And it didn't happen for my brothers—she couldn't do it again. But she made it happen for me. But for me, going to college was—it was liberty. It was total change of life . . .
>
> So it was an urban environment versus a rural environment. Rural isolation versus urban mania. It was hugely different, radically different. It was a complete shift. Since I could drive—since age sixteen I was going with my high school friends into Atlanta—midnight movies, hanging out, um, Atlanta was an hour away—it's what we did. So as soon as I was able I knew I wanted to live in the city. And I went to school, lived in dormitories downtown, and it was like living in the city. So I had complete liberty. I didn't have to take care of my brothers. I was alone for the first time. I had absolute liberty. I could choose what I wanted to do and I just totally loved it.
>
> Question: What did you find at college that had been lacking where you grew up?
>
> Humanity. Urban culture. Um . . . I could go to a bar because drinking age was eighteen, so I could go to a bar. Um, and just my

classmates. In my class there were kids from all over the USA. People from all over! I met Jews, I met Catholics. We talked about the difference in religion, difference in culture. I met people from Seattle, from Chicago *[says with a Chicago accent]* . . .

There was definitely a gay culture in my college and at the university [in the 1980s]. And it was fairly open. Um, there were very flamboyant students at my college. And I thought, oh, they're really out. They're really over the top. So that was my chance to really get in touch with the gay community. The different bars have their little cliques. I kind of learned about, you know, the subcultures within the gay culture. You know, there's leather and there's disco and there's preppy and there's— there's no rock and roll; you have to go somewhere else for rock and roll. But there were gay people there too; it was just more mixed and it was—it was a whole new adventure. Learning about my gayness and about other gay people.

As in the case of geographic mobility, as the population of "out" same-sex couples has grown from 1990 to 2000, the profile of the same-sex couples has become more similar to that of same-race married couples. Between 1990 and 2000, the average educational attainment of the young same-sex couples declined, while the average educational attainment of same-race married couples increased. As a result of these two trends, the educational gap between traditional heterosexual same-race married couples and same-sex couples was narrow (though still statistically significant) in 2000.[46] Another explanation for this trend is that as U.S. society becomes more tolerant of homosexuals, gay couples who are middle class and working class are increasingly able to be "out," whereas in the past only the more financially secure gay couples had the confidence to be "out."

Gay Couples and Interraciality

By treating both same-sex unions and interracial unions as two consequences of the independent life stage, I am explicitly arguing that these two kinds of unions, usually analyzed separately, are part of the same fabric of family and social change. This does not imply that individuals experience homosexuality and interracial unions in similar ways or that homosexual desire and interracial desire are correlated.

Racial segregation may be just as powerful within the gay community as outside of it. Tolerance for homosexual rights in the United States appears to be lower in the black and Hispanic communities, for instance, than in the white community.[47]

In their ethnographic study of the lesbian community of Buffalo, New York, Kennedy and Davis argued that lesbians were more tolerant of and more likely to participate in interracial unions than the wider Buffalo society.[48] Kennedy and Davis implied that the lesbians' willingness to date interracially derived from the women's experience with surviving the consequences of breaching the norm of heterosexuality. In Kennedy and Davis's view, being gay made the lesbians of Buffalo social outsiders, and being social outsiders made them less averse to dating across racial lines. However, several of my gay and racially nonwhite interviewees complained that the racial divisions within the gay community mirrored the racial divisions of the wider society. One gay black man with a white husband complained that political meetings to promote marriage equality were nearly all white and that no effort was made to diversify the movement. He attended one meeting, surveyed the crowd, and remarked: "Excuse me, it's looking very pale in here. . . . I mean it's not the same people who are outwardly discriminatory but it can get very 'holier than thou.' And I say look fellas, where are the women? Where are the Asians? Where are the transgenders?"

Even if being gay had no effect on an individual's view of race, there are several structural reasons why same-sex unions might be more likely to be interracial. Same-sex unions and interracial unions are both associated with geographic mobility and urban residence. The family pressure and community norms that suppress interracial unions and same-sex unions may not be the same pressures and norms, but they are overcome in the same manner—by moving away. Leaving home, going away to college and then moving to the city nullifies the traditional familial barriers to all types of transgressive unions. Same-sex unions and interracial unions may be correlated because both types of nontraditional union are correlated with the independent life stage. The independent life stage may not alter individual mate preferences, but it does alter the set of potential mates to which the young adult is exposed. Young adults who enjoy the freedoms of the independent life stage are more able to mate with a

also due to cruising for ♂ too more limited pool

what gender breakdown?

partner despite parental disapproval. The correlation between inter-raciality and homosexuality is not a correlation of desires, but rather a correlation of structural opportunities.

Table 5.9 shows the percentage of couples in each group that were interracial. Among young heterosexual married couples in 1990, 5.68 percent were interracial compared with 9.64 percent for heterosexual cohabiting couples and 14.52 percent for same-sex couples. The odds of being interracial were 2.82 times as high for same-sex couples as for heterosexual married couples in 1990. The odds ratio is symmet-rical, meaning that the odds of being in a same-sex couple were 2.82 times higher for interracial couples than for same-race couples in 1990. The association between interraciality and same-sex couples sup-ports the contention that the two kinds of nontraditional unions have a common root in the independent life stage.

Between 1990 and 2000, the interraciality of young heterosexual couples increased sharply, and the interraciality of same-sex couples declined from 14.52 percent to 12.41 percent (the adjusted same-sex sample shows a less significant decline) so that the gap in interraciality between same-sex couples and heterosexual couples was much lower in 2000 than in 1990. If we think of heterosexual cohabitation as being a trial period before marriage, it makes sense that family pres-sure and social norms would intervene to reduce the percentage of interracial couples who go on to marry. If we think of heterosexual cohabitation as an alternative kind of union in its own right, with greater geographic mobility and much greater urban concentration than heterosexual married couples, it follows that heterosexual co-habiting couples should be more likely to be in interracial unions compared with heterosexual married couples.[49]

Age at Marriage and Interracial Unions

In Chapter 2, I suggested that increased age at first marriage was associated with extended independence of young adults and de-creased parental control. Unfortunately, the 1990 and 2000 censuses did not include questions about age at first marriage or even number of times married. In order to test the relationship between age at marriage and nontraditional unions, one has to go back to the 1980 census, since the 1980 census did record age of first marriage for all

Table 5.9 Rates of interracial unions for young couples by type of couple, 1990–2000

| | 1990 | | 2000 | |
Type of couple	Percent interracial	Odds ratio of interraciality compared with (1)	Percent interracial	Odds ratio of interraciality compared with (1)
(1) Heterosexual, married	5.68		9.06	
(2) Heterosexual, cohabit	9.64	1.77***	14.02	1.64***
(3) Same-sex, cohabit	14.52	2.82***	12.41	1.42***

* $p < .05$ ** $p < .01$ *** $p < .001$, two-tailed test.

Sources: Weighted 1990 and 2000 5% microdata via IPUMS.

Note: All couples are composed of U.S.-born individuals, ages 20–29. Interracial couples have partners with different races, where race is defined by the four categories; non-Hispanic white, non-Hispanic black, Hispanic, non-Hispanic Asian and all others (including those who identify as multiracial in 2000). Percentage of interraciality for all heterosexual couples (a weighted average of categories 1 and 2): 6.21% in 1990, and 10.19% in 2000. Adjusted estimate (dual marital status recodes excluded) for same-sex couples in 2000: 14.25% interracial.

persons who had ever been married.[50] In order to control for the changing social climate of racial attitudes, I examine U.S.-born men and women who were recently married at the time of the 1980 census, that is, couples who were married for the first time in the 1970s. Two alternative hypotheses are possible:

On the one hand, if parental control is a key factor in promoting traditional same-race marriage, and if parental control wanes as young adults spend more time in post–secondary education and living away from home, then later age at first marriage should be associated with a higher percentage of interracial marriages.

On the other hand, studies of attitudes in the United States suggest the opposite hypothesis. Studies of attitudes about race demonstrate that racial tolerance is inversely associated with age.[51] The older the person, the earlier the birth cohort, the less receptive the person is likely to be toward civil rights for minorities. The literature on individual racial attitudes suggests that the youngest people should be the most likely to form interracial unions.

Figure 5.2 shows the percentage of first marriages that are interracial for U.S.-born men and women who married for the first time in the 1970s. As before, interracial here means marriage across the racial groups of non-Hispanic white, non-Hispanic black, Hispanic, Asian and others. The patterns for both men and women show relatively low rates of interraciality for couples who married young. Only about 4.5 percent of marriages were interracial if the husband or wife was a teenager at marriage, or ages 20–24. For individuals who married in their late twenties, early thirties, or late thirties, the rate of interraciality was significantly higher. For women, the probability of interraciality peaked at 5.4 percent for those who were in their early thirties at first marriage. For men, the rate of interraciality peaked at 6.8 percent for those who were in their late thirties at first marriage.

The median age of first marriage for U.S.-born women in the 1970s was roughly twenty-two years, and for men the median age was roughly twenty-four years (see Chapter 3, Figure 3.6). Those who were substantially older than the median age at first marriage were more likely to be in an interracial marriage, up to a point. For the small number of individuals who married for the first time in their forties or fifties, the percent of interracial marriages declined sharply. The inverted U-shaped curves of Figure 5.2 provide some support for both hypotheses

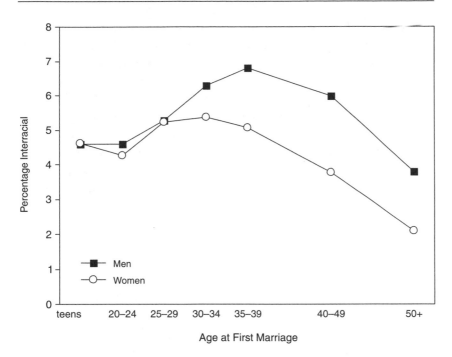

Figure 5.2. Interracial marriages for U.S.-born men and women married for the first time in the 1970s, by age at marriage. Source: 1980 5% census microdata via IPUMS. Interracial marriage is any marriage between the four racial groups: non-Hispanic white, non-Hispanic black, Hispanic, and Asian and all others.

about age and interracial marriage. In the age groups in which first marriage was most likely, increasing age at marriage was associated with more interracial marriage, which supports the theory of declining parental control with later age at marriage.[52]

By a certain age (the mid thirties) young adults are as independent from their parents and families as they ever will be. Beyond the age of full adulthood increasing age does not make much difference in independence from family, but the cohort effect on racial attitudes comes into play.[53] The lower rates of interracial marriage for the oldest marriage cohorts supports the hypothesis that individuals from earlier birth cohorts (in this case cohorts that came of age before the civil rights movement) would be less open to interracial unions.

Even though surveys of racial attitudes show that young people are the most liberal on issues of race, Figure 5.2 shows that the youngest married couples are *not* the most likely to be interracial. The reason that young married couples are relatively less likely to be interracial is that marriage outcomes are a function of more than individual tastes and preferences. Marriage outcomes are also a function of the potential mates to which a person is exposed, the implicit or explicit family pressure to choose a certain type of mate, and the young person's ability or willingness to be independent from family pressure. Individual mate selection choices are, in other words, embedded within families and communities.

Changes in attitudes are not sufficient by themselves to explain the rise of interracial and same-sex unions, for two reasons. First, one must still explain the source of the changing attitudes. Second, research on attitudes about race and homosexuality views these attitudes as coming fundamentally from *individuals*. Granovetter has argued that binary exchanges between presumably independent individual actors could not be understood without considering the web of norms and network ties (both historical and expected) in which each individual actor was embedded.[54] Granovetter's "embeddedness" argument is a classic sociological argument because it emphasizes the importance of social context even for interactions that appear to involve only two people. Mate selection often appears to be a simple binary agreement between two partners, but any study of mate selection patterns quickly reveals the powerful underlying effects of social structure and social context. Children are socialized to race and heterosexuality primarily by their family, and children are embedded in a physical and social environment chosen by their parents. Mate selection depends on exposure and opportunity as well as on individual preferences and attitudes.[55]

Mates come from a field of potential or eligible candidates.[56] For sociology, the most interesting question is not how individuals select their mates from among the field of eligibles—that conscious selection among explicit options is grist for advice columns and popular dramas. The more interesting question is how the small field of eligibles arises, as if by magic, from the vast sea of a national or even world population.

When we think of mate selection, we usually think of how the mate was selected from the small field of eligibles. The eligibles include friends, friends of friends, colleagues, neighbors, schoolmates, other members of the church choir, and coworkers—in other words the people whom one might know well enough to fall in love with. At any one time, the field of eligible mates might number in the dozens or, perhaps, as many as a hundred. Because modern life and the independent life stage afford young people the opportunity to choose their mates fairly freely from among the small field of eligibles, scholars and writers have wrongly assumed that love and compatibility were the only criteria for mate selection in the modern era.[57] In fact, the usually invisible filter that reduces a racially heterogeneous population of millions to a more racially homogenous field of several dozen eligibles is a much more selective filter than the filter that selects one mate from several dozen eligible candidates. The more selective first filter, which creates the field of eligibles from the general population, is the filter of social structure. This first filter represents the effects of racial segregation, gender role expectations, economic class, geographic region, religion, age, national origin, and other social structural forces that affect our lives but whose real impact is often invisible to us.

Conclusions

The independent life stage is a relatively new stage in the life course, which is reshaping the social fabric by promoting diversity in the kinds of romantic unions that young people form. Whereas the acknowledged and accepted American couples of the past were nearly always same-race heterosexual couples, in the late twentieth century, interracial and same-sex couples have become visible and important minorities.

The idea of social control and parental control as a limiting factor in mate selection runs through many distinct social science literatures, but it has rarely been quantified or empirically tested.[58] The literature on same-sex unions has devoted the most attention to the theory of social and parental control, but the attention has been historical and ethnographic rather than quantitative.[59] There are historical discus-

sions of parental control over mate selection in the literature on interracial unions and the literature on gender and family history.[60]
Literature on the family in the American colonies takes the question
of parental and social control as a central theme, but these studies
simply do not have data on the different kinds of marital outcomes
for the children.[61] The fabric of social control was so much stronger
in the colonial family than in the modern family that even if good
data were available on marriage choices in the colonies, few, if any,
interracial unions and same-sex unions would be registered. My analysis provides the beginning of a quantitative empirical basis for long-
standing theories and speculations about social control, family control, and nontraditional unions.

Elizabeth Bott studied twenty families with small children around
London in the 1950s.[62] In Bott's research, "traditional" couples were
couples whose husband worked and whose wife stayed home to care
for children, clean the house, and prepare meals. Nontraditional couples had more egalitarian or more varied sex roles. Bott found that
the nontraditional couples were almost always geographically farther
away from where they had grown up, and they had much less contact
with their extended families and the social networks of their youth.
Traditional couples tended to settle near where they had grown up,
which embedded them in the dense social network of family and
friends. The dense social network reinforced traditional norms and
made it much harder for couples to deviate from what was expected
of them. Bott's research was intensive, but her sample was small, and
she expressed hope that subsequent research would subject her con-
clusions to quantitative testing.

My intention is to use the enormous sample size and historical span
of the U.S. census to create empirical tests of theories that have not
previously been tested on large nationally representative samples and
to draw the different theoretical perspectives and different disciplinary views of the family together. Interracial unions and same-sex
unions have been separately studied by different scholars who apply
different theoretical frameworks. Yet both interracial unions and
same-sex unions are nontraditional kinds of families that the social
structure effectively suppressed in the past. Interracial unions and
same-sex unions share a common root in the independent life stage;
that is why same-sex unions are more likely to be interracial, and

interracial unions are more likely to be same-sex unions. The parental controls and social controls that in the past prevented gay people from being "out" were fundamentally the same kinds of parental controls and social structures that prevented people from choosing mates of another race. Individuals who experience the independent life stage, who live on their own, who travel, who support themselves, who postpone marriage, and who have access to higher education are individuals who have greater exposure to different kinds of potential mates and greater ability to choose a mate over the objections of their parents.

The more independent and geographically mobile young people are, the more likely they are to be involved in a nontraditional union. Same-race heterosexual married couples are the least geographically mobile. Heterosexual cohabiting couples are more geographically mobile than same-race married couples. Interracial couples are more geographically mobile than same-race couples. Same-sex couples are even more geographically mobile and interracial same-sex couples are the most geographically mobile. Compared with U.S. natives, immigrants are more likely to be in a same-sex relationship.

Although nontraditional couples are drawn to the urban cores of the largest and most cosmopolitan U.S. cities, geographic mobility is not *only* a result of the attraction of the great cities. Nontraditional couples are geographically mobile in part because they are moving away from disapproving parents and extended families. There is, in other words, an important "push" effect. Even in rural areas, nontraditional couples are more likely to have moved away from the state of their birth. The association between geographic mobility and nontraditional unions is robust. Multivariate tests show that the association between geographic mobility and nontraditional unions remains strong and statistically significant even when controlling for age, education, urban residence, and exposure to potential nontraditional partners.

The evidence of a strong correlation between geographic mobility and transgressive unions sheds some light on the forces that underlie the formation of couples and, therefore, on the nature of social reproduction. Parents not only are responsible for the direct socialization of their young children, but they also play a role in selecting the schools and neighborhoods in which secondary socialization takes place. If one wants to understand how social norms and traditions are reproduced from generation to generation, one must start with the family. The key transitional moment in the cyclical pattern of social reproduction is the moment when young adults start their own families. In the past, this transitional moment was carefully controlled by law and custom and by direct intervention of the parents. In the age of the independent life stage, parents have lost much of their ability to influence their children's choice of mate. The loss of parental control has led to the growth of same-sex unions and interracial unions, the kind of unions that were never permitted in the past.

By saying that same-sex unions and interracial unions were prohibited in the past, I do not mean to suggest that there were no homosexual or interracial sexual relations in the past. On the contrary, human expressions of sexuality have always found ways to transgress against social norms and values. In the past, however, interracial couples and same-sex couples or partners were unacknowledged and hidden from view. When slave masters had sexual relations with their slaves, the masters generally did not acknowledge their mixed-race progeny, and the old South created a legal and social system based on the "one drop rule" to ensure that children of mixed race or uncertain race parentage could not be considered "white."[63] Similarly, most adult homosexual activity in the past was carried on furtively by people who were married or quietly and carefully by adults who remained unmarried. That is to say, most adult homosexual activity took place in what we now euphemistically call "the closet." Transgressive sexual relations were not so menacing to the social order as long as the social stigma against the behavior was strong enough to force the transgressors to be nearly invisible.

Between 1990 and 2000, the geographic mobility and urbanization of same-sex couples in the United States appear to have declined sharply, though the data are not entirely comparable. The geographic mobility and urban concentration of heterosexual cohabiting couples declined from 1990 to 2000. From 1970 to 2000, the geographic mobility of interracial couples also declined. The pattern of declining geographic mobility and declining urban concentration of transgressive couples over time suggests that the strength of social stigma against cohabitation, interraciality, and homosexuality have declined in the United States. Not only are the numbers of nontraditional couples growing, but also American families seem to be less inclined to expel and marginalize and disown their children who take nontraditional mates. The American family (and therefore American society) seems to be becoming not only more diverse but also more tolerant. If American society is indeed becoming more tolerant of transgression, it is natural to ask why.

SIX

Childhood

THE RISE OF THE INDEPENDENT LIFE STAGE is a natural explanation for the new diversity of families and unions, since mate selection often takes place while young adults are living independently, traveling away from home, and enjoying their freedom. The rise of nontraditional unions in the United States is certainly important, but the vast majority of romantic unions are still of the traditional type: same-race heterosexual marriages. What is the effect of the independent life stage on the general population, most of whom will never be part of an alternative union? In this chapter, I extend the discussion of the independent life stage by exploring the effects of the independent life stage on the relationship between parents and children.

The family is a small society. There are rules, the parents are the leaders, and the children are the followers. The experience of the small and personalistic society of the family is the child's first and most influential preparation for the child's eventual participation as an adult in the wider society. This does not mean that childhood socialization is necessarily functional, because parents have never had an easy time determining which skills and ideas will serve their children best as adults, nor do parents necessarily know how to teach those required skills or instill the proper ideas in their children. Nonetheless, parents have usually understood their role as, in part, preparing their children for the future, and so parental socialization of children is usually *intended* to have a functional purpose.

Because effective childhood socialization is designed to prepare children for the specific adult reality envisioned by their parents, changes in the adult world are usually accompanied by changes in childhood socialization. Although it is not easy to compare child-rearing practices across time, between cultures, or even between social classes in the same time and place, the way societies socialize children (and the way that socialization of children changes over time) has much to teach us about the nature of society (and how society changes).[1]

In the individual life course, childhood precedes adolescence, which precedes adulthood. An individual's childhood experience influences that individual's outlook as an adult. At the familial or societal level, the arrow of intergenerational influence points in the other direction: parents and adult society in general shape the lives of children to conform to the parents' expectations. Social changes in adulthood generally precede social changes in childhood, because childhood is structured and managed by adults. As young adults have become more independent from their parents, parenting styles have changed as well, in order to prepare children for the independent life stage. Scholars have described a general trend in parenting strategies over time, from patriarchal and authoritarian to more permissive and tolerant.[2] I hypothesize that the independent life stage influences parents to raise their children with more tolerance and permissiveness because their parenting goal is a relatively new goal: to produce independent young adults.[3]

The parent-child relationship in the United States began changing in interesting ways beginning around 1960, as the independent life stage was emerging. For instance, the modern awakening of interest in child abuse can be dated to a landmark 1962 article by C. Henry Kempe in the *Journal of the American Medical Association*.[4] Kempe and his colleagues attempted to show that a wide range of childhood injuries that had previously been inexplicable were actually due to physical abuse by parents and guardians. In Kempe's view, the cause of the injuries had remained mysterious because physicians could not bring themselves to think that the parents were responsible for such injuries. Following Kempe's seminal article, laws were passed and bureaucracies were created (such as the 1973 U.S. Child Abuse Prevention and Treatment Act and the National Center on Child Abuse and Neglect) to intervene into the family and protect children from potential abuse by parents.[5]

Child Rearing in the Colonies

Modern scholarship usually views the preindustrial family as an authoritarian and patriarchal productive unit with less room for the kinds of love, affection, and companionship that constitute the ideal (if not the reality) for modern couples.[6] In addition to child labor, infanticide was common in premodern times, and physical discipline that would now be viewed as child abuse may also have been common.[7] The Puritans, who had a special flair for rigorous discipline, were known to tie restless children into balls and kick them and to force children to wear pointed sticks that jabbed them as a constant reminder of their misdeeds, among other creative punishments; older children were simply whipped.[8]

Cotton Mather, one of Puritan New England's most influential figures, quoted and endorsed the biblical passages from the Book of Proverbs that encouraged parents to discipline their children with the rod or the whip, but he urged that the blows should be given not in anger but with calm conviction and dedication to the task at hand.

> Yea, there may be occasion for you, to consider that word of God, in Prov 13:24, He that spareth his rod, hateth his son, but he that loveth him, chasteneth him betimes; and that Word, in Prov 19:18, Chasten thy son while there is hope, and let not thy soul spare for his crying; and that word, in Prov 23:13 Withold not correction from the child; for if thou beatest him with the rod, he shall not dy; thou shalt beat him with the rod, and shalt deliver his soul from hell. But if it must be so, remember this council; never give a blow in passion. Stay till your passion is over; and let the offenders plainly see that you deal thus with them, out of pure obedience unto God, and for their true repentance.[9]

The theology of the Puritans insisted that children were inherently devilish and disobedient, and therefore they were in need of strict correction.[10] "Your children are born with deadly wounds of sin upon their souls. . . . There is a corrupt nature in thy children, which is a fountain of all wickedness and confusion."[11]

For colonial parents like Cotton Mather, strictness and physical correction were part of the nurturing role of parenthood. Colonial parents could not properly prepare their children for adulthood without instilling in them a degree of obedience and deference to their elders. There were in the colonies, just as there are today, parents who abused their children and treated them with profound cruelty. For most colonial parents, however, the application of physical correction to children was not only normative but also it was a direct consequence of parental concern for the children's welfare, and all members of the family would have understood it as such.[12]

The Quakers of the colonial Delaware Valley had a less punitive view of child rearing than the Puritans. Unlike the Puritans of New England or the Anglicans of Virginia, the Quakers avoided putting their children into servitude, choosing instead to keep their children with their parents. The Quakers, who were among North America's first pacifists and opponents of slavery, had an unusually egalitarian and permissive domestic life. George Keith sparked a schism among American Quakers in the late seventeenth century in part by demanding that Quakers impose stricter discipline over their children, but Keith's demands for greater rigor and discipline were eventually rebuffed by Quaker leaders in the Delaware Valley. The permissive Quaker view of child rearing was, however, a rather isolated exception to the general social custom of strict discipline punctuated by occasional "physical correction," which was the custom in most of England's colonial possessions in North America.[13]

Child Rearing in the Nineteenth Century

In the late nineteenth century, family reformers led by temperance activists and feminists created the first societies for the prevention of cruelty to children. These anticruelty societies, led by upper-class women volunteers, did manage to bring the issue of child abuse before the public and before the courts for a while.[14] The volunteer class of women reformers did not have the institutional power, however, to fundamentally change the way American society treated its children.

A New York girl named Mary Ellen, discovered savagely beaten by her (adoptive) parents in the year 1874 is often cited as the 'first recorded case' of child abuse. Mary Ellen was removed from her home following a lawsuit brought by the American Society for the Prevention of Cruelty to Animals. (The law of this era afforded more in the way of formal protection to animals than to children as such.)[15]

Two late nineteenth-century American figures, G. Stanley Hall and L. Emmett Holt, defined that time's divergent and unsettled perspective on child rearing.[16] Holt was a traditionalist and a pediatrician who represented one side of the new scientific approach to parenting advice. Holt helped introduce new guidelines to govern the milk supply in order to reduce the chance that children would be sickened by bacteria in milk. Holt's worldview was one of order, discipline, and regimentation. Psychologist G. Stanley Hall, though also a believer in a certain degree of order and discipline, had a view of childhood that warmly embraced the unpredictable passions of children. Hall's book on adolescence is widely credited with introducing into the popular literature the idea that adolescence was an inherently turbulent and uncertain life stage.[17]

Child Rearing in the Early Twentieth Century

The standard manual on infant care in the early twentieth century was a small government publication titled simply *Infant Care*, first published by the U.S. Department of Labor's Children's Bureau in 1914 and heavily influenced by L. Emmett Holt's work.[18] *Infant Care* has been through twelve editions and more than 50 million copies. According to the first edition of *Infant Care*, playing with the infant was overindulgent behavior likely to spoil the child, so the advice was simple: "The rule that parents should not play with the baby may seem hard, but it is without doubt a safe one."[19]

Modern psychology recoils at the idea that playing with babies could be harmful. According to the attachment school of child psychology, the constant presence of the nurturing mother imprints upon infants an essential sense of confidence and security that they carry with them for the rest of their lives.[20] Modern research in child development and psychology supports the idea that nurtured infants grow into more secure adults and that no amount of tenderness is too much for an infant.[21]

Early versions of *Infant Care* carried forward an eighteenth-century Calvinist notion that children were imbued with devilish spirits that needed to be conquered if the child were to grow into a successful adult. Infant thumb sucking and masturbation were seen as expressions of devilment, and the suggested treatment was tying the child's arms down or pinning the shirt sleeves to prevent the self indulgent behavior.[22] The warning about masturbation was particularly dire in the first edition of *Infant Care:* "This is an injurious practice which must be eradicated. . . . Children are sometimes wrecked for life by habits learned from vicious nurses, and mothers can not guard too strictly against this evil."[23]

The infant's inherent willfulness was supposed to be conquered not by physical discipline (which could not appropriately be directed at a child of less than one year) but rather by rigid regularity. *Infant Care* advocated strict adherence to schedules for feeding and napping. Toilet training was to start as early as one month after the child's birth.[24] The rationale behind the rigid scheduling and the early toilet training was that the mother was assumed to have sole responsibility for child care as well as care of the home and preparation of the meals. Money was assumed to be tight, space was limited, and time was short. The first edition of *Infant Care* was full of step-by-step advice on how to make such things as diapers and child's bedding from available materials like old tablecloths and wooden baskets.[25] For an overworked working class mother in the early twentieth-century United States, the child's regularity of schedule and obedience to parents was essential to the family's sense of well-being.

Child Rearing after 1940

Dr. Benjamin Spock's 1946 *Common Sense Book of Baby and Child Care* was explicitly critical of the kind of rigid and controlling traditional advice offered in the government's pamphlet *Infant Care.*[26] Dr. Spock also took a dim view of corporal punishment in his first edition, and each successive edition was more explicit about the harm that spanking does to children.[27] Whereas physical discipline of the child was accepted without question and even recommended a few generations ago, now middle-class white morality strongly discourages corporal punishment. In seven editions, Spock's *Baby and Child Care* has sold more than 50 million copies, making it by far the most influential child-care manual of the post–World War II era. In addition to writing the best-selling manual on child care in the post–World War II era, Dr. Spock was a political free thinker, an outspoken critic of the Vietnam War, an early leader of the movement against the proliferation of nuclear weapons, and a minor party presidential candidate.[28]

What is radical about *Baby and Child Care*, or what came to be perceived by conservatives as radical, was the book's message of tolerance, permissiveness, and nonviolence within the family. Political conservatives understood that a permissive upbringing free of corporal punishment and unburdened by a strict sense of parentally imposed order might create young adults who would be less responsive to external authority.[29] Dr. Spock's insistent and outspoken political activism in the 1960s gave conservatives further evidence, if conservatives needed any further evidence, for the inherent political and antitraditional ramifications of Spock's child-rearing advice. In the late 1960s, as youth culture challenged adult society in brazen new ways, liberals and conservatives alike wondered whether the disorder in the streets was "all Dr. Spock's fault."[30]

Rather than struggling to impose toilet training on unwilling or uncomprehending young children, Spock advised parents to wait and let the children come to toilet training when the children were ready for it. Spock's manual always emphasized an appreciation for the independent spirit of young children and a Freudian resistance toward the repression of children's natural urges.[31] At age two, Spock argued, children feel that the bowel movement is the product of their own work and creativity, and they do not want their parents to control how and where they do it. In Dr. Spock's view, forcing young children to submit to parental regimentation is potentially damaging to the child's sense of independence and self-worth, and it is usually counterproductive in achieving successful toilet training. As for masturbation in young children, Dr. Spock advised parents that it was perfectly natural and the parents should not interfere.[32]

The first edition of Dr. Spock's *Infant and Child Care* (published in 1946) made no mention of homosexuality. The absence of homosexuality from Spock's first edition is one sign of the shroud of silence that covered homosexuality before Kinsey and before Stonewall. Though Spock would later earn a place in the pantheon of liberal leaders, Spock's view of gender roles had some catching up to do in the 1960s and the 1970s.[33] In the most recent (1998) version of *Baby and Child Care*, Spock applied his permissive and tolerant perspective to homosexuality, and cautioned parents to be supportive rather than repressive toward or fearful of their children whose gender or sexual identity does not fit the traditional mold.

> Although gays and lesbians are now more visible in our popular culture . . . many people still have an unreasonable fear of homosexuality. This fear is called homophobia. In its most common form, it is the fear heterosexuals have that they could be gay.[34]

Spock cautioned parents not to be anxious if their boy plays with dolls or if their daughter plays sports with boys.

> A mother who is overly anxious about her own femininity and sexual attractiveness to men may put too much emphasis on her daughter's feminine development. If she only gives her dolls and cooking sets to play with, and always dresses her in cute, frilly clothes, she is sending a distorted message about female identity.[35]

Rather than shaping children to accommodate their parents, Spock believed that parents should give children the chance to choose their own path (within certain boundaries) and that parents should adapt to and support their children's different personalities. Spock advocated "child-centered" parenting,[36] which was necessarily tolerant of the diversity of childhood personalities. Children who are allowed individuality and freedom of personal expression tend to become adults who have a higher appreciation for individual liberty and personal privacy. Politically conservative parenting authorities, in contrast, argue that parents need to instill the proper gender identities in their children in order to minimize the possibility of adult outcomes, such as homosexuality, that the conservatives view as undesirable.[37]

To combat what they perceived as political and social chaos brought on by too much permissiveness, political conservatives in the 1970s hurried into print with their own child-rearing advice, emphasizing discipline, including an enthusiastic endorsement of corporal punishment, and strict enforcement of traditional gender roles.[38] The modern wave of conservative Protestant advice to parents echoes Cotton Mather's biblically grounded advice from an earlier age.[39] Yet even some of the harshest critics of the new permissiveness shy away from identifying themselves with the old authoritarianism. Richard Nixon was fond of denouncing permissive parenting and spoiled adolescents on the campaign trail, but Mrs. Nixon was careful to explain that "Dick . . . never said a harsh word to the girls."[40]

Child-care advice in the United States evolved from local sources such as Cotton Mather in colonial times, to the simply written government pamphlet *Infant Care* in the first half of the twentieth century, to Dr. Spock's tome, which started at 500 pages in 1946 and grew to more than 900 pages. Along with Dr. Spock's sizeable tome, bookstores are now inundated with a greater number and variety of child-care books than ever before.[41] Cotton Mather's pamphlet, in contrast, was eighty-six pages long and had little competition. Of Mather's eighty-six pages, only thirty-seven pages were directed to the parents, and the remainder was an old-fashioned fire-and-brimstone oration directed to children about the dangers of disobedience. The various editions of *Infant Care* have each been fewer than 100 pages long.

The changing nature of child-care advice is due both to the expanding literacy of the U.S. population and to the increasingly rapid pace of social change. Parents in static traditional societies do not need a manual on child rearing, because parents simply raise children the way they themselves were raised (and if the parents do not remember, they ask their elders). The greater the rate of social change in a society, the less parents can rely on their own experience as a guide for raising children, and the more parents need comprehensive guidance from experts like Dr. Spock. Despite Dr. Spock's admonition to parents that "You know more than you think you do," the opening line of his manual,[42] the size of the book (more than 900 pages) cannot help but convince parents of the exact opposite, that is, that their instincts are entirely insufficient.[43]

Privacy within the Family

Whereas in colonial times it was typical for the parents to share a one-room house (and perhaps two beds) with half a dozen children and a servant or two,[44] now the parents have their own bedroom and in middle-class families the adolescent children usually have their own rooms as well. The physical layout of the modern American home promotes sexual privacy. Young adults who grow up with some measure of privacy for themselves tend to be hesitant to allow the government to impinge on the privacy of others.[45] Dr. Spock's advice to parents with a newborn is not to let the baby sleep with the parents, but rather to put the child in his or her own room so that the baby might learn to put himself or herself to sleep when tired, and so that the parents might preserve their own personal privacy. This advice assumes, of course, that the parents have an extra room to give to the baby.[46]

Census data on the number of rooms and the number of bedrooms per house only extend back to 1960. Since 1960, American families with U.S.-born heads of household have been having fewer children and living in larger homes. Table 6.1 shows that the number of children per household (in households with children) has declined steadily, and the number of bedrooms per household has increased steadily since 1960.[47] The result of these two trends is that the average

Table 6.1 Number of bedrooms per child, U.S. households with children, 1960–2000

Year	A Number of children per household	B Number of bedrooms per household	C = B − 1 Available bedrooms	C/A Number of available bedrooms per child
1960	2.38	2.61	1.61	0.68
1970	2.37	2.85	1.85	0.78
1980	1.97	2.96	1.96	0.99
1990	1.87	2.95	1.95	1.04
2000	1.87	3.01	2.01	1.07

Sources: 1960–2000 1% weighted microdata via IPUMS.

Note: All households have at least one resident child (age < 18), and head of household born in the United States. Available bedrooms equals total bedrooms minus one, assuming that the head of household and his or her partner occupy one bedroom and the remaining family members are distributed into the remaining rooms.

number of bedrooms per child has increased from 0.68 to 1.07, which is to say that children of U.S.-born parents are increasingly likely to grow up with their own room and their own private space.

Social Class and Parenting

Not all American families have large enough homes to provide each child with his or her own room. Socioeconomic class is, and has always been, an important factor in both the life experience of adults and in the way adults raise their children. Dr. Spock's books are influential and widely read, but most of the readers are white and at least middle class. The U.S. government's *Infant Care* manual has been targeted toward a more working-class audience, and *Infant Care* incorporated permissive and tolerant advice more slowly than Dr. Spock did. Research suggests that the traditional authoritarian parenting style is more widely practiced in the working classes than in the middle classes.[48]

According to one view, working-class parents hold onto traditional values longer (including the traditional authoritarian style of parenting) because working-class parents are less well educated and, therefore, have less exposure to the newest ideas.[49] Melvin Kohn's research into social class, parenting, and social attitudes argued that the working-class attachment to authoritarian parenting was not a vestige of earlier times, but rather a practical adaptation to the kind of occupational careers working-class parents experienced and therefore expected for their children.[50]

In Kohn's view, men who worked doing physical labor were always subject to the arbitrary authority of bosses and supervisors. Authoritarian parenting as practiced by working-class parents reasonably prepared children for an adult work experience of following orders, being closely supervised, and being subject to arbitrary demands. Middle-class parents experienced more autonomy at work and more freedom from direct supervision, so the daily experience of being middle class inclined parents toward instilling independence and self-motivation in their children.

Evidence of Changing Child-Rearing Strategies

The changing nature of child-rearing advice, from Cotton Mather to *Infant Care* to Dr. Spock, suggests a historical transformation from authoritarian parenting to permissive "child-centered" parenting. Extrapolating from expert advice to common practice is problematic, however. Reliable data on popular attitudes about parenting do not extend very far into the past. Dr. Spock's own research on child-rearing practices showed how stubbornly parents resisted external advice.[51] In this section, I examine the limited available historical survey data on parents' own views about child-rearing priorities, in order to ascertain if parenting styles really have changed over time (as the prior literature review has suggested) and, if so, when the greatest changes have taken place.

In 1924, as part of their landmark study of a Midwestern town they called *Middletown*,[52] Robert and Helen Lynd offered 141 mothers a list of traits, and they asked them which three traits were the traits they most desired for their children.[53] In order to capture generational change, the Lynds also asked the mothers which three traits their own mothers had emphasized the most. In 1978, Theodore Caplow and his colleagues returned to Middletown and repeated the survey with 324 women.[54] Table 6.2 is adapted from Duane Alwin's 1988 paper comparing the 1924 results with the 1978 results.[55] Despite some methodological problems—the 1924 sample was small and non-random, since random sampling had not yet been invented—the comparison between the 1924 data and the 1978 data is instructive.

Table 6.2 reflects the parenting values of four generations of women from Middletown: the women of 1924 and 1978 themselves and each group's retrospective recollection of their mothers' values. The earliest generation, the mothers of the 1924 interviewees, valued (according to their daughters interviewed in 1924) three traits in their children far above all others: loyalty to the church (69.3 percent), strict obedience (64.4 percent), and good manners (40.6 percent). This first generation, the mothers of the 1924 interviewees, were raising children around 1900. The priorities of the Middletown mothers of 1900 were the kind of traditional parenting values advocated by Cotton Mather and by the authors of *Infant Care*. Few of the Middletown mothers of 1900 valued either tolerance (5 percent) or independence (15.8 percent) in their children.[56]

The 1924 interviewees had the same three most-favorite priorities for their children (loyalty to the church, strict obedience, good manners) as their own mothers had, but with reduced unanimity (50.4 percent, 45.4 percent, and 30.5 percent respectively). The inter-

Table 6.2 Percent choosing a trait as among the three most desired traits for children to have, 1924 and 1978

Trait	1924		1978	
	Mother	Self	Mother	Self
Tolerance (respect for opinions opposed to one's own)	5.0	5.7	21.9	46.8
Independence (ability to think and act for oneself)	15.8	24.8	34.4	75.8
Strict obedience	64.4	45.4	43.8	16.8
Loyalty to the church	69.3	50.4	35.0	22.4
Good manners	40.6	30.5	40.4	23.3
Frankness in dealing with others	24.8	27.0	16.7	25.5
Desire to make name in the world	5.0	5.0	6.6	0.9
Concentration	4.0	9.2	4.1	7.7
Social-mindedness (a sense of personal responsibility for those less fortunate)	6.9	12.8	17.3	25.7
Appreciation of art, music, and poetry	5.0	9.2	3.3	4.8
Economy in money matters	21.8	24.8	26.0	16.8
Knowledge of sex hygiene	2.0	14.9	5.1	7.8
Curiosity	1.0	0.7	2.6	9.9
Patriotism	16.8	20.6	8.3	4.5
Getting very good grades in school	14.9	19.1	23.6	6.3
N	101	141	313	324

Source: Adapted from Alwin, Duane F. "From Obedience to Autonomy: Changes in Traits Desired in Children, 1924–1978." Public Opinion Quarterly 52:33–52, Table 1, © 1988 by the American Association for Public Opinion Research, Published by the University of Chicago Press, reprinted with permission.

Note: Most desired traits are the top three traits parents most strongly desire for their children, from the list of fifteen traits.

viewees of 1924 were more likely (24.8 percent) to value independent children than their parents were.

The third generation of Middletown mothers were the mothers of the 1978 interviewees, who would have been raising their children around 1955. The Middletown mothers of 1955 valued, according to their daughters, strict obedience, good manners, and loyalty to the church as their three most favorite traits in children (43.8 percent, 40.4 percent, and 35 percent respectively). The Middletown mothers of 1955 were not so different from the Middletown mothers of 1900, except that between 1900 and 1955 the changing world made the mothers of Middletown a bit less certain of the advantages of teaching children to be obedient to parents and loyal to their church. An increasing minority of Middletown mothers of 1955 valued tolerance and independence for their children.

The major change in child rearing in Middletown was between the mothers of 1955 and the mothers of 1978, two generations on opposite sides of the historical divide of 1960. The mothers interviewed in 1978 valued independence above all other traits in their children— 75.8 percent of the 1978 interviewees thought that independence was a most desired trait. The women of 1978 rated independence more highly than any of the three previous generations had rated any trait. The women of Middletown in 1978 were also much more interested (46.8 percent) in teaching their children to be tolerant than the previous generation had been. Compared with earlier generations, the Middletown mothers of 1978 were much less interested in teaching their children strict obedience or loyalty to the church.

The data from Middletown supports the thesis that the relationship between parents and children has fundamentally changed since 1960. The old authoritarian style of parenting, carrying forward values from the premodern family such as obedience to parents and loyalty to church, was still the norm in Middletown in the 1950s. After 1960, the old pattern of intergenerational relations was overturned and the parents of Middletown began preparing their children to be independent and tolerant.

SEVEN

◆ ◆ ◆

The Rise of Tolerance

My parents came to Africa to visit me [says Charles, gesturing to Lula] and they met her and then they went back home to the U.S. A few weeks later they called me and they said, "well, we want to encourage you to not see her anymore." That made me really angry, made me feel angry. That was the point, I think everybody in their life goes through—the point where what their parents think doesn't matter any more.

CHARLES IS A TALL WHITE MAN with an easy laugh. He makes his living writing computer software. He was working for a defense contractor in Arizona after graduating from college but did not find the work very rewarding or interesting. He wanted to travel. He had a friend who was working in a remote village in southern Africa, so he wrote to the friend, quit his job, and bought a one-way plane ticket to Africa.

Charles's father was a history professor from a small and conservative Midwestern town of German immigrants. Charles's mother was a suburban housewife who came into adulthood during the civil rights movement and had moderate views on race. They sent Charles to a public elementary school that had a substantial number of black students. When Charles's parents initially had objections to Lula, they were very careful to say that Lula's race was not the problem. Rather, they said, Lula was too rural and unsophisticated and spoke too little English.

Lula grew up with her uncle and thirty family members in simple farm shacks on tribal land in Africa. Lula had been keeping up an erratic correspondence with her distant father, an exiled rebel fighter, but she longed to spend some more time with him. Charles heard Lula's story and decided that he would try to find her father for her. Charles traveled across the country, into rebel territory, found Lula's father and brought him a letter from his daughter. Lula's father wrote a reply, which Charles brought back to Lula. The reply asked Lula to come and spend some time with him in the hospital, because his health was failing and he wanted to get to know his daughter. Lula's uncle and extended family received the letter from Lula's father with distrust. First, they did not want bright young Lula, who had lived such a sheltered life, to venture so far from home. Second, Lula's uncle did not want Charles, an outsider and a white man, to play the role of family intermediary. Lula pleaded and bargained with her uncle to let her visit her father, and her uncle agreed but only on the condition that Lula return within a week. Lula stayed with her father for six months, and this was the beginning of an estrangement from her uncle and his clan. When she returned home after being with her father, her uncle beat her severely.

Lula invited Charles to visit her in the village in order to show him what traditional life was like. The visit did not go well. Lula's uncle intuited that Charles was Lula's boyfriend, and he called the police to arrest Charles. The police came and heard the uncle's complaint, but because Charles and Lula's relationship broke no laws, the police took no action. Lula's uncle dedicated himself to keeping Lula and Charles apart. No one in the village was allowed to give Charles food. Charles spoke only English and so he could not communicate with the villagers. After two days, Charles had no choice but to leave. Lula's uncle forbade Lula to leave the village. At one point, Lula was chained to the house. Charles went to the human rights office in a nearby town and complained about Lula's confinement. The human rights officials went to Lula's uncle and told him that Lula could not be chained to the house. Lula's uncle relented and made a deal with Lula. She would be allowed to leave the village only to pursue her education. Charles sent letters but they were intercepted by Lula's family. A few months later, Lula received an acceptance letter from the national university, and she left the suffocating confinement of her village to pursue her education in the capital city.

Charles was already teaching in the capital city, so Charles and Lula finally had a chance to be together away from the powerful controls of her family. Lula loved the university, and she adored Charles as well. Charles felt confident enough in the relationship to invite his parents to come from the United States to Africa and to introduce them to Lula. He considered his parents to be liberals, and he expected them to be supportive. But they were not. His parents advised him to stop seeing Lula, but Charles and Lula had been through difficult times together already. Charles's parents went back to the United States and Charles and Lula remained in Africa together, quite independent from the influence of both families and perfectly happy.

Lula did well enough at the university to get a scholarship to go to the United States to continue her studies. She went back to the village to ask her uncle if she had his permission to accept the scholarship. Lula's uncle was struck dumb by his own inability to intercede. He knew his niece was going whether he liked it or not. The scholarship sent her to a small state college in Ohio, where she finished her college degree.

By this time, Lula had earned a college degree and spoke fluent English, and Charles's parents had had time to reassess the situation. Once they saw that Charles intended to marry Lula, Charles's parents made a practical and logical decision: they endorsed the marriage and they participated fully in the wedding. Charles and Lula had a traditional southern African wedding in Ohio, complete with traditional dress and music. After the ceremony, they marched singing and dancing down the middle of the street from the church to the bride's house, as is the custom in Lula's village.

Lula was not at all surprised that her uncle tried to prevent her from seeing Charles. Not only is social control of the elders fundamental to village life, but also the social coherence of the village depends in part on marriage within the clan. In contrast to Lula, Charles expected his parents to support him in any major decision he made, and he was surprised by his parents' initial negative reaction to Lula. Charles had experienced college, had lived on his own, had worked for a company far from where he grew up, and had traveled in Africa. These experiences of social freedom had taught Charles to never doubt his own judgment. It seems somewhat paradoxical, but Charles's parents raised Charles to be open-minded, and the result was that Charles came into conflict (temporarily) with his parents because on matters of race he was more liberal than they were.

It is a fundamental assumption in the fields of child development and child psychology that the parent-child relationship remains influential as children grow into adulthood. Freudian psychoanalytic theory, which has lost some of its influence within the academy in recent decades, is nonetheless an important intellectual root (though not always acknowledged as such) in many fields of psychology, especially child development and child psychology. One of Freud's key insights into human nature was that childhood and adolescent experiences influence adults in important ways beyond the conscious awareness of the adults. Mid-twentieth-century studies of political tolerance and intolerance, such as Adorno's *The Authoritarian Personality*, were influenced by Freud.[1] Adorno and his colleagues argued that authoritarianism within adult society is a direct product of old-fashioned authoritarian child rearing. According to Else Frenkel-Brunswick, fathers who raised their children to believe that the father was always right and needed to offer no explanations for his edicts, raised their children to be both receptive to authoritarian political leaders (who would take the place of the strong father of their youth) and mistrustful of social deviance and political minorities.[2] The political outlook of adults, in other words, was thought to have been largely determined by the way in which the adults had been raised as children.

In the second half of the twentieth century, as the social sciences became more quantitative, the sweeping psychological and historical theories influenced by Freud fell out of favor because Freudian theories were difficult to quantify.[3] Researchers have had a difficult time quantifying the effect of family environment because so many other variables (school, neighborhood, genetics, individuality, intrafamily dynamics) are difficult to control and because the key variables (family environment, adult character) are difficult to measure consistently.[4]

The attachment school of child development, led by John Bowlby and Mary Ainsworth, became influential in the 1960s and 1970s by arguing that children need an absolutely consistent nurturing bond with their mother in order to grow into self-confident and secure adults.[5] The attachment school emphasized the family environment, and specifically the parent-child relationship, as the most important determinant of the child's future character and personality. More recent scholarship has balanced the attachment school's emphasis on family environment with a new appreciation for the importance of biological and genetic factors in determining childhood character.[6]

Human character is too complicated to yield to simple causal explanations, yet there are some things we know with a high degree of certainty. Children who are subjected to violence are themselves more likely to resort to violence as adults.[7] Even scholars who are critical of the attachment school's emphasis on nurture over nature in determining childhood character admit that substandard family environments have long-term negative consequences for children, consequences whose residue carries forward to adulthood.[8] The debate, then, is over what kind of child-rearing practices ought to be encouraged.[9] Even Judith Harris, whose book *The Nurture Assumption* suggests that parents have no direct effect on their children's characters, admits that children are enormously influenced by their peer groups and that parents choose peer groups for their children by choosing the neighborhoods in which they live and by choosing schools for their children.[10]

In their 1951 study *The Lonely Crowd*, David Riesman and his colleagues explored the new family and the kinds of personalities it produces.[11] Riesman referred to the modern character type as "other-directed." Other-directed people are raised in family settings that would have been considered overly permissive in earlier generations. Other-directed people look to their peer group rather than to their parents for direction and guidance.

Compared with earlier social and personality types, Riesman described the other-directed person as somewhat lazy, lacking in ambition, perhaps a bit spoiled, and interested more in consumption than in production or making a difference.[12] The other-directed person has one advantage (in Riesman's view) over his predecessors, however: the other-directed person is tolerant rather than moralistic by nature.[13] The other-directed person's character is formed by interactions with a broad peer group rather than by the more single-minded forge of the parents. Modern middle-class parents raise their children toward an eventual goal of independence, and, as a result, modern parents tolerate a degree of dissent and disobedience from children that would probably not have been tolerated two or three generations ago. The modern family, in the age of other-directedness and with the independent life stage as its fulcrum, nurtures, listens to, and negotiates with children, rather than breaking their will to ensure obedience.

Most experts, regardless of political or academic orientation, agree that childhood experience (broadly understood) influences the personality of children, and hence the personality and dispositions of the adults that the children become. In this chapter I argue that post-1960 changes in popular attitudes are partly due to the changing structure of the American family. As children in the United States are less likely to be exposed to the old authoritarian style of parenting, and as more and more young adults experience the independent life stage, Americans have become more tolerant of social differences.

Changing Attitudes

American popular attitudes toward racial and sexual minorities have become more tolerant in the past thirty years. According to the literature on racial attitudes in the United States,[14] there has been a steady decline over time of attitudes that David O. Sears referred to as "old-fashioned racism,"[15] including a steady decline in the percentage of whites who believe that interracial marriage should be illegal. There is debate, however, about the depth and importance of the secular changes in racial attitudes. Some scholars argue that the observed secular shifts in racial attitudes, although still important, are partly superficial.[16] Despite the low percentage of whites who say they believe that interracial marriage should be illegal, in the privacy of the voting booth a different sentiment emerges. Nearly half of the voters in southern states voted to keep anti-intermarriage laws on the books thirty years after the Supreme Court made such laws null and void.[17]

Although white Americans support civil rights for blacks in vague and general ways, whites continue to resist government interventions, such as affirmative action and school busing, that might directly benefit blacks, but possibly at the expense of whites.[18] Sears found that whites opposed school busing regardless of whether they themselves had school-aged children. Sears concluded that white opposition to school busing was not a rational response to a policy that would affect them directly, but rather a subtle new form of racism he called "symbolic racism."[19]

Given complicated and paradoxical public opinions about loaded subjects such as race or sexuality, the problem is how to describe and understand public opinion. The word "liberal" is used very broadly to mean so many different things, from tolerance, to support for civil rights, to support of multiculturalism, to support of free markets, or finally to the opposite of the equally vague term "conservative."[20] American attitudes about race and homosexuality are full of seeming paradoxes because on some questions, public opinion seems remarkably liberal, and on other questions, the same respondents give answers that are surprisingly conservative.

I use the word "tolerance" the way the Lynds used it in their survey of Middletown women,[21] to mean respect for opinions opposed to one's own or willingness to allow unpopular groups to exercise their rights. I define liberalism more narrowly than most authors. I will use liberalism to mean a more generous and open spirit; liberalism embraces difference, diversity, and multiculturalism in ways that tolerance does not. True liberals not only support civil rights for minorities, but also welcome the practical ramifications of minority rights.

Vermont Governor Howard Dean welcomed the 1999 Vermont Supreme Court decision in Baker v. State, a decision that forced the Vermont state legislature to craft the first civil unions bill for gay couples in the United States.[22] But after welcoming the decision and promising to support the passage of a civil unions bill, Dean said this about gay marriage: "It makes me uncomfortable, the same as anyone else."[23] Dean's stated position in this case was more tolerant than liberal.

Although the post-1960 changes in U.S. public opinion on issues of race and sexuality have often been described as "liberalizing," public opinion is still remarkably conservative on many social and sexual issues.[24] Politically, the United States is more conservative and individualistic than Canada, the country whose European roots are the most similar.[25] Although there is no doubt that some of the many changes in American society since 1960 are truly politically liberal in nature, many other changes are due to an increase in tolerance more than to an increase in liberalism. Take, for example, U.S. popular attitudes about homosexuality and gay rights.

The General Social Survey, or GSS, was first fielded in 1972 and has become the leading source for data about trends in social, political, and cultural opinions in the United States. The GSS surveyed a random sample of about 1,500 households (1973–1993) and a larger sample of about 3,000 households in 1994–2002, and uses the same questions year after year in order to capture changing attitudes.[26]

Figure 7.1 shows trends in U.S. attitudes about homosexuals and homosexual rights. At the top of Figure 7.1 are trend lines for two survey questions that reflect tolerance of basic gay rights. The first question is, "Suppose an admitted homosexual wanted to make a speech in your community. Should he be allowed to speak or not?" The percentage of respondents who said that an admitted homosexual should be allowed to speak in their community rose from 62 percent in 1973 to 85 percent in 2002.

The bottom two trend lines in Figure 7.1 reflect answers to the question, "What about sexual relations between two adults of the same sex—do you think it is always wrong, almost always wrong, wrong only sometimes, or not wrong at all?" The percentage of respondents who gave the liberal response that consensual homosexual sex was not wrong at all rose from 11 percent in 1973 to 34 percent in 2002. Among adults with at least some college education, the percentage with a liberal attitude toward gays is slightly higher than for the population as a whole. Although popular opinion toward homosexuality has become more liberal in recent years, adults who hold a liberal view of homosexuality are still very much in the minority. In fact, the most popular answer to the question about consensual homosexual sex is that it is "always wrong." The percentage of adults in the United States who thought consensual homosexual sex between adults was "always wrong" was 74 percent in 1973, remained steady at roughly the same level and only began to decline in the late 1990s, reaching 54 percent in 2002 (not shown in Figure 7.1). Attitudes in the United States toward gay sex and gay people remain surprisingly illiberal.

Survey data demonstrate an impressive gap between the high levels of tolerance toward basic gay rights and the low levels of liberalism toward homosexuals (low even among the college educated). Many of the respondents who believe that a gay person should have the right to speak in their community also believe that homosexual sex is "always wrong." Scholars have noted the paradox of U.S. public opinion about gays and gay rights, that is, the substantial popular

Figure 7.1. Tolerance and liberalism toward homosexuality, 1973–2002. *Source:* Weighted GSS data 1973–2002, "Don't know" and "No answer" responses excluded. Questions: (1) Suppose an admitted homosexual wanted to make a speech in your community. Should he be allowed to speak or not? (2) If some people in your community suggested that a book he [a homosexual man] wrote in favor of homosexuality should be taken out of your public library, would you favor removing this book, or not? (3) What about sexual relations between two adults of the same sex—do you think it is always wrong, almost always wrong, wrong only sometimes or not wrong at all?

[handwritten margin note: but what abt by age cohorts?]

support for some civil rights for gays but continued disapproval of homosexuals and homosexuality.[27]

Determinants of Tolerance toward Homosexual Rights

I have been arguing that the increasing tolerance of U.S. society is partly a function of the independent life stage and the more permissive child-rearing practices that have become the norm since 1960. The time has come to demonstrate with empirical data that education, urban residence, geographic mobility, family structure, life stage, and the cohort experience of coming of age before or after 1960 all have a pronounced effect on tolerance at the individual level. Table 7.1 describes some of the many factors that influence tolerance toward homosexual rights, in this case agreement that an "admitted homosexual" should be allowed to make a speech in the respondent's community.[28]

According to General Social Survey data for 1973–2002, the more formal education a person had, the more tolerant of gay rights they were. Adults with five or more siblings were substantially less tolerant than adults that came from smaller families. People living in rural areas and very small towns (population less than 10,000) were the least tolerant, whereas people living in cities of more than 1 million inhabitants were the most tolerant. Jews and atheists were more tolerant than Protestants. Biblical literalists (people who believe the Bible is the actual word of God and is to be taken literally word for word) were substantially less tolerant of gay rights than people who thought the Bible was simply an ancient book of fables and legends. People who lived their whole life in one community were less tolerant than people who had traveled or moved.

Among the predictors of tolerance in Table 7.1, formal education appears to be the strongest because educational groups have the largest differences in tolerance, from 51.8 percent to 92.6 percent. Among persons with less than a high school education, only 51.8 percent agreed that homosexuals should have the right to speak in their community. Every level of formal education substantially increased tolerance toward homosexual rights. Persons with postgraduate education were the most tolerant, with 92.6 percent believing that homosexuals should have the right to speak in their communi-

[handwritten margin note: stronger than age cohort?]

Table 7.1 Predictors of tolerance toward the right of a homosexual to speak, from GSS 1973–2002

	Pct tolerant	Odds ratio	Adjusted odds ratio
Education			
Less than high school	51.8	—	—
High school degree	72.9	2.49***	1.62***
Some college	83.4	4.65***	2.51***
Bachelor's degree	89.7	8.07***	3.68***
Post-graduate	92.6	11.64***	5.82***
Number of siblings			
No siblings	80.5	—	—
1–2 siblings	82.5	1.14	1.00
3–4 siblings	74.6	0.71***	0.80**
5–10 siblings	64.0	0.43***	0.68***
11 or more siblings	59.0	0.35***	0.64***
Population size of community			
Less than 10K persons	64.6	—	—
10K–99K persons	77.0	1.84***	1.42***
100K–999K persons	79.3	2.10***	1.83***
1 million or more persons	81.0	2.33***	2.11***
Religion			
Protestant	70.0	—	—
Catholic	79.4	1.65***	1.43***
Jewish	91.0	4.32***	2.86***
None	81.9	1.94***	1.43***
Attitude toward the Bible			
Biblical literalist	60.9	—	—
Bible is important	85.3	3.65***	—
Bible is a book of legends	91.3	6.30***	—
Lived whole life in this community?			
Yes	60.9	—	—
No	73.8	1.80***	—

* $p < .05$ ** $p < .01$ *** $p < .001$, two-tailed test.
Source: General Social Survey 1973–2002.
Note: Odds ratios are calculated separately for each variable. Adjusted odds ratios are calculated jointly for all variables using multivariate logistic regression (with "tolerance of a homosexual to speak in your community" as the dependent variable) which includes all the listed variables as predictors (except for biblical attitudes and how long lived in the community, which are not available for all survey years) along with race, survey year, age, age squared, family income, and gender. Adjusted odds ratios account for the oversample of blacks in 1982 and 1987, and also for interviewee household size.

ties. The difference in tolerance between the highest educational level (92.6 percent tolerant) and the lowest educational level (51.8 percent tolerant) is impressive. The odds ratio for the comparison is 11.64,[29] which means that the odds of being tolerant of free speech rights for gays were more than 11 times higher for people with postgraduate education compared with people with less than a high school degree.

The observed difference in tolerance between the least educated and the most educated suggests a causal relationship between education and tolerance, namely that education transforms students into more tolerant adults. The relationship between education and tolerance, however, could be misleading. Other social factors could be effecting both tolerance and higher education. For instance, we know that educational attainment has increased over time and tolerance of gay rights has also increased over time, so the observed relationship between education and tolerance could be nothing more than the confounding effect of the passage of time on both education and tolerance. Similarly, people with education beyond college were more likely live in major cities, were more likely to come from smaller families, were less likely to be biblical literalists, and so on.

Multivariate analysis allows for the odds ratios to be reestimated taking all the variables and additional controls simultaneously into account. The "adjusted odds ratios" column in Table 7.1 uses multivariate logistic regression to predict the odds of being tolerant toward gay rights, using education, number of siblings, population size, and religion as predictors along with age, age squared, survey year, race, family income, and gender. The adjusted odds ratios for education's influence on tolerance are smaller than the unadjusted odds ratios, but they are still statistically significant and substantially larger than one. The adjusted odds ratios suggest that education did have a direct and powerful effect on individual tolerance, even after the passage of historical time, differences in individual age, family income, and urban residence are taken into account.

All respondents in the GSS are at least eighteen years old, which is to say all respondents are young adults or adults. The number of siblings is interesting not because family size makes a difference to adults, but rather because family size tells us something important about the experience of childhood that produced the adults. The modern "child-centered" family, with children permitted to follow

their own independent spirits, is only possible if the number of children is small. The ability of parents to give adolescent children their
own bedrooms and to save money for their children's college educations declines as the number of children increases. This is what
economist Gary Becker refers to as the tradeoff between quantity and
"quality" in children.[30]

The larger the number of children, the more the parents or guardians must resort to authoritarian rule as a matter of practical necessity.[31] Three children with minds of their own may be quaint, but
twelve children with each making separate demands is chaos. Parents
in colonial times needed large numbers of children workers to make
the family unit economically viable.[32] Parents in charge of such an
army could brook little dissent from the children if the family was to
succeed. Early twentieth-century editions of the government manual
Infant Care emphasized rigid and regular training and feeding of the
infant in order to ensure that the mother (who was assumed to be
home by herself with several children) could manage her many du-
ties.[33] The number of siblings is a crude proxy for something that is
otherwise quite difficult to measure retrospectively: the nature of the
childhood experience. Table 7.1 shows that adults with none or one
to two siblings were the most tolerant of the rights of a homosexual
to speak in their community (80.5 percent and 82.5 percent tolerant,
respectively). Tolerance declined a bit for adults with three or four
siblings, and tolerance dropped off rather sharply for adults with five
to ten and eleven or more siblings (64.0 percent and 59.0 percent
tolerant, respectively). The adjusted odds ratios in Table 7.1 show that
the difference in tolerance between adults raised in small families and
adults raised in large families remained statistically significant even
after education, urban residence, religion, income, the passage of historical time, and other factors were taken into account.[34]

Respondent age and historical time also matter in determining tolerance toward gay rights. Because individual age and historical time
increase in lock step (every passing year of historical time increases
each individual's age by exactly one year), sociologists and demographers have a notoriously difficult time disentangling life-course effects
from historical effects.[35]

Figure 7.2 shows the percent of adults who were tolerant of a homosexual's right to speak in their community, by respondent age and

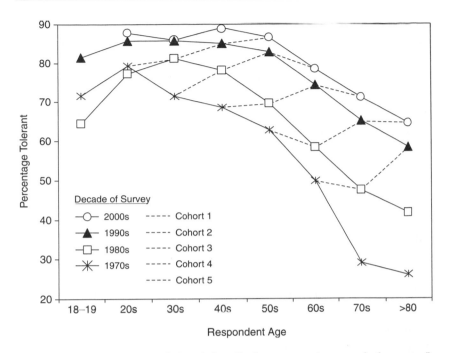

Figure 7.2. Tolerance toward the right of a homosexual to speak, by age of respondent and decade of survey, GSS 1973–2002. *Source:* Weighted GSS data 1973–2002. "Suppose this admitted homosexual wanted to make a speech in your community. Should he be allowed to speak, or not?" Cohort 1 is the highest dotted line, cohort 2 is the second highest, and so on.

by survey decade. The dark lines connect age groups within each decade of GSS surveys. The dotted lines follow birth cohorts over time. The highest dotted line (cohort 1) connects respondents who were in their twenties in the 1970s to respondents who were in their thirties in the 1980s to respondents who were in their forties in the 1990s, to respondents who were in their fifties in the early part of the first decade of the new millennium. The second-highest dotted line corresponds to cohort 2, the third-highest to cohort 3, and so on. The GSS is a random survey of several thousand Americans every two years or so. Like the U.S. census microdata, the GSS is not a longitudinal study, meaning the GSS interviews a different random sample of people every two years, rather than finding and reinterviewing the same sample over and over. Researchers sometimes call these "synthetic cohorts" to distinguish them from true cohort studies built from repeated interviews with the same set of subjects.

The dark lines of Figure 7.2 show an inverted "U" pattern of tolerance by age. Tolerance of gay rights was highest for respondents who were in their twenties and thirties. Respondents who were eighteen and nineteen years old had lower rates of tolerance, and older Americans, especially Americans older than fifty, had much lower rates of tolerance. If one examined only the dark lines, one might assume that individuals are most tolerant during the independent life stage and become less tolerant as they age. Making a life-course inference from cross-sectional data can, however, be very misleading. The reason older people were substantially less tolerant, especially older people surveyed in the 1970s and 1980s, was that these people were from earlier birth cohorts. People in their fifties in the 1970s were born around 1920, and they came of age long before the independent life stage became the norm and long before the civil rights movement (along with the independent life stage) changed the way Americans think about individual rights.

If one follows the dotted lines of synthetic cohorts from the 1970s to the 2000s, one sees that tolerance toward homosexual rights actually went *up* over the life course; every cohort had higher tolerance in 2000 and 2002 than they had thirty years earlier in the 1970s. Cohorts 4 and 5 had declining tolerance between the 1970s and the 1980s, but these declines were reversed between the 1980s and the 1990s. Tolerance was generally stable or increasing over the life course, which is just the opposite of what cross-sectional data (the dark lines of Figure 7.2) and popular wisdom suggest.

Why are eighteen- and nineteen-year-olds so much less tolerant than people in their twenties surveyed at the same time? People who are eighteen and nineteen have not yet finished their formal educations, have not yet traveled, and have not yet experienced the full power of the independent life stage. Not all eighteen- and nineteen-year-olds attend college or move away from home or travel the world, but in the post-1960 era many do. The independent life stage makes young adults more appreciative of their own freedoms and more tolerant of the freedoms of others.

One of the factors that makes the United States more tolerant of individual rights over time is a process that Norman Ryder referred to as "demographic metabolism."[36] The arrival of the new generation of young people may have less effect on the society than the death of the oldest generation. In the 1970s, GSS respondents who were eighty years of age or older were the most intolerant of any group toward gay rights—only 26 percent thought that a homosexual speaker should have the right to speak in their community. This is the lowest level of tolerance recorded for any group—much lower than high school dropouts, much lower than biblical literalists, much lower than adults with eleven or more siblings, and much lower than people who had lived their whole lives in the same place. Among the predictors of tolerance listed in Table 7.1, every category (averaged over all respondent ages and all survey years) had at least 50 percent tolerance.

At the upper left-hand corner of Figure 7.2, where the tolerance graphs peak, the dark lines are fairly close together. This is because young adults who came of age in the 1970s, 1980s, and 1990s had comparable experiences. At the bottom right-hand corner of Figure 7.2, the dark lines are much farther apart because the older respondents came of age long before 1960 and their formative experiences were fundamentally different from what the post-1960 cohorts experienced.

Political scientist Ronald Inglehart has argued that a slow but steady change is overtaking the political values of all developed Western nations.[37] Because these societies have eliminated hunger (though not inequality), individuals have come to have a greater interest in personal fulfillment and individual privacy. The changes in political culture are slow, however, because they are fundamentally birth cohort changes. It takes half a lifetime or more for the children and adolescents who are raised under new conditions to become adults and assume positions of power, and, similarly, many decades must pass before the adults who were raised under earlier conditions retire from their positions of authority, cease voting and participating, and eventually expire. As life expectancy in the West has risen, and as retirement ages are increasing, the pace of social change driven by cohort replacement has slowed even further. Despite the slow pace of political change driven by cohort replacement, the effects over two or three generations can be (and have been) quite dramatic.

Table 7.2 compares the tolerance toward the right of a gay speaker

Table 7.2 Birth cohort and tolerance toward the right of a homosexual to speak, from GSS 1973–2002

Birth cohort	When reached age 20	Pct tolerant	Tolerance odds ratio compared with born before 1900	Tolerance odds ratio Compared with born in 1930s	Adjusted odds ratio tolerance compared with born in 1930s
Pre-1900	Pre-1920	26.1	—	0.13***	0.20***
1900–1929	1920–1949	57.8	3.89***	0.49***	0.66***
1930s	1950s	73.5	7.96***	—	—
1940s	1960s	81.2	12.21***	1.53***	1.29***
1950s	1970s	82.7	13.50***	1.70***	1.40***
1960s	1980s	82.2	13.04***	1.64***	1.26***
After 1970	After 1990	87.4	19.70***	2.48***	1.87***

***$p < .001$, two-tailed test.

Source: General Social Survey 1973–2002.

Note. Odds ratios control for interviewee household size and black oversample. Adjusted odds ratios control for race, survey year, family income, size of respondent's community, gender, and education using multivariate logistic regression, with tolerance of gay speaker as the dependent variable.

to make a presentation in the respondent's community, across birth cohorts. Persons born before 1900 (interviewed beginning in 1973) were the least tolerant: only 26.1 percent believed that a known homosexual should have the right to speak in their community. The most recent birth cohorts, those who were born in 1970 or later and who turned twenty years old in 1990 or later were the most tolerant—87.4 percent believed a known homosexual should have the right to speak in their community.

The first column of odds ratios in Table 7.2 compares the tolerance of each birth cohort with the oldest and least tolerant cohorts, those born before 1900. Since the pre-1900 birth cohorts were so intolerant, this comparison is impressive but not terribly instructive. The last two columns of Table 7.2 use as the reference case the birth cohorts of the 1930s, who reached age twenty in the 1950s, just before the family revolution of the 1960s. Table 7.2 shows that people in the United States who reached age twenty after 1960 were substantially more tolerant than those who had reached the age of twenty before 1960, even taking income, education, and other factors into account.

Cohorts who came of age after 1960 are more tolerant than cohorts that came of age before 1960 because family structure, the nature of childhood, and the independent life stage have all changed since 1960. Our outlook on the world, and on the rights of others, is shaped by how we experience family as children and as young adults.

Over the next forty years, demographic metabolism will eliminate all the birth cohorts that reached twenty years of age before 1960 (that is, everyone born before 1940) and replace them with newer and more tolerant birth cohorts. Cohort replacement has already increased societal tolerance for individual rights in the United States. It is likely that cohort replacement will continue to increase societal tolerance in the United States even if the tolerance level of every individual in the society remains fixed during their lives.

EIGHT

Privacy and the Law

SINCE 1960, the Supreme Court of the United States has recognized a series of new personal privacy rights: the right of access to birth control, the right of heterosexual couples to marry across racial lines, the right of abortion, and the right of adult gay couples to have consensual sex.[1] Conservative critics have complained that the new privacy rights have no explicit textual basis in the U.S. Constitution.[2] If the new personal privacy rights do not come from the text of the U.S. Constitution, where do they come from?

Laws against sodomy were part of the common law that prevailed in colonial times, and these laws were adopted into the laws of most states as a matter of course, even though the laws were rarely enforced.[3] State laws against racial intermarriage and against abortion were first introduced in the nineteenth century.[4] Laws against birth control tended to be more recent only because the practical technology of birth control is of more recent vintage. The new privacy rights, in other words, reverse a long tradition. The argument of legal traditionalism—for example, the argument that the states should be allowed to criminalize interracial marriage because they had done so for more than a century—did not persuade the Warren Court in 1967.[5] Why did the old tradition of state control over individual sexuality, supported by case law and unmentioned in the U.S. Constitution, suddenly become unacceptable after 1960?

The change in family structure and the rise of the independent life stage may be part of the answer. The independent life stage has given young adults a taste of freedom and independence that previous gen-

156

a comp intl framework would be very useful

erations never experienced. The new freedoms of young adulthood undoubtedly shape the way young adults see the world.[6] Adults who were raised in the tolerant style and who experienced the independent life stage have come to have a very different outlook on individual privacy than their ancestors had.

This is not to say that the United States has suddenly become a politically liberal country and that all old traditions have been swept aside. Adults still harbor aversion to homosexuality, and whites still harbor resentment about black political gains.[7] The United States is, by some measures, still quite socially and politically conservative. The new independent life stage has, however, increased popular tolerance for personal privacy and for individual rights. Even though most adults in the United States believe that homosexuality is "always wrong," an increasing percentage of them believe that homosexuals are entitled to privacy and to basic rights.[8]

The rise in legal recognition of individual privacy rights is not limited to the United States. A similar pattern of increasing individual *exactly* rights, especially in mate selection, women's rights, and gay rights, has been described for much of the Western world. The independent life stage exists in some form in every developed Western country.[9] The less-developed countries have slowly adopted greater legal protections for gays in order to satisfy requirements of international political and economic treaties, which originate in the more economically developed Western countries.[10] Although much has been written about the new individualism, the literature has not offered an entirely satisfactory explanation for the timing of the new individual privacy rights. Why has the revolution in individual privacy rights occurred in the post-1960 era and not during the industrial revolution? If the cultural and intellectual roots of the new individualism can be traced back to the Protestant Reformation,[11] shouldn't modern privacy rights have been recognized centuries before 1960? The timing of the revolution in individual privacy rights owes something, I believe, the post-1960 changes in family structure. The justices of the Warren court and their successors on the high court (except for the most recent) all came of age before 1960.[12] It is not the justices' own experiences of independent young adulthood that reshaped American law in the 1960s and 1970s, but rather their sensitivity to the rapidly increasing American appetite for individual privacy.

The right to privacy is not found in the U.S. Constitution, and this absence of specific textual legal support for privacy makes the rise of individual privacy rights all the more interesting. Our eighteenth-century ancestors, including the framers of the Constitution, clearly believed in much more state control over sex, marriage, and procreation. The central critique of conservatives against the new privacy rights is that the new privacy rights are the result of the imagination of activist liberal judges rather than a product of strict constitutional interpretation. In the issue of individual privacy rights, however, conservatives are swimming against a demographic tide.

Privacy and Birth Control

Estelle Griswold was the executive director of the Planned Parenthood League of Connecticut. In 1958, Connecticut adapted an old law (first passed in Connecticut in 1879) that made birth control illegal in the state. In 1961, Griswold and her medical director were arrested and convicted for giving married persons information, medical advice, and prescriptions for contraception. Because Connecticut's law against birth control was rarely enforced, Planned Parenthood had a difficult time attracting the attention of the police in order to be charged and convicted, so that the organization would then be able to challenge the constitutionality of the law. The state of Connecticut and its defenders argued that the infrequent application of the law made the law hardly invasive to personal privacy. Critics of the law responded that the law's rare and arbitrary application made the law less reasonable and less just, not more.[13] Griswold sued Connecticut to try to overturn the law against birth control. Griswold lost in the Connecticut courts, but in 1965, the U.S. Supreme Court heard Griswold's appeal, and in June 1965, the Supreme Court handed down a decision nullifying Connecticut's law.

The Supreme Court decision in Griswold v. Connecticut ushered in a new but controversial era of sexual privacy rights, and it swept aside state laws against birth control that had been in place since Anthony Comstock's late nineteenth-century anti-vice campaigns.[14] The majority opinion, written by Justice Douglas, held that the Connecticut statute was an unconstitutional invasion of the privacy of married persons: "Would we allow the police to search the sacred precincts of marital bedrooms for telltale signs of the use of contraceptives? The very idea is repulsive to the notions of privacy surrounding the marital relationship."[15] Justices Black and Stewart dissented, arguing that the U.S. Constitution offered no such privacy protections and therefore the Connecticut law against birth control, although "offensive" (in Black's view) and "uncommonly silly" (in Stewart's view), was not unconstitutional. Justice Black wrote, "The Court talks about a constitutional 'right of privacy' as though there is some constitutional provision or provisions forbidding any law ever to be passed which might abridge the 'privacy' of individuals. But there is not."[16]

In 1972, in the case of Eisenstadt v. Baird, the Supreme Court extended the new privacy rights from married couples to individuals.[17] William Baird had been arrested for distributing contraceptive foam after he gave a talk on birth control to students at Boston University. Massachusetts law allowed access to birth control only to married people. Baird had no way of knowing which of the Boston University students in his audience were married, but the local prosecutor assumed that Baird must have known that many were not married. The state of Massachusetts argued that the ban on birth control for unmarried persons advanced a compelling interest by dissuading unmarried people from having sex. Justice Brennan, writing for the majority of the Supreme Court, argued that Massachusetts's ban on birth control for unmarried persons infringed individual privacy too much:

> It is true that in *Griswold* the right of privacy in question inhered in the marital relationship. Yet the marital couple is not an independent entity with a mind and heart of its own, but an association of two individuals each with a separate intellectual and emotional makeup. If the right of privacy means anything, it is the right of the *individual*, married or single, to be free from unwarranted governmental intrusion into matters so fundamentally affecting a person as the decision whether to bear or beget a child.[18]

Since the court gave the new privacy rights to individuals, individuals also had the right of access to birth control. Between 1965 when *Griswold* was decided and 1972 when *Eisenstadt* was decided, Justice Black had retired and Justice Stewart had joined the majority in supporting the new privacy rights; only Chief Justice Warren Burger offered a dissenting opinion in the *Eisenstadt* case.[19] Burger's dissent in

Eisenstadt took a familiar form: "I see nothing in the Fourteenth Amendment or any other part of the Constitution that even vaguely suggests that these medicinal forms of contraceptives must be available in the open market."[20]

In 1973, the Supreme Court extended personal privacy rights to the right of abortion in Roe v. Wade.[21] Jane Roe (a pseudonym) was a pregnant single woman in Texas who desired, but could not obtain, an abortion. Elective abortions were illegal in Texas at the time. The American Medical Association had campaigned against abortion and helped to make abortions illegal for the first time in the late nineteenth century.[22] Part of the American Medical Association argument against abortion in the nineteenth century was that abortion, as then practiced, was dangerous to women. By 1973, medical abortions had become quite safe. The state could no longer claim it was "protecting women's health" by making abortion unavailable. Since the states no longer had a compelling public health justification for preventing abortion, the Supreme Court ruled that laws criminalizing first- and second-trimester abortions were an unconstitutional infringement on the privacy rights of women. Justice Brennan, writing for the majority, wrote:

> This right of privacy, whether it be founded in the Fourteenth Amendment's concept of personal liberty and restrictions upon state action, as we feel it is, or, as the District Court determined, in the Ninth Amendment's reservation of rights to the people, is broad enough to encompass a woman's decision whether or not to terminate her pregnancy. The detriment that the State would impose upon the pregnant woman by denying this choice altogether is apparent.[23]

Justice Rehnquist's dissent in *Roe* made the usual complaint that the court had found a new privacy right that was neither explicitly mentioned in the Constitution nor intended by the Fourteenth Amendment's authors: "To reach its result, the Court necessarily has had to find within the scope of the Fourteenth Amendment a right that was apparently completely unknown to the drafters of the Amendment."[24]

The court's decision in Roe v. Wade not only struck down the Texas anti-abortion law, but the *Roe* decision also set explicitly narrow standards for when during a pregnancy and under what circumstances of maternal health the states would be allowed to prohibit abortions.

Because the *Roe* decision was so explicit and specific, nearly all the states' abortion laws had to be rewritten to bring them into compliance with the new national standard.[25] Since 1973, the opponents of abortion rights have held the political initiative and used Roe v. Wade as a symbolic rallying point.[26]

Why has Roe v. Wade sparked such a dedicated and persistent backlash, whereas most of the other Supreme Court decisions that have advanced individual privacy and the rights of sexual expression have created hardly a whimper of organized public opposition? The right of a pregnant woman to have an abortion conflicts not only with the state's traditional right to regulate behavior, but also with the rights (however ill-defined) of the fetus. Abortion opponents concentrate their rhetoric on the rights of the defenseless fetus rather than on the right of the state to prevent abortion. No one marches with signs defending the traditional right of the state to regulate personal and sexual behavior. Both sides of the abortion debate advance individual rights arguments, though the two sides have different individuals in mind. Legal scholar Mary Ann Glendon has argued that the rhetoric of individual rights, what she refers to as "rights talk," has become nearly universal in the post-1960 period.[27] No one's rights are infringed by birth control, and therefore adult access to birth control has fewer organized opponents. Post-1960 changes in law and sexuality are driven by an increased appreciation for individual rights. Sexual expression between consenting adults (interracial marriage, homosexuality) is increasingly legal, whereas acts that transgress against another individual's rights (such as rape or domestic violence) have been increasingly reported, stigmatized, and punished in the United States and around the world since 1970.[28]

Racial Intermarriage

Mildred Jeter, a black woman, and Richard Loving, a white man, had grown up together in rural Virginia. They fell in love and wanted to marry, but they knew that Virginia had a law against interracial marriage. In 1958, Jeter and Loving traveled to Washington, D.C., got married, and returned home to Virginia. In that same year, the district attorney of Caroline County, Virginia, obtained warrants for the arrest of the Lovings, arrested them in their bed at night, and took them off to jail. Unbeknownst to the Lovings, Virginia's law applied to Virginia residents even if their marriage had been legally celebrated in another state.[29]

In 1959, the Lovings pleaded guilty to violating Virginia's Racial Integrity Act of 1924. Virginia Circuit Court Judge Leon Bazile sentenced the Lovings to one year each in jail. The sentence was suspended for twenty-five years on the proviso that the Lovings leave Virginia and never return as husband and wife. The Lovings did leave Virginia, but they found it difficult to be away from their families. Mildred Loving returned to Virginia for the births of all three children, but the law prevented her husband from accompanying her. In 1963, the Lovings decided to return to Virginia and challenge the law. The case came back to Judge Bazile who emphatically reaffirmed his initial decision and endorsed the anti-intermarriage law as a matter of urgent state policy. The Lovings had no success in the appeals courts of Virginia, but in 1967 the U.S. Supreme Court heard the Lovings' appeal and reversed the decisions of the Virginia courts.

In Loving v. Virginia,[30] Chief Justice Earl Warren wrote a decision for the unanimous court, finding in favor of the Lovings and striking down all state anti-intermarriage laws as unconstitutional. Warren avoided the legally uncertain territory of privacy rights and based his decision on the "equal protection" clause of the Fourteenth Amendment to the U.S. Constitution. Virginia had argued that the anti-intermarriage laws did not discriminate by race because it treated both racially intermarried partners with equal severity. The Supreme Court disagreed, noting that the Lovings' marriage was only criminal in Virginia because of their races. Chief Justice Warren wrote, "Marriage is one of the 'basic civil rights of man,' fundamental to our very existence and survival."[31]

At the time of the *Loving* decision, sixteen states (all of the Deep South along with Oklahoma, Texas, West Virginia, Delaware, and Tennessee) had laws on the books barring racial intermarriage. Between World War II and 1967, fourteen other states including California, had repealed their laws against racial intermarriage.[32] Prior to 1967, the Supreme Court had avoided several opportunities to tackle the constitutionality of the anti-intermarriage laws.[33] The National Association for the Advancement of Colored People (NAACP) and other leading civil rights organizations had been reluctant to make an issue of intermarriage, because they feared white backlash and they were not sure that more than a handful of people were affected by the laws.[34] The Lovings' case was initially argued not by the NAACP (which wrote a strong amicus brief when the case came before the Supreme Court), but by two lawyers affiliated with the American Civil Liberties Union (ACLU). When the justices of the Supreme Court believed that white public opposition to intermarriage had softened just enough to make a national revolt against the court unlikely, the court struck down the anti-intermarriage laws.[35]

Virginia had argued in their brief before the Supreme Court that the Fourteenth Amendment ought to be understood and applied the way its framers and supporters understood it and applied it in the nineteenth century—this is the legal doctrine of original intent.[36] The Fourteenth Amendment, adopted in 1868, promised equal protection under the law to all persons. The first section of the Fourteenth Amendment reads:

> All persons born or naturalized in the United States, and subject to the jurisdiction thereof, are citizens of the United States and of the state wherein they reside. No state shall make or enforce any law which shall abridge the privileges or immunities of citizens of the United States; nor shall any state deprive any person of life, liberty, or property, without due process of law; nor deny to any person within its jurisdiction the equal protection of the laws.

The Thirteenth Amendment (which made slavery illegal), the Fourteenth Amendment, and the Fifteenth Amendment (which declared that voting rights could not be denied or abridged on account of race) were the key parts of the constitutional guarantees made to blacks in the aftermath of the Civil War. The sweeping guarantees the Fourteenth and Fifteenth Amendments made to blacks were unfulfilled, especially in the South, for nearly a century.

In arguments before the court in *Loving*, Virginia based its claim on original intent. In other words, Virginia noted that in 1868 when the Fourteenth Amendment was ratified, many of the states that ratified it had anti-intermarriage laws; Virginia did not see the Fourteenth Amendment as inconsistent with those laws, so why should the Fourteenth Amendment be inconsistent with similar laws a hundred years later? When the Supreme Court decisively struck down the anti-intermarriage laws in 1967 as inconsistent with the Fourteenth Amendment, the unanimous decision skirted the question of original intent.

Many aspects of life changed in the United States between 1868 and 1967. One change that has been little appreciated but has powerful consequences is the change in the structure of the family, especially the relationship between generations. The changing structure of the family makes interventions in marital decisions, interventions that were once commonly accepted and widely endorsed, seem suddenly unjust and inappropriate.

The language of the Fourteenth Amendment speaks of the lofty ideals of liberty, due process, and equal protection. To modern eyes, the words of the Fourteenth Amendment seem quite inconsistent with the actual legalized discrimination that blacks were subject to in the late nineteenth and early twentieth centuries. Slavery coexisted for three quarters of a century with the United States Constitution, at the time the most liberal and democratic constitution in the world. One of the fundamental problems for historians of the United States is how to reconcile the great and sweeping idealistic liberties of the Constitution with the illiberal reality of slavery and Jim Crow segregation. Can it be that nineteenth-century white Americans were simply extraordinary hypocrites? Some hypocrisy was undoubtedly present, but it is also important to recognize that nineteenth-century Americans understood "freedom" and "liberty" in narrower ways than we do today. Modern family life and the independent life stage has given us a different understanding of personal freedom, so we understand the language of the Constitution differently from our ancestors.

Privacy and Homosexuality

In 1986, in the case of Bowers v. Hardwick,[37] the Supreme Court, in a 5–4 decision, reaffirmed the passing remarks from Justice Goldberg's concurring opinion in the *Griswold* case that the new privacy rights did not extend to consensual sexual relations between adults of the same gender.[38] Michael Hardwick was a Georgia resident whose home was entered by the police acting on an erroneous search warrant. The police found Mr. Hardwick engaged in oral sex with another man and arrested Hardwick under Georgia's anti-sodomy law.[39] The local district attorney did not want to prosecute Mr. Hardwick because the anti-sodomy law was rarely enforced.

Defenders of the anti-sodomy laws argued, as defenders of Connecticut's anti-birth control law had argued two decades earlier, that the laws were rarely enforced and therefore did not represent an invasion of privacy. Why would a state insist so vigorously in keeping a law that the state itself was unwilling to enforce? The answer is that the anti-sodomy laws were used to cast homosexuals under a presumptive cloud of criminality, which was then used to limit gay rights and force gays to live in fear of prosecution. Connecticut's law against birth control, overturned in the *Griswold* case, had managed (without arresting anyone) to keep Planned Parenthood from opening a clinic in Connecticut.[40]

Despite the hesitancy of the local district attorney in Georgia, Hardwick sued the attorney general of Georgia, Michael Bowers, to try to overturn the law anyway. The Supreme Court upheld Georgia's law in 1986. Chief Justice Burger wrote, in a concurring opinion, "I join the Court's Opinion, but I write separately to underscore my view that in constitutional terms there is no such thing as a fundamental right to commit homosexual sodomy."[41]

In 2003, in Lawrence v. Texas,[42] the Supreme Court overruled the earlier *Bowers* decision and finally extended the new privacy rights and sexual freedoms to gay couples. As was the case with Hardwick in Georgia years earlier, Lawrence was arrested in his home by police who were responding to an erroneous search warrant. They found Mr. Lawrence and his partner Mr. Garner having sex and arrested them for violating Texas's anti-sodomy law. Writing for the court majority, Justice Kennedy wrote:

> Resolution of this case depends on whether petitioners were free as adults to engage in private conduct in the exercise of their liberty under the Due Process Clause. . . . Although the laws involved in *Bowers* and here purport to do not more than prohibit a particular sexual act, their penalties and purposes have more far-reaching consequences, touching upon the most private human conduct, sexual behavior, and in the most private of places, the home. They seek to control a personal relationship that, whether or not entitled to formal recognition in the

law, is within the liberty of persons to choose without being punished as criminals. The liberty protected by the Constitution allows homosexual persons the right to choose to enter upon relationships in the confines of their homes and their own private lives and still retain their dignity as free persons.[43]

Justice Kennedy's majority decision in Lawrence v. Texas did not argue that American public opinion about homosexual sex had changed fundamentally in the seventeen years since the Bowers v. Hardwick decision upheld Georgia's anti-sodomy law. Although tolerance toward homosexual rights has increased in the United States since 1986, popular attitudes are still not very liberal toward homosexuality. Several states had retired their sodomy laws between 1986 and 2003, but that was also not the basis of the Lawrence decision. The basis of the Lawrence decision (consistent with Griswold, Eisenstadt, Roe, and Loving) was that the individual right to privacy was more important than community standards, more important than popular opinion, and more important than the original intent of the framers of the U. S. Constitution.

The five-vote majority in Lawrence v. Texas comprised four justices who were added to the Supreme Court after the Bowers v. Hardwick decision (Kennedy, Souter, Ginsburg, and Breyer), along with Justice Stevens, who had sided with Mr. Hardwick against the state of Georgia in 1986. Justice Sandra Day O'Connor concurred with the court majority in finding that Texas's sodomy law was unconstitutional, but she dissented against overruling the Bowers decision.[44] The court's change from 1986 to 2003 on the rights of homosexuals to privacy was not due so much to a changing of minds as to a turnover in personnel, the juridical equivalent of cohort replacement.

The steady advance of judicially endorsed privacy and sexual rights has horrified hard-line conservatives.[45] Robert Bork, a conservative constitutional literalist, opposed the 1965 U.S. Supreme Court decision in Griswold v. Connecticut, the decision that struck down state laws that prohibited married couples from using contraception and that started the modern privacy revolution in the courts. Bork's position is that the court in Griswold overreached by drawing on privacy rights not found in the Constitution. Even though Bork's position has some legal merit, and the concurring and dissenting opinions in *Griswold* agree with Bork at least in part, the tide of post-1960 life experience has enshrined privacy as a fundamental right. Bork's nomination to the Supreme Court in 1987 was defeated by the largest negative Senate vote in the history of Supreme Court nominations. Bork's defeat in the U.S. Senate was widely seen as a political coronation of the new privacy rights that Bork had relentlessly attacked.[46]

The new privacy rights recognized by the last thirty years of jurisprudence are not to be found, at least not explicitly, in the U.S. Constitution. In attempting to understand where the new rights do come from, it may be useful to consider some of the ways in which changing family life has affected our privacy and individual rights. We experience more privacy and our childhood individuality is more readily tolerated because the nature of parenthood is different than it used to be. Whereas once physical discipline of children was recommended, now it is strongly discouraged. Whereas in the colonies large families of six or more children and several servants often shared only one room, now typical American couples average one or two children each, and each child is likely to have his or her own bedroom. Parenthood in the past was more authoritarian because economic necessity demanded it. Parents in past generations needed to raise their children to be obedient because parents needed obedient children to support the parents in their old age. Colonial society required parents to take a firm hand with their children because outside of family government there was hardly any government at all.

Modern parenting prepares children to be independent. Modern parents expect their children to grow up, move out, and make their own way in the world. In the past, young adults usually lived with their parents (or were subject to family government as servants in another household) until they married. Since 1960, however, the reality in the United States is that more and more young adults live on their own, work, and pursue their education beyond the reach and control of family government. Parenting styles have adapted to the new relationship between the generations. Individual attitudes about privacy and tolerance have changed as a result of the changing structure of the family, and the law has in turn changed to reflect the new demographic reality of the post-1960 era. Of course, society and individual attitudes have changed in many ways since 1960; no one theory could possibly explain the full breadth of social change in a society as complex as the United States. Nonetheless, theories of social change that ignore the family are ignoring a crucial social context that shapes how we all view the world.

NINE

Same-Sex Marriage and the
Future of the American Family

THE FRONTIER OF INDIVIDUAL PRIVACY and sexual rights in the U.S. has advanced a long way since 1960. Same-sex marriage, the individual privacy and sexual rights issue that currently embroils American politics, would have seemed quite improbable in 1960. In order to understand how the debate over same-sex marriage arose, and in order to assess the future prospects for same-sex marriage, it is useful to review the historical and demographic forces that brought us to this point.

The social and legal history of interracial marriage in the United States, which can be viewed advantageously by hindsight, has much to teach us about the social and legal question of same-sex marriage. In this chapter, I examine the current status and the future of same-sex marriage in light of the history of interracial marriage. The number of interracial marriages and the number of same-sex unions in the United States have both grown in recent years for some of the same demographic and social reasons. The fear of same-sex marriage and the fear of homosexuals that is still prevalent is not so different from the fear of interracial marriage and the fear of blacks that was once openly and widely expressed by white leaders in the United States.

Interracial marriage had been a politically untouchable subject for most of U.S. history up to the early 1960s, and it became a legal right in 1967.[1] Since 1967, the public opposition to the legality of interracial marriage has mostly melted away. Same-sex marriage had been a politically untouchable subject until the early 1990s in the United States, but this is beginning to change.[2] The justifications for maintaining laws against racial intermarriage are especially worth reviewing because many of the arguments against same-sex marriage appeared in similar form, several decades ago, as arguments against racial intermarriage.

Virginia's Arguments against Interracial Marriage

Original Intent

In its 1967 brief before the Supreme Court in Loving v Virginia, the state of Virginia defended its law against racial intermarriage with legal, constitutional, moral, historical, scientific, and public policy arguments.[3]

Virginia argued original intent, that is, that the Fourteenth Amendment to the U.S. Constitution could not be inconsistent with laws against racial intermarriage since the Fourteenth Amendment had been adopted by states that had laws against racial intermarriage at the very time of the Fourteenth Amendment's adoption.[4]

Defense of Tradition

Virginia argued that the weight of tradition was on its side. Laws prohibiting racial intermarriage had been upheld dozens of different times in many different jurisdictions.

Judicial Review

What right do judges have to overturn laws passed by democratically elected legislatures and signed into law by democratically elected executives? Some of the founding fathers intended the courts to act as a balance against legislatures and against the tyranny of the majority.[5] Regardless of the intentions of the framers of the U.S. Constitution, the Supreme Court in 1803 (in the celebrated case of Marbury v. Madison), gave itself the power to review acts of the legislative and executive branches.[6]

The Scientific and Biological Basis

In the early twentieth century, scientific opinion generally supported the contention that blacks were biologically inferior and that racial intermarriage was therefore a threat to the racial integrity of white America.[7] The intellectual credibility of white racial supremacy eroded over the course of the twentieth century. Hitler's fanatical embrace of Germanic racial supremacy, the mobilization of the United States to fight against Nazi Germany, and the subsequent revelations of the extraordinary atrocities committed by the Third Reich all served to discredit the old theories of inherent racial difference and white racial supremacy. By 1967, the racial theories of black biological inferiority that had supported the laws against racial intermarriage were in a state of intellectual disrepute. Virginia claimed (and North Carolina in a friend of the court brief agreed[8]) that the scientific debate on the biological differences between the races and on the dangers of racial intermarriage was unresolved. Both Virginia and North Carolina, in their briefs before the Supreme Court, acknowledged implicitly that some experts had abandoned or rejected the old racial theories, but they asserted that other experts still supported the idea that racial mixing was necessarily detrimental to the genetic vitality of human society.[9] The attorney general of Virginia argued that "scientific breeders have long ago demonstrated that the most desirable results are secured by specializing types rather than by merging them."[10]

God's Will

Before the landmark case of Loving v. Virginia was heard by the U.S. Supreme Court, the Virginia state courts first ruled against the Lovings and in favor of the laws against racial intermarriage. In his decision turning back the Lovings' appeal, Virginia circuit court Judge Leon Bazile (who had convicted the Lovings in an earlier trial and whose decision the state of Virginia defended before the U.S. Supreme Court) wrote: "Almighty God created the races white, black, yellow, malay and red, and he placed them on separate continents. And but for the interference with his arrangement there would be no cause for such marriages. The fact that he separated the races shows that he did not intend for the races to mix." [11]

Protecting the Children

Virginia argued that its law against racial intermarriage was essential for the protection of children from the harm and confusion of being raised by an interracial couple. Arguments for defending vulnerable children from corruption and harm have proved to be especially effective as the basis for social control and social reform movements over the years.[12]

> Inasmuch as we have already noted the higher rate of divorce among the intermarried, it is not proper to ask, "Shall we then add to the number of children who become the victims of their intermarried parents?" If there is any possibility that this is likely to occur—and the evidence certainly points in that direction—it would seem that our obligation to children should tend to reduce the number of such marriages.[13]

Despite the fact that Virginia's arguments were based on substantial legal and historical precedents, the Warren court unanimously dismissed Virginia's arguments and decided the case in favor of the plaintiffs. The legality of interracial heterosexual marriage in the United States is now settled law. White voters in the South may still harbor resentment over the legality of racial intermarriage, but elected conservative political leaders are unwilling to make these objections explicit.[14]

The arguments against same-sex marriage recycle many of the arguments that were used to oppose interracial marriage: that same-sex marriage runs counter to the original intent of the framers of the U.S. Constitution; that same-sex marriage would overturn a long historical tradition of marriage exclusively for heterosexuals;[15] that same-sex marriage is promoted by activist judges against the democratic will of the people;[16] that same-sex marriage trespasses against science, biology, and evolution; that same-sex marriage is contrary to God's will;[17] and that same-sex marriage would injure children.[18]

Same-Sex Marriage and Children

Children are at the center of all public policy debates about marriage and family, including the debate over same-sex marriage. Opponents of same-sex marriage argue that children are better served by heterosexual parents.[19] Supporters of same-sex marriage argue that gay parents can raise children just as well as straight parents can and, furthermore, that gay parents already have children who need the protection of the law.[20] There is, inevitably, a lack of nationally representative longitudinal data on the social adjustment of children raised by gay parents. Opponents of same-sex marriage argue that no further rights should be granted to same-sex couples until nationally representative data on gay families demonstrate the suitability of gays as parents.[21] Supporters of same-sex marriage respond that long-term studies of gay couples and their children depend on the willingness of gay couples to participate, which in turn depends on the willingness of the state to give gay couples equal rights.[22] The one fact that is not hard to establish about same-sex couples and their children is that their numbers are growing.

Table 9.1 shows that the number of minor children living with same-sex cohabiting parents seems to have grown substantially between 1990 and 2000. In 1990 there were 68,000 children living with

Table 9.1 Children living with same-sex cohabiting parents

	Census year:		
	1990	2000, Adjusted	2000, Unadjusted
(A) Number of children in the United States	63,400,000	73,400,000	73,400,000
(B) Number of children living with same-sex cohabiting parents	68,000	126,000	426,000
(B/A) Fraction of children living with same-sex cohabiting parents	1/934	1/571	1/172

Sources: 1990 and 2000 5% weighted U.S. census microdata via IPUMS.

Note: Children are all persons under eighteen years of age. Adjusted data for 2000 excludes from the same-sex cohabiting category all couples whose marital statuses were both recoded by the census bureau, and is therefore more comparable with the 1990 census data.

same-sex cohabiting parents, representing 1 out of every 934 children in the United States. The adjusted data from 2000 are more comparable with the 1990 data, and these indicate 126,000 children living with same-sex cohabiting couples. The unadjusted 2000 census data are less comparable with the 1990 data (since the Census Bureau expanded their definition of same-sex cohabiting couples), but the unadjusted data from 2000 are supposed to give a more accurate picture of gay families in 2000.[23] According to the unadjusted data from the 2000 census, there were 426,000 children, or 1 out of every 172 children, living with same-sex cohabiting parents.

Consider the case of Pascal and Mark, two of my interviewees. Pascal and Mark are two gay white men who are married to each other, live in San Francisco, and are the parents of two adopted black boys. Everyone in the family speaks French. When seen walking down the street, Pascal and Mark's family challenges almost every outwardly visible notion of the traditional family. And yet, Pascal and Mark's family is utterly conventional. Pascal and Mark enjoy taking their sons to the park. They volunteer in their sons' preschool. They arrange their work schedules to maximize the time they can spend with their sons.

Pascal and Mark want the same thing that most parents want: to provide for their children the most secure and most nurturing environment possible. Pascal and Mark's ability to provide for their children is limited, however, by the current second-class legal status of gay marriage. Pascal is a citizen of France, whereas Mark is a citizen of the United States. If Pascal were a woman, Mark and Pascal's marriage would allow Pascal to become a U.S. citizen. Because Pascal and Mark are both men, their marriage was never recognized by the U.S. federal government.[24] As a result, Pascal stays in the United States thanks to a work visa, which forces him to leave the country in order to reapply every two years. Every two years, Pascal and Mark's life is put on hold as they prepare themselves for the possibility that Pascal's visa renewal will be denied and that they will have to close their business, sell their belongings, and leave the United States on short notice.

The Hawaii Precedent

In 1990, Ninia Baehr and Genora Dancel applied for a marriage license in Hawaii and were denied, on account of their both being women. Baehr and Dancel began a legal journey that would result in eventual victory at trial against the state of Hawaii, followed by defeat as Hawaii citizens passed a constitutional amendment to prevent same-sex marriage. Although Baehr and Dancel were never allowed to marry, their victory at trial in 1996 changed the legal landscape for same-sex marriage.[25] At first, the Hawaii courts turned away Baehr and Dancel's complaint. In 1993, the Hawaii Supreme Court heard Baehr and Dancel's appeal, sent the case back to the lower courts, and ordered that the burden of proof rested on the state of Hawaii to show a compelling state interest in preventing same-sex couples from marrying.[26] The case (renamed Baehr v. Miike) finally came to trial in 1996, in the Hawaii Circuit Court of Judge Kevin Chang.[27]

In Baehr v. Miike, the suitability of gays and lesbians as parents was on trial. Hawaii based its claim of compelling interest on the claim that same-sex parents could not do as good a job as heterosexual married parents in raising Hawaii's children.[28] At trial, Hawaii presented physicians and social scientists as witnesses, who argued that the state had an interest in favoring heterosexual marriage. But even the state's own witnesses had to admit that "parents' sexual orientation does not disqualify them from being good, fit, loving, or successful parents."[29] The state of Hawaii offered only one witness who categorically denied that same-sex couples could be adequate parents, but because this witness objected to all social science, psychology, and the theory of evolution, Judge Chang did not lend this witness much credence.[30] The trial demonstrated that within the academy and within the health-care professions, absolute objection to gay rights had become an isolated and marginal position. Since the state could find very little credible evidence that same-sex marriage was necessarily detrimental to children, and since all of the plaintiff's witnesses argued that same-sex parentage was no inherent disadvantage to children, the weight of the evidence was clear. Judge Chang found that the state of Hawaii had not proven a compelling interest in preventing same-sex couples from marrying, and he ordered the defendant, Lawrence Miike, Hawaii's Department of Health director, not to deny marriage licenses to same-sex couples.

The rejection at trial of Hawaii's arguments about the inferiority of gay parents has proved to be a thorn in the side of those who have subsequently argued that any state government has an interest in preventing gay marriage.[31] The attorney general of Vermont, in de-

fending Vermont's right to deny marriage to same-sex couples, dis-
tanced himself from the ultimately unpersuasive claims that Hawaii
had made about the inadequacy of gay parenting, which left Vermont
defending heterosexual exclusivity in marriage on rather narrow
grounds:

> Appellants mischaracterize the nature of the State's justification in this
> regard. They contend it is the same as that offered by the State of
> Hawaii in *Baehr, that is,* that children reared in a marital setting turn
> out "better" than a child raised in a different setting. By setting up this
> straw they find an easy target to shoot down. Unlike Hawaii, the State
> [of Vermont] is not asserting that children raised by same-sex couples
> will develop differently in any measurable psychological way. Rather,
> the State's interest goes to the intangible benefit of teaching children
> that both men and women share responsibilities in child rearing and
> participate together in any number of endeavors. The State furthers
> this interest through its treatment of marriage.[32]

Vermont's attorney general had little choice but to concede that same-
sex couples could possibly raise children as well as heterosexual married couples. By conceding the potential fitness of gays as parents,
however, Vermont's attorney general had painted himself into a legal
corner. The plaintiffs in Baker v. State won at least a partial victory
because the state could identify few compelling reasons for preventing the legal union of gay couples.[33]

The Scientific Basis of Antigay Discrimination

Prior to the 1970s in the United States, homosexuality was officially
considered a mental disorder in the American Psychiatric Association's official *Diagnostic and Statistical Manual of Mental Disorders.*[34] In
other words, prior to the 1970s, discrimination against homosexuals
had the imprimatur of the scientific community, just as racism against
blacks had had the imprimatur of science until the middle of the
twentieth century. Until the 1950s, the consensus of psychiatrists and
psychologists was that homosexuals were deeply disturbed people.
The evidence for the disturbed nature of homosexuals was due to the
biased nature of the sample: most homosexuals who were referred to

professional treatment were referred from prisons or from mental hospitals where mental illness was prevalent. Homosexuality in the general population was so hidden and closeted at the time that psychologists and psychiatrists were generally unaware of the existence of a mentally well-adjusted homosexual population. In 1957, Evelyn Hooker did the first controlled experiment of psychological adjustment of homosexual and heterosexual men, using contacts with the Mattachine Society to find gay men outside of the penal institutions and the mental hospitals. Hooker matched the heterosexual and homosexual groups for IQ, age, and education, and she administered a standard set of psychological tests to each group. Hooker's samples were all men from the general population who were not in therapy. Hooker showed that psychiatric professionals were unable to distinguish clinically between her sample of heterosexuals and homosexuals.[35] Hooker's conclusion was that "homosexuality as a clinical entity does not exist."[36] In subsequent years, Hooker's results were repeated by other scholars, and the prior scientific consensus (that homosexuality was a form of mental deviance) began to crumble.[37]

In the 1970 meetings of the American Psychiatric Association (APA) in San Francisco, gay activists protested panels and heckled speakers whose clinical work included therapy with homosexuals to convert them to heterosexuality, which the clinicians presumed to be the only healthy sexual orientation.[38] Leaders of the medical and psychiatric professions were at first taken aback by the protests, but over the next three years, the urgency and passion of the activists won them over. In the 1973 APA national meetings in Honolulu, opponents and supporters of the increasingly discredited mental deviance theory of homosexuality battled over what the association's official policy should be.[39] The politically progressive psychiatrists won the battle and recommended a new official statement on homosexuality, which began: "Whereas homosexuality per se implies no impairment in judgment, stability, reliability, or general social or vocational capabilities, therefore, be it resolved that the American Psychiatric Association deplores all public and private discrimination against homosexuals."[40]

In 1975, the American Psychological Association adopted a position similar to the psychiatrists' and "urged all mental health professionals to help dispel the stigma of mental illness that had long been associated with homosexual orientation."[41] The national organization of social workers soon followed. The increasing visibility and political activism of gays in the United States helped to change the scientific and professional consensus on homosexuality. The changing scientific consensus has removed one of the key pillars that supported legalized discrimination against homosexuals in the past.

As a result of the post-1973 reevaluation of homosexuality in the social sciences, states like Hawaii and Vermont have had a difficult time finding credible expert witnesses to defend the idea that the state has a compelling interest in preventing same-sex marriage. With most of the credible experts in academia and in the health professions aligned in favor of homosexual rights, the states have little ammunition with which to fight same-sex marriage, and that is why Hawaii lost at trial in Baehr v. Miike and why Baker v. State was decided against the state of Vermont.

Acts of Marriage

In February 2004, the newly elected mayor of San Francisco, Gavin Newsom, ordered his county clerk to stop denying marriage licenses to gay couples. Hundreds of gay couples converged on city hall, not knowing how long they would have the opportunity to marry.[42] My interviewees Pascal and Mark already had two sons, but they had never thought they might be able to get married. When Pascal heard what was happening at city hall, he called Mark and proposed marriage. Mark remembers:

> So he calls me up at the office and says come down to city hall. I'm on my cell phone and he says, "Come down to city hall and marry me!" And I just said no—you cannot propose on the telephone.
>
> I want the knee and the ring, you know. Still no ring, by the way. But um, I said no. Not gonna do it. And then we learned that there was a seventy-two-hour period and there would be a court injunction, which is why we did it. I had long given up on the idea. . . . I wanted to get the families to come and have the little ceremony and then the dinner and all that fanfare.
>
> But instead we stood in line. . . . It was pouring rain, pouring. The line went around the building. We were sort of nicely dressed but once we got in it went from being cold and wet to being like a sauna. . . .

And then we just looked bad. You had to apply, then you had to do a ceremony, then you had to wait for your license. But it was great. There was so much positive energy.

San Francisco married more than 4,000 same-sex couples in the following weeks.[43] Because California law expressly disallowed same-sex marriage (due to statewide voter initiative Proposition 22 passed in March 2000), the legal status of San Francisco's same-sex marriages was uncertain. Pascal and Mark were among those who assumed that even if the courts forced San Francisco to halt gay marriages, the courts would not strip already married persons of their marital status. They were wrong. In August of 2004, California's Supreme Court decided that Mayor Newsom had overstepped his authority, and the court voided all of San Francisco's gay marriages and ordered San Francisco to return the $30 license fee to each couple.[44] The court left the question of the constitutionality of California's gay marriage ban for a later time, so the issue remains unresolved.

My students and I interviewed Pascal and Mark in July of 2004, one month before the California Supreme Court voided their marriage. During our interview, both Pascal and Mark described their marriage as having more emotional meaning than they had expected it to have. Mark said: "It's sort of like, when you're traveling back from someplace far, far away; you're not home yet when you take this long plane flight and you land at the airport. You're home after the cab ride. And it's the cab ride which was our marriage. You know, and then we were home."

The state of Massachusetts began marrying gay couples in the spring of 2004, following the Massachusetts Supreme Court's decision in Goodridge v. Department of Public Health.[45] The first recognized gay marriages, which took place in several states in 2004 but had the most legal recognition in Massachusetts, activated a conservative religious backlash. In the 2004 general elections, eleven states easily passed referenda changing their laws or their state constitutions to prevent gay marriages, and the popular opposition to gay marriage was credited by some with delivering the presidential election to George W. Bush. The election results of 2004, along with prior constitutional amendments banning same-sex marriage in Hawaii and Alaska and

the 1996 federal Defense of Marriage Act (which received bipartisan
support and was signed by President Clinton) are all manifestations
of a powerful political backlash against gay rights and especially
against same-sex marriage.[46]

Same-Sex Marriage in Light of Historical Precedent

What do the historical precedents mean for the future of civil unions
and marriage for same-sex couples in the United States? The experience of pioneer states offers one clue. In the sixteen months between
May 2004, when same-sex couples were first legally married in Massachusetts, and September 2005, when the Massachusetts legislature
considered (and rejected) a proposed constitutional amendment to
ban gay marriage, opposition to gay marriage in Massachusetts dwin-
dled precipitously.[47] Opponents of gay marriage had promised that
gay marriage would have disastrous and immediate consequences for
the social fabric of Massachusetts, but after sixteen months and 6,600
gay marriages, no such harmful effects were detected. Lawmakers in
Vermont had a similar experience. When civil unions for gay couples
were first enacted in Vermont in 2000, the immediate political backlash was ferocious. Two years later, however, opposition to civil unions
was no longer a cause that galvanized large crowds in Vermont, and
several legislators who had been elected on the wave of initial opposition to civil unions were themselves subsequently turned out of office.[48]

If same-sex marriage follows the trajectory of interracial marriage,
there will be slow incremental growth in the number of states granting
same-sex marriage licenses. Several states may follow Massachusetts's
pioneering example. When the pioneer states have been granting
same-sex marriage licenses for several years without tearing the social
fabric in any obvious way, other states may follow. States whose elec-
torates are most influenced by fundamentalist Christian activism (including the southern states that retained their laws against interracial
marriage the longest) have already reinforced their state laws or rewritten their state constitutions to ban same-sex marriages.

Despite the political backlash against same-sex marriage, there are
now thousands of gay married couples in Massachusetts and thousands
of same-sex couples with state-recognized civil unions in Vermont and

maybe he doesn't
entertain objections to
Same-Sex Marriage and the Future of the American Family   181   many

in other states. The growing number of same-sex marriages will lend
credibility and normalcy to gay parents and gay couples. Opposition
arguments against same-sex marriage that now sound reasonable may
in the future sound strained, strident, and intolerant, like the last
gasps of state arguments against interracial marriage in the mid-1960s.
The current legal landscape for same-sex couples is a confusing state-
by-state legal checkerboard, something akin to the situation that faced
interracial couples before 1967. Eventually, after years of legal and
legislative struggles at the state level, and after the initial political
passions have cooled, the U.S. Supreme Court may weigh in and force
all the states to recognize same-sex marriage on the same basis as
heterosexual marriage. That is the most favorable scenario from the
perspective of gay rights. The eventual legality of same-sex marriage
is made more likely by the rise of same-sex unions, by the increasing
tolerance for gay rights that is partly a consequence of the new post-
1960 family structure, by the declining intellectual credibility of antigay arguments, by a string of state court decisions, and by the 2003
U.S. Supreme Court decision in Lawrence v. Texas, which swept aside
state laws against homosexual sex. Antonin Scalia's dissent in
Lawrence v. Texas complained that the majority decision in that case
left "on pretty shaky grounds state laws limiting marriage to opposite-
sex couples."[49]

Limits to the Civil Rights Analogy

The interracial marriage analogy, despite its usefulness, is an imper-   exactly
fect analogy for same-sex marriage. One reason the political establishment in the United States moved so swiftly to advance civil rights
for blacks in the 1960s was the cold war.[50] The cold war made the
political perspectives of third-world nations relevant to the United
States for the first time. People in Africa, Asia, and Latin America
naturally sympathized with the plight of blacks, Asians, and Hispanics
in the United States. One reason that the United States gave political
and social rights to racial minorities in the 1960s for the first time
was that world opinion demanded it. There is no analogous worldwide
public opinion pressure in favor of same-sex marriage. On the contrary, in most of the third world, religious and cultural opposition to
gay rights is even stronger than it is in the United States.

note — he never does intersectional anal. of race & sex politics
i.e. the whiteness of gay as category

When the Episcopal Church of New Hampshire ordained as bishop in 2003 V. Gene Robinson, a divorced man in a same-sex union, many third-world Episcopalians threatened to secede from the worldwide Anglican communion. Opposition to the ordination of a gay bishop was especially strong among Anglican leaders in Africa.[51] The Anglican Church commission in England issued a strongly worded rebuke of New Hampshire's ordination of a gay man as bishop, but the commission disappointed conservative church leaders by not calling for Bishop Robinson's resignation.[52]

lots of diff
key
hist pol tical
yes!
of the white
of wedge politics

It is possible that, if same-sex marriage rights spread across Europe, European public opinion will increase the pressure for same-sex marriage rights in the United States, but this is only a future possibility. At the present moment, there are few external pressures on the United States to legalize same-sex marriage, and this is one of the key differences between the status of gay rights at present and the status of racial minorities in the 1960s.

It is also worth noting that, from a legal perspective, same-sex couples are further from legal recognition in the United States than interracial couples were at any time in the twentieth century. At the time of the *Loving* decision in 1967, interracial marriages were legal in more than half of the states. The anti-intermarriage laws had their greatest influence in the United States between 1913 and 1948, and even during that period, only thirty of the forty-eight states banned racial intermarriage.[53] The federal government recognized racial intermarriages, and even states that outlawed racial intermarriage were obliged to recognize the unions of interracial couples who traveled through their territory.[54] In 2005, same-sex couples could legally marry only in Massachusetts. The federal Defense of Marriage Act of 1996, passed in response to Hawaii's Baehr v. Miike, allows states and the federal government to disregard same-sex marriages regardless of where they are celebrated.[55]

Looking to the Future

The 2004 national elections in the United States were clearly a setback for gay rights, and there may be further electoral and legislative setbacks to come.[56] Popular opinion in the United States still runs strongly against gay marriage. The courts, however, are finding arguments against gay marriage less persuasive over time. The 1996 Baehr v. Miike decision in Hawaii was the first court decision that found that gay couples had a constitutional right to marry. The *Baehr* decision set a precedent that has already been persuasive to state courts in Alaska, Vermont, and Massachusetts. In 1948, when the California Supreme Court decided Perez v. Sharpe in favor of the interracial plaintiffs' right to marry, interracial couples were still widely reviled in the United States. It took two decades for the pioneering decision in Perez v. Sharpe to become the law of the entire United States and several decades more for interracial marriage to begin to become normalized. It may take two decades or more after *Baehr* for same-sex marriage to be widely legal in the United States.

Could the political backlash against gay marriage hold sway for more than two decades? In the early nineteenth century, historians note, the spirit of the young republic and the possibility of free land to the west gave young white citizens the ability to make informal unions without the formal blessing of church or state.[57] Informal unions were the rule for a while, but eventually a conservative Christian and state bureaucratic backlash forced couples to go to the county courthouse for a marriage license or else disinherit their children.[58] The same backlash eventually led, in the late nineteenth century, to the first laws in the United States against abortion and to the Comstock Act, which was used to persecute sexual nonconformists and political freethinkers.[59] The nineteenth-century backlash (a backlash against informal unions and what religious leaders viewed as loose morality) lasted more than a century and did not fully die out until the 1920s. I do not believe the backlash against gay marriage will be as powerful in 2050 as it is today, for one simple reason: the demography of family structure and the independent life stage are slowly draining the base of support from those who would oppose gay rights.

Conservative critics are right about one thing: the new personal and sexual freedoms are revolutionary. Scholars have tended to overstate the rate of family change in the past, during the industrial revolution for instance, which has indirectly made the post-1960 changes seem less dramatic than they really are. The conservative view that post-1960 changes in family life are a decisive break from the past is more correct than scholars have usually been willing to admit. Abortion, divorce, birth control, cohabitation, interracial unions, and homosexual unions are all drastically more common or more available than fifty years ago. The American family system managed to suppress all types of families except heterosexual same-race marriages until quite recently. The sweeping changes to family life in the United States since 1960 have made strong political reaction from conservatives all but inevitable.

Notwithstanding the conservative backlash, however, gay rights have made impressive gains in recent years. Since 1990, Vermont, Hawaii, California, and New Jersey enacted civil union legislation for gay couples, and scores of municipalities and hundreds of corporations have followed suit. In 2004, mayors in San Francisco and small towns in Oregon, New York, and New Jersey challenged state laws by providing marriage licenses to gay couples, though these local rebellions were later blocked by state courts.[60] Following the 2003 Massachusetts state Supreme Court decision in Goodridge v. Department of Public Health, Massachusetts began marrying same-sex couples in 2004.[61] The U.S. Supreme Court swept away the laws against sodomy in 2003. Outside of the United States, civil unions of one sort or another for gays have been enacted since 1990 in many countries, including Denmark, Norway, Sweden, France, and Germany. The Netherlands has had marriage equality for gays since 2001.[62] Canada and Spain both adopted marriage equality for same-sex couples in 2005.[63]

One logical question about the gay rights revolution is: why now? If homosexuals have been part of every society, and if homosexuals have been widely mistreated across societies for more than a thousand years, and if modern traditional marriage has its roots in the customs of the Middle Ages, and if the idea of individual rights has its roots in the Protestant Reformation, then why did the gay rights revolution not take place hundreds of years ago? A key part of the answer is demography. The independent life stage, which is common to the developed first-world countries but absent in less-developed countries, gives young adults an unprecedented degree of independence from their parents.

Although scholars have written about changes in how young people experience the transition to adulthood,[64] the relevance of the independent life stage to the *kind* of families young people form has never been systematically explored. Other demographic trends such as the birth rate, divorce rate, total population size, or life expectancy are the subject of constant reports, regular academic attention, and popular commentary. The independent life stage, however, leaves no official record behind. Without historically consistent data on who lives with whom, our view of the subject tends to be colored by personal experience and historical myopia. Thus, it is commonly believed that Americans are "returning to the parental nest" in greater and greater numbers. The data, however, show that the popular conception of Americans returning to the nest is misguided. In fact, we have been tricked by an old social paradox—we notice customs more when they are breached than when they are observed. Now that young people are expected to get an education and live independently, young adults in their twenties attract special attention by moving back into their parents' homes. In the past, when nearly all unmarried young adults lived with their parents, the phenomenon of intergenerational co-residence was not worthy of notice.

The independence of young adults from their parents has contributed to a quiet revolution in the nature of family life. The rise in the number of self-identified same-sex couples in the United States is not due to a sudden upsurge in homosexual desire. Rather, the rise in the number of same-sex couples is a consequence of the decline in the power of parental social control, which kept young people from forming same-sex unions in the past and kept previous generations of gay couples hidden from view in what was euphemistically called "the closet."

The independent life stage has an important influence over the kind of unions we form, how parents raise their children, and how we think about personal liberty and privacy. Parents now raise their children to be independent rather than subordinate. Parents who raise their children with Dr. Spock's recommended degree of tolerance, privacy, and permissiveness are producing adults whose childhood experience makes them value freedom, privacy, and individual liberty more than previous generations could. The independent life stage has helped shape the social context for sweeping decisions by the U.S. Supreme Court, such as recognizing individual sexual privacy rights (birth control, abortion, interracial marriage, consensual gay sex) that are not specifically enumerated in the Constitution and were not recognized by our ancestors.

Scholars across many disciplines have described an increase in individualism in the United States and in other parts of the developed world in the post-1960 period. As it relates to family life, Edward Shorter makes the following analogy: in premodern times, the nuclear family was like a boat tied to the dock of extended family and communal society. In the modern era, the boat that represents the couple has been unmoored from social expectations, and it now sails freely away.[65] Modern couples make their own rules rather than living within traditional rules and expectations. The implicit and patriarchal contract of marriage, which was based on several hundred years of English and American common law, has been overturned and replaced by a more gender-neutral marriage contract.[66] Women's labor market access and no-fault divorce have made it easier (though perhaps no less painful) for either spouse to end a marriage.

Some scholars see the new independence and individuality as a sign of emancipation.[67] For these scholars, the democracy and relative gender equality of the modern family create for the first time the historical conditions within which true love—the love between equals—can thrive. Other scholars are not so sanguine. If every modern romantic relationship is fundamentally unmoored from tradition and requires constant communication and renegotiation, how strong can our personal commitments be? The critics see the new individualism leading us down a pathway to unhappiness, unrealistic expectations, and divorce.[68] Whichever view one takes of the merits of the new individualism, there is general agreement that post-1960 U.S. society is a fundamentally more individualistic society.[69]

If one wants to understand how social norms, customs, and traditions are reproduced from generation to generation, one must start (as politically conservative thinkers always have) with the family.[70] Demographic evidence shows that family structure, especially the bonds between parents and their young adult children, has changed in fundamental ways since 1960. Whereas young adults used to live with their parents until marriage, now single young adults usually live on their own. Parental control over adult children in the past was based on co-residence. In the post-1960 era, young adults choose partners and make social and sexual decisions far from the watchful eyes of their parents.

The age at first marriage, especially for women, is higher than it has ever been before. Later age at marriage increases the probability that young people will find mates who are outside the social circle of their childhood neighborhood. In the past, because young women had few career options, they had to marry when young in order to have a husband's financial support. Since World War II, women have steadily increased their presence in the formal labor force. Because women in the post-1960 era are increasingly confident they can obtain an education and can support themselves economically, women marry later and are less likely to subordinate their own mate preferences to the preferences of their parents. Greater independence from parental control makes young adults more likely to form nontraditional unions.

By reducing parental control and oversight, the independent life stage has increased the number interracial unions and the number of same-sex unions in the United States. Increased numbers of same-sex unions and of interracial unions create a visibility and normalcy for alternative unions that deflates the formerly pervasive argument that such unions were "unnatural." In the recent past the number of "out" same-sex couples and the number of interracial married couples were so small that few people outside the unions were exposed to them. One reason we are living in the midst of a gay rights revolution is that gay couples are more numerous and more visible than ever before.

The rising number of alternative unions increases their visibility to strangers. Increased visibility of interracial or same-sex unions creates greater exposure, which can lead to alternative unions becoming more accepted. Visibility of alternative unions to strangers, however, can also lead to backlash, harassment, and hate crimes. Nearly all of the interracial and same-sex couples I interviewed are still cautious about how they present themselves when traveling. Many of the interracial and same-sex couples (especially those who have been together for many years) have been harassed by strangers. The influence of alternative unions on their closest circle of friends, parents, siblings, aunts, and uncles is more important than the influence of alternative unions on strangers, since strangers can have negative reactions. Many of my interviewed couples reported that their parents' attitudes had changed over time as a result of their children's mate selection choices. As the number of same-sex couples and interracial couples has grown, the percentage of Americans who have interracial couples or same-sex couples within their circles of friends and relatives has grown rapidly.

Scientific advances in birth control have certainly played an important role in post-1960 changes in the American family. Without medically safe abortions, there would be no abortion rights. The birth control pill has allowed women to have greater control over their own fertility. Better family planning has allowed women to postpone marriage and to have fewer children over their life course. Smaller families make possible the kind of permissive child rearing that was not feasible a century ago. Although the birth control pill has undoubtedly shaped the modern American family, "the pill" is only influential to the extent that it is legal and readily available. The legality and availability of birth control is a consequence of judicial decisions of the late 1960s and early 1970s. The judicial decisions that swept aside state restrictions to birth control (Griswold v. Connecticut; Eisenstadt v. Baird) were judicial reflections of a new American attitude toward individual privacy. The change in American attitudes toward privacy is, I have argued, partly a result of the new way Americans experience childhood and young adulthood.

Before World War II, higher education was available mainly to the rich and the social elite. Now, college education is a practical goal for most middle-class Americans. Young people who attend college, who travel, who live in cities, and who settle far from home are much more likely to be involved in an interracial union or a same-sex union. The geographic mobility and economic freedom of the independent life stage has a powerful and demonstrable effect on the kinds of unions young people form.

Technological and social change has proceeded so rapidly in the post–World War II era that parents are no longer experts in the world their children grow into. Educational attainment and educational requirements have grown so quickly that by their early twenties young adults are likely to be more educated than their parents. Rapid social, technological, and economic change naturally favors the young over the old and, therefore, naturally undermines the authority (even the moral authority) of the parental generation in the eyes of their young adult children.[71]

In the past, the marriages of young people were carefully controlled by law and custom and by direct intervention of the parents. In the age of the independent life stage, parents have lost much of their ability to influence their children's choices of mates, and the number of same-sex unions and interracial unions has grown as a result. Changes in the basic demographic structure of the family have had a slow but steady and important effect on how new families are created and how we think about formerly taboo subjects, such as racial intermarriage and homosexuality.

Americans who came of age before 1960 are much less tolerant of homosexual rights than are Americans who came of age after 1960. Every year, as a new cohort of young adults moves away from home and as older Americans die, demographic metabolism replaces earlier birth cohorts that never experienced the independent life stage with a new cohort that will. Because of the way family structure has changed, the passage of time undermines opposition to gay rights. By the year 2050, there will be no one left who came into adulthood before 1960. Demographic changes in family life make it very likely that homosexuals in the United States will be admitted into the circle of full citizenship, a circle that necessarily includes the right to marry, before 2050.

Homophobia will not disappear. The civil rights victories of the 1960s did not eliminate racism from the United States. Blacks still face discrimination, but they have rights that before 1960 were considered unattainable. Before the U.S. Supreme Court struck down the laws against racial intermarriage in 1967, opposition to racial intermarriage, especially white opposition, was thought to be insurmountable.[72] Since the 1967 *Loving* decision, opposition to interracial marriage has not disappeared, but the opposition has been relegated to the political margins. Some whites, especially in the South, still harbor resentment against the legality of interracial marriage.[73] Interracial couples still face more parental opposition than same-race married couples do, but parental opposition does not have the force it once had. By the middle of the twenty-first century, homosexuality may still be controversial but same-sex marriage will likely have been legal for some time.

terms diff of alternative "of the man" - doesn't consider diversity of

- lacks intersectional anal of sex, race — the whiteness of "gay"
  presumes essential "homosexual"

- ignores 19th utopian experiments & polyg.
  - doesn't differentiate ♂ & ♀ gays sufficiently or do enough gender anal in data

Appendix Tables

Appendix tables A.1–A.9 follow on pages 192–202.

Table A.1 Selected family characteristics that changed during the industrial revolution in the United States

	1850	1860	1870	1880	1890	1900	1910	1920	1930	1940	1950	1960	1970	1980	1990	2000
Pct of households who farm	57.6	52.5	44.9	46.8		42.5	37.0	33.1		25.1	16.9	9.5	4.5	2.7	1.8	1.2
Pct who live in urban center	7.9	12.3	13.4	15.0		23.0	27.9	32.0		33.5	31.2	37.0	34.5	29.2	22.3	27.1
Mean household size	5.54	5.3	4.99	4.8		4.56	4.32			3.63	3.36	3.35	3.13	2.73	2.57	2.49
Life expectancy at birth						47.3	50.0	54.1	59.7	62.9	68.2	69.7	70.9	73.7	75.4	77.0
Divorce rate		1.2	1.5	2.2	3.0	4.0	4.6	8.0	7.5	8.8	10.2	9.2	14.9	23.9	22.2	20.1
School enrollment ages 5–19	54.0	57.8	47.5	51.2		54.9	63.4	68.6		74.1		84.3	88.0	88.8	88.9	93.4

Sources: Percent of households who farm is percentage of households with U.S.-born head, which included at least one full-time farmer, from weighted census data (via IPUMS). Percent of persons living in urban center excludes the suburbs and is derived from weighted census microdata (via IPUMS). Household size from weighted census microdata for U.S. born persons in non-group quarters. Life expectancy from *Historical Statistics* (Washington D.C.: U.S. Bureau of the Census, 1975, p. 55) and for 1980–2000 from *Statistical Abstract of the U.S.* (Washington, D.C.: U.S. Bureau of the Census, 2003). Divorce rate is number of divorces per thousand married couples, number of divorces 1920–1970 from *Historical Statistics*, p. 49. Divorce rate 1860–1900 from Jacobson, *American Marriage and Divorce* (New York: Rinehart and Company, 1959, p. 90). School enrollment from weighted census microdata for U.S.-born persons ages 5–19.

Table A.2 The stability or reinforcement of family government during the industrial revolution and the decline in family government since 1960

	1880	1890	1900	1910	1920	1930	1940	1950	1960	1970	1980	1990	2000
Median age at first marriage:													
Women	22.0		22.4	22.4	21.9		22.0	20.8	20.2	21.0	22.5	24.3	25.5
Men	25.4		26.1	25.6	25.4		25.0	23.5	22.5	22.8	24.5	26.6	27.4
Pct of unmarried young adults living with their parents:													
Women	68.4		70.2	70.8	73.1		71.1	65.4	56.1	49.6	39.1	38.9	36.2
Men	59.0		60.4	61.1	68.4		74.9	66.0	56.3	51.6	45.3	45.1	41.6
Pct of unmarried young adults who head their own household													
Women	2.4		2.2	2.4	1.8		2.9	5.2	10.8	18.2	30.4	30.4	35.6
Men	4.5		4.6	4.0	2.6		2.7	2.8	7.6	14.5	26.8	24.3	28.0
Pct of young men unattached	5.7		6.5	5.5	3.8		3.5	2.7	4.7	8.9	22.0	27.8	35.1

Sources: All data are author's tabulations from weighted census microdata (via IPUMS).

Note: Median age of first marriage is calculated for U.S. born men and women. Unmarried young adults are U.S.-born, ages 20–29, never married. Unmarried young adults who head their own households excluded those who lived with their parents. Unattached heads of household were ages 20–39, lived in non-group quarters, and were neither married nor living with parents.

Table A.3 The number of interracial marriages in the United States, 1880–2000

	1880	1890	1900	1910	1920	1930	1940	1950	1960	1970	1980	1990	2000
Black–white married couples (*n*)	8,367		10,624	28,469	12,410		53,805	44,362	55,089	67,685	132,603	236,908	345,652
Asian–white married couples (*n*)	100		759	1,526	5,853		5,270	11,443	49,110	115,150	308,914	478,754	579,190
Hispanic–non-Hispanic white married couples										526,559	838,685	1,158,123	1,530,117

Sources: All data are author's tabulations from weighted census microdata (via IPUMS). Couples include individuals of all ages and all national origins. Whites and blacks include Hispanics for consistency with pre-1970 data.

Table A.4 The fraction of each racial or ethnic group married to other races, 1880–2000

	1880	1890	1900	1910	1920	1930	1940	1950	1960	1970	1980	1990	2000
Intermarriage to blacks per 1,000 married white													
Men	0.5	0.6	0.2	0.3	0.3		1.0	0.6	0.8	0.6	0.7	1.4	2.0
Men (in legal states only)	0.6		0.2	0.1	0.3		0.7	0.5	0.6				
Women	0.6		0.5	1.5	0.4		1.1	0.8	0.7	1.0	2.3	3.7	5.4
Women (in legal states only)	0.6		0.6	0.8	0.4		0.8	0.6	0.6				
Intermarriage to whites per 1,000 married black													
Men	4.9		4.3	11.5	3.6		12.4	9.0	8.2	12.6	29.2	50.1	64.0
Women	3.7		1.6	2.4	2.9		11.2	7.3	9.8	7.6	9.4	20.0	25.5
Intermarriage to Asians per 1,000 married white													
Men				0.0	0.1		0.0	0.1	0.8	1.8	4.8	7.5	9.2
Women				0.1	0.2		0.2	0.2	0.5	1.0	2.0	3.1	3.4
Intermarriage to whites per 1,000 U.S.-born married Asian													
Men				30.3	105.7		193.7	70.1	59.6	145.3	211.3	267.8	249.9
Women				51.1	92.5		60.9	68.2	92.0	158.9	282.5	325.2	338.1

Table A.4 (continued)

	1880	1890	1900	1910	1920	1930	1940	1950	1960	1970	1980	1990	2000
Intermarriage to Hispanics per 1,000 non-Hispanic white													
Men										6.9	10.1	14.5	16.2
Women										6.6	9.6	13.2	18.8
Intermarriage to non-Hispanic whites per 1,000 U.S.-born married Hispanic													
Men										84.0	254.2	300.1	263.7
Women										88.9	245.4	296.9	269.6

Sources: All data are author's tabulations from weighted census microdata (via IPUMS). Individuals are married persons of all ages. Individuals include persons of all national origins, except as noted. Whites and blacks include Hispanics unless otherwise specified for consistency with pre-1970 data. Laws against racial intermarriage were unconstitutional and therefore unenforceable in the United States after 1967; see Peter Wallenstein, *Tell the Court I Love My Wife* (New York: Palgrave Macmillan, 2002).

Table A.5 The log odds ratios of racial intermarriages, 1880–2000

	1910	1920	1930	1940	1950	1960	1970	1980	1990	2000
Log odds ratios for black-white intermarriage										
All couples	−12.29	−13.74		−11.30	−12.15	−11.91	−11.73	−10.71	−9.62	−8.82
Young couples				−11.65	−12.15	−12.78	−11.39	−10.10	−8.68	−7.65
Log odds ratios for Asian-white intermarriage										
All couples				−12.10	−10.93	−9.17	−8.13	−7.26	−7.03	−7.16
Young couples						−9.76	−7.42	−6.34	−5.79	−5.56
Log odds ratios for Hispanic–non-Hispanic white married couples										
All couples							−6.64	−6.22	−5.85	−5.80
Young couples							−6.20	−5.13	−4.55	−4.51

Sources: All data are author's tabulations from weighted census microdata (via IPUMS). Log odds ratios are derived from the cross product of 2×2 tables, excluding other races. The mcre negative the log odds ratio, the more uncommon was intermarriage between the two groups relative to the sizes of both groups. See Rosenfeld and Kim, "The Independence of Young Adults and the Rise of Interracial and Same-Sex Unions." Whites and blacks include Hispanics unless otherwise specified for consistency with pre-1970 data. "Young couples" are U.S.-born, ages 20–29. "All couples" includes individuals of all ages and all national origins.

Table A.6 Urban residence for young white couples by type of couple, 1990–2000

| | 1990 | | 2000 | |
| | Percent living in city | Odds ratio of urban residence compared with (1) | Percent Living in City | Odds ratio of urban residence compared with (1) |
Type of couple				
(1) White, heterosexual, married	15.2		15.0	
(2) White, heterosexual, cohabit	26.1	1.97***	23.9	1.78***
(3) White, cohabit, same-sex	60.6	8.58***	29.4	2.36***

*** $p < 0.001$, two-tailed test.

Sources: 1% Metro Sample 1990, 5% sample 2000 census via IPUMS.

Note: All couples are composed of U.S.-born non-Hispanic whites, ages 20–29. Households whose urban residence is unknown (a larger group in 2000 than in 1990) are excluded from the sample. Adjusted estimate of urban concentration for white same-sex couples in 2000 (dual marital status recodes excluded): 36.3%.

Table A.7 Geographic mobility (all ages) by rural/urban/suburban residence, 1990–2000

	1990		2000	
Type of couple	Percent geographic mobility	Odds ratio of mobility Compared with (1)	Percent geographic mobility	Odds ratio of mobility compared with (1)
Rural:				
(1) Heterosexual, same-race, married	44.0		42.7	
(2) Heterosexual, interracial, married and cohabit	63.3	2.20***	63.3	2.31***
(3) Same-sex, cohabit	54.1	1.50***	46.6	1.17***
(4) Same-sex, interracial, cohabit	69.8	2.94***	70.0	3.13***
Suburban:				
(1) Heterosexual, same-race, married	54.5		52.6	
(2) Heterosexual, interracial, married and cohabit	63.8	1.47***	61.3	1.43***
(3) Same-sex, cohabit	67.8	1.75***	59.2	1.31***
(4) Same-sex, interracial, cohabit	#		68.0	1.91***
Urban:				
(1) Heterosexual, same race, married	55.7		53.9	
(2) Heterosexual, interracial, married and cohabit	63.5	1.38***	64.5	1.56***
(3) Same-sex, cohabit	77.6	2.76***	67.3	1.76***
(4) Same-sex, interracial, cohabit	77.4	2.73**	74.5	2.50***

* $p < .05$ ** $p < .01$ *** $p < .001$, two-tailed test

Sources: 1% Metro Samples 1990 (because the 5% microdata from 1990 did not have urban/suburban distinctions) and 5% 2000 census via IPUMS. 1990 rural couples are from 5% 1990 sample non-metropolitan. All couples are composed of U.S.-born individuals.

Note: Households whose central city or metropolitan status is unknown (a larger group in 2000 than in 1990) are excluded from the sample. Geographically mobile couples live in a different U.S. state than the birth state of one or both partners. Geographic mobility for same-sex couples (regardless of race) excluding dual marital status recodes in 2000: 56.3% mobility in rural areas, 65.5% in suburbs, 71.7% in cities.

insufficient data.

Table A.8 Predictors of same-sex cohabitation for partnered men in 2000, odds ratios and summary statistics from logistic regressions

	Model 0	Model 1	Model 2	Model 3	Model 4
Log likelihood	−157,560	−157,303	−156,047	−153,937	−152,027
Δ −2LL		514	2,512	4,220	3,820
df	7	8	15	16	17
Independent variables:					
Constant	.009***	.008***	.03***	.015***	.014***
Education					
<5 years	1.42***	1.42***	1.84***	1.85***	1.72***
5–8 years	.96	.97	1.24***	1.33***	1.32***
9	1.05	1.05	1.16**	1.20***	1.18***
10	1.08*	1.08*	1.14***	1.17***	1.15***
11	1.09*	1.10*	1.07	1.08	1.04
High school (reference)					
Some college	1.20***	1.17***	1.14***	1.07***	1.07***
BA or more	1.39***	1.31***	1.33***	1.18***	1.14***

200

Table A.8 *(continued)*

	Model 0	Model 1	Model 2	Model 3	Model 4
Geographic mobility	1.32***	1.32***	1.37***	1.27***	1.28***
Age					
<20 (reference)					
20–29			.39***	.38***	.39***
30–39			.37***	.36***	.37***
40–49			.29***	.29***	.30***
50–59			.21***	.21***	.22***
60–69			.17***	.17***	.18***
70–79			.18***	.18***	.19***
>80			.20***	.19***	.20***
Pct gay men in metro				1.91***	1.81***
Live in city					2.52***

* $p < .05$ ** $p < .01$ *** $p < .001$, two-tailed test.

Sources: 2000 5% census microdata, via IPUMS. Logistic regression models use data weighted by household weights.

Note: Adjusted odds ratios (dual marital status recodes excluded) for geographic mobility's influence on same-sex cohabitation: 1.59 (Model 1), 1.71 (Model 2), 1.58 (Model 3), 1.60 (Model 4), all statistically significant. Unweighted N: 2,706,642.

Table A.9 Effect of geographic mobility on different nontraditional unions for men in 2000

Base population	Dependent variable	Model 1 Mobility, education	Model 2 Model 1 + age	Model 3 Model 2 + exposure	Model 4 Model 3 + live in city
Married white men	Marriage to black women	1.56***	1.68***	1.63***	1.62***
	Δ −2LL		1,060	276	576
Married white men	Marriage to Asian women	2.58***	2.69***	2.44***	2.44***
	Δ −2LL		1,752	8,956	576
Married white men	Marriage to Hispanic women	1.54***	1.64***	1.40***	1.41***
	Δ −2LL		7,794	24,706	276
Partnered men	Same-sex cohabitation	1.32***	1.37***	1.27***	1.28***
	Δ −2LL		2,512	4,220	3,820

* $p < .05$ ** $p < .01$ *** $p < .001$, two-tailed test.

Source: 2000 5% census microdata, via IPUMS. Logistic regression models use data weighted by household weights.

Note: Data shown are odds ratios and summary statistics from logistic regressions. Model numbers correspond to models in the previous table. Unweighted Ns: married white men, 2,285,604; partnered men (married and cohabiting men), 2,706,642. Adjusted odds ratios (dual marital status recodes excluded) for geographic mobility's influence on same-sex cohabitation: 1.59 (Model 1), 1.71 (Model 2), 1.58 (Model 3), 1.60 (Model 4), all statistically significant. Blacks are non-Hispanic black and whites are non-Hispanic white. Geographically mobile individuals live in a different state from the state of their birth. All individuals in the base populations are U.S. born of any age. Δdf = 7 (Model 2 − Model 1); Δdf = 1 (Model 3 − Model 2); Δdf = 1 (Model 4 − Model 3).

Notes

1. Introduction

1. William N. Eskridge, Jr., *Equality Practice: Civil Unions and the Future of Gay Rights* (New York: Routledge, 2002); Brause v. Bureau of Vital Statistics Alaska, WL 88743 (1998); Baehr v. Miike, WL 694235 Hawaii Circuit Court (1996).

2. Andrew Koppelman, *The Gay Rights Question in Contemporary American Law* (Chicago: University of Chicago Press, 2002); Baker v. State, 170 Vermont 194 (1999).

3. Lawrence v. Texas, 539 U.S. 558 (2003).

4. Dean E. Murphy, "San Francisco Married 4,037 Same-Sex Pairs from 46 States," *New York Times,* March 18, 2004, A:1; Goodridge v. Department of Public Health Massachusetts SJC-08860 (2003); Thomas Crampton, "Court Says New Paltz Mayor Can't Hold Gay Weddings," *New York Times,* June 8, 2004, B:6; Thomas Crampton, "Issuing Licenses, Quietly, to Couples in Asbury Park," *New York Times,* March 10, 2004, B:5; Matthew Preusch, "Oregonians Look to One Suit to Settle Gay Marriage Issue," *New York Times,* March 25, 2004, A:16.

5. Eskridge, *Equality Practice;* William N. Eskridge, Jr., *Gaylaw: Challenging the Apartheid of the Closet* (Cambridge, Mass.: Harvard University Press, 1999); Koppelman, *The Gay Rights Question in Contemporary American Law.*

6. John D'Emilio, *The World Turned: Essays on Gay History, Politics, and Culture* (Durham, N.C.: Duke University Press, 2002).

7. Robert J. Sickels, *Race, Marriage, and the Law* (Albuquerque: University of New Mexico Press, 1972); Loving v. Virginia, 388 U.S. 1

(1967); Rachel Moran, *Interracial Intimacy: The Regulation of Race and Romance* (Chicago: University of Chicago Press, 2001); Peter Wallenstein, *Tell the Court I Love My Wife: Race, Marriage, and Law—An American History* (New York: Palgrave Macmillan, 2002).

8. Examples of scholarship that examine the independent life stage include Jeffrey Jensen Arnett, *Emerging Adulthood: The Winding Road from the Late Teens through the Early Twenties* (Oxford: Oxford University Press, 2004); Richard A. Setterstein, Jr., Frank F. Furstenberg, Jr., and Rubén G. Rumbaut, eds., *On the Frontier of Adulthood: Theory, Research, and Public Policy* (Chicago: University of Chicago Press, 2005); John Modell, *Into One's Own: From Youth to Adulthood in the United States, 1920–1975* (Berkeley: University of California Press, 1989); Marlis Buchmann, *The Script of Life in Modern Society: Entry into Adulthood in a Changing World* (Chicago: University of Chicago Press, 1989); Frances K. Goldscheider and Calvin Goldscheider, *The Changing Transition to Adulthood: Leaving and Returning Home* (Thousand Oaks, Calif.: Sage Publications, 1999); Frances K. Goldscheider and Calvin Goldscheider, *Leaving Home before Marriage: Ethnicity, Familism, and Generational Relationships* (Madison: University of Wisconsin Press, 1993).

9. The landmark case was Loving v. Virginia. See Moran, *Interracial Intimacy*.

10. Douglas S. Massey and Nancy A. Denton, *American Apartheid: Segregation and the Making of the Underclass* (Cambridge, Mass.: Harvard University Press, 1993).

11. The counts of different kinds of nontraditional unions are given here with different temporal endpoints because the U.S. census began identifying the different populations at different times; see Steven Ruggles et al., "Integrated Public Use Microdata Series: Version 3.0," in *Historical Census Projects* (Minneapolis: University of Minnesota, 2004), http://www.ipums.org. Same-sex cohabiting couples and heterosexual cohabiting couples were first distinguished from roommates in the 1990 census. Hispanic self-identification was first allowed in the 1970 census. The distinction between black, white, and Asian can be traced with some degree of consistency in the U.S. census back to the nineteenth century.

12. U.S. Bureau of the Census, "Technical Note on Same-Sex Unmarried Partner Data from the 1990 and 2000 Censuses" (2001), http://landview.census.gov/population/www/cen2000/samesex.html (accessed February 7, 2004).

13. Paul Spickard, *Mixed Blood: Intermarriage and Ethnic Identity in Twentieth-*

Century America (Madison: University of Wisconsin Press, 1989), p. 291.

14. Wallenstein, *Tell the Court I Love My Wife.*

15. Edmund S. Morgan, *The Puritan Family: Religion and Domestic Relations in Seventeenth-Century New England* (New York: Harper, [1944] 1966).

16. Morgan, *The Puritan Family,* pp. 144–145.

17. Morgan, *The Puritan Family;* David Hackett Fischer, *Albion's Seed: Four British Folkways in America* (New York: Oxford University Press, 1989); Richard Godbeer, *Sexual Revolution in Early America* (Baltimore: Johns Hopkins University Press, 2002).

18. Tamar Lewin, "For More People in 20's and 30's, Home Is Where the Parents Are," *New York Times,* December 22, 2003, B:1; Abby Ellin, "You Earned Your Wings, So Return to the Nest," *New York Times,* June 16, 2002, 3:10.

19. Goldscheider and Goldscheider, *Leaving Home before Marriage.*

20. Jessie Bernard put this observation more strongly: every marriage is really "two marriages, his and hers." Jessie Bernard, *The Future of Marriage* (New Haven, Conn.: Yale University Press, 1972), pp. 4–5.

21. Alexis de Tocqueville, *Democracy in America,* vol. 1, trans. Henry Reeve, Francis Bowen, and Phillips Bradley (New York: Vintage, [1835] 1945); Ellen Rothman, *Hands and Hearts: A History of Courtship in America* (New York: Basic Books, 1984); Frank F. Furstenberg, Jr., "Industrialization and the American Family: A Look Backward," *American Sociological Review* 31, no. 3 (1966): 326–337.

22. Steven Mintz and Susan Kellogg, *Domestic Revolutions: A Social History of American Family Life* (New York: Free Press, 1988); Paula S. Fass, *The Damned and the Beautiful: American Youth in the 1920's* (New York: Oxford University Press, 1977); Christine Stansell, *City of Women: Sex and Class in New York, 1789–1860* (Urbana: University of Illinois Press, 1982); Steven Mintz, *Huck's Raft: A History of American Childhood* (Cambridge, Mass.: Harvard University Press, 2004); Nan Enstad, *Ladies of Labor, Girls of Adventure: Working Women, Popular Culture, and Labor Politics at the Turn of the Twentieth Century* (New York: Columbia University Press, 1999); Carole Shammas, "Anglo-American Household Government in Comparative Perspective," *William and Mary Quarterly* 52, no. 1 (1995): 104–144.

23. As parents become more tolerant of their children's nontraditional choices, nontraditional unions start appearing even before the independent life stage. Teenagers start having openly gay or openly interracial relationships while still living at home; Professor David John Frank, personal correspondence, October 22, 2005.

24. Doug McAdam, *Political Process and the Development of Black Insurgency, 1930–1970* (Chicago: University of Chicago Press, 1982).

25. Frances Fox Piven and Richard Cloward, *Poor People's Movements: How they Succeed, How They Fail* (New York: Pantheon, 1977).

26. See especially Doug McAdam, *Freedom Summer* (Oxford: Oxford University Press, 1990); Todd Gitlin, *The Sixties: Years of Hope, Days of Rage* (New York: Bantam, 1993).

27. Students for a Democratic Society, "Port Huron Statement" (New York: Students for a Democratic Society, 1962).

28. To mention but one other example, the leaders of the American Revolution were far younger than their opponents in the loyalist movement. The loyalist leaders had been around long enough to rise to prominence within the colonial system, whereas the young revolutionaries were young enough to see that a radical change in government could catalyze their own political and economic ambitions. See Mintz, *Huck's Raft*, p. 69.

29. Randy Shilts, *The Mayor of Castro Street: The Life and Times of Harvey Milk* (New York: St. Martin's Press, 1982).

30. Martin Duberman, *Stonewall* (New York: Plume, 1993).

31. Ibid., p. 207.

32. It does not even begin to scratch the surface, but examples include Gitlin, *The Sixties: Years of Hope, Days of Rage;* Sara Evans, *Personal Politics: The Roots of Women's Liberation in the Civil Rights Movement and the New Left* (New York: Vintage, 1980); McAdam, *Freedom Summer;* Milton Viorst, *Fire in the Streets: America in the 1960s* (New York: Simon and Schuster, 1979); Duberman, *Stonewall;* John D'Emilio, *Sexual Politics, Sexual Communities: The Making of a Homosexual Minority in the United States, 1940–1970* (Chicago: University of Chicago Press, 1998).

33. Ruggles et al., "Integrated Public Use Microdata Series: Version 3.0."

34. James Allan Davis, Tom W. Smith, and Peter V. Marsden, *General Social Surveys, 1972–2000: Cumulative Codebook* (Chicago: National Opinion Research Center, 2000).

35. Steven Ruggles, "The Transformation of the American Family Structure," *American Historical Review* 99, no. 1 (1994): 103–128.

36. Peter L. Berger and Thomas Luckmann, *The Social Construction of Reality: A Treatise in the Sociology of Knowledge* (New York: Doubleday, 1966); Nancy F. Cott, *Public Vows: A History of Marriage and the Nation* (Cambridge, Mass.: Harvard University Press, 2000); John D'Emilio and Estelle Freedman, *Intimate Matters: A History of Sexuality in America* (New York: Harper and Row, 1988); Godbeer, *Sexual Revolu-*

tion in Early America; Michael Grossberg, *Governing the Hearth: Law and the Family in Nineteenth-Century America* (Chapel Hill: University of North Carolina Press, 1985); Moran, *Interracial Intimacy.*

37. Sidney Kaplan, "The Miscegenation Issue in the Election of 1864," *Journal of Negro History* 34, no. 3 (1949): 274–343.

38. Laud Humphreys studied men who had sex with men in public restrooms. Since most of these men were married and their homosexuality was a carefully guarded secret whose revelation would have threatened their social standing, Humphreys had to resort to very clever deceit (or in the view of some critics, unethical methods) in order to study this group. See Laud Humphreys, *Tearoom Trade: Impersonal Sex in Public Places* (New York: Aldine de Gruyter, 1975). In general, covert or closeted behavior is beyond the reach of nationally representative surveys.

39. William Julius Wilson, *The Truly Disadvantaged: The Inner City, the Underclass, and Public Policy* (Chicago: University of Chicago Press, 1987); Lee Rainwater and William L. Yancey, *The Moynihan Report and the Politics of Controversy* (Cambridge, Mass.: MIT Press, 1967); Herbert G. Gutman, *The Black Family in Slavery and Freedom, 1750–1925* (New York: Vintage, 1976).

40. There is a substantial literature on interracial unions. See Milton Gordon, *Assimilation in American Life: The Role of Race, Religion, and National Origin* (New York: Oxford University Press, 1964); Matthijs Kalmijn, "Trends in Black/White Intermarriage," *Social Forces* 72 (1993): 119–146; Matthijs Kalmijn, "Intermarriage and Homogamy: Causes, Patterns, Trends," *Annual Review of Sociology* 24 (1998): 395–421; Zhenchao Qian, "Breaking the Racial Barriers: Variations in Interracial Marriage between 1980 and 1990," *Demography* 34 (1997): 263–276; Maria P. P. Root, *Love's Revolution: Interracial Marriage* (Philadelphia: Temple University Press, 2001); Michael J. Rosenfeld, "Measures of Assimilation in the Marriage Market: Mexican Americans 1970–1990," *Journal of Marriage and the Family* 64 (2002): 152–162; Moran, *Interracial Intimacy;* Renee C. Romano, *Race Mixing: Black-White Marriage in Postwar America* (Cambridge, Mass.: Harvard University Press, 2003); David Heer, "Intermarriage," in *Harvard Encyclopedia of American Ethnic Groups,* ed. Stephan Thernstrom, Ann Orlov, and Oscar Handlin (Cambridge, Mass.: Harvard University Press, 1980), pp. 513–521; David Heer, "The Prevalence of Black-White Marriage in the United States, 1960 and 1970," *Journal of Marriage and the Family* 36 (1974): 246–258; Randall Kennedy, *Interracial Intimacies: Sex, Marriage, Identity and Adoption* (New York: Pantheon,

2003); Spickard, *Mixed Blood: Intermarriage and Ethnic Identity in Twentieth-Century America.*

Literature on same-sex couples includes Allan Bérubé, *Coming Out under Fire: The History of Gay Men and Women in World War Two* (New York: Free Press, 1990); Lillian Faderman, *Surpassing the Love of Men: Romantic Friendship and Love between Women from the Renaissance to the Present* (New York: Harper Collins, [1981] 1998); Lillian Faderman, *Odd Girls and Twilight Lovers: A History of Lesbian Life in Twentieth-Century America* (New York: Penguin, 1991); George Chauncey, *Gay New York: Gender, Urban Culture and the Making of the Gay Male World, 1890–1940* (New York: Basic Books, 1994); John D'Emilio, "Capitalism and Gay Identity," in *The Lesbian and Gay Studies Reader,* ed. Henry Abelove, Michele Aina Barale, and David M. Halperin (New York: Routledge, 1993), pp. 467–478; D'Emilio, *Sexual Politics, Sexual Communities;* Elizabeth Lapovsky Kennedy and Madeline D. Davis, *Boots of Leather, Slippers of Gold: The History of a Lesbian Community* (New York: Routledge, 1993).

Among the sources above that discuss both same-sex couples and interracial couples are Romano's *Race Mixing* and Kennedy and Davis's *Boots of Leather, Slippers of Gold.*

Recently, a few social scientists and legal scholars have been working on the intersection of sex and race. One example is Joane Nagel, *Race, Ethnicity, and Sexuality: Intimate Intersections, Forbidden Frontiers* (New York: Oxford University Press, 2003). Nagel's argument is mostly about the sexual stereotypes and gender power dynamics in heterosexual interracial unions, but she also discusses sexual identity and homosexuality. Legal scholarship on gay rights and same-sex marriage usually discusses interracial marriage because the court decisions on interracial marriage (especially Loving v. Virginia) are a key legal precedent for the question of same-sex marriage in the United States. See Eskridge, *Equality Practice;* Koppelman, *The Gay Rights Question in Contemporary American Law;* Mark Strasser, "Family, Definitions, and the Constitution: On the Antimiscegenation Analogy," *Suffolk University Law Review* 25 (1991): 981–1034.

41. Andrew Sullivan and Joseph Landau, eds., *Same-Sex Marriage: Pro and Con* (New York: Vintage, 1997); Strasser, "Family, Definitions, and the Constitution"; D'Emilio, *Sexual Politics, Sexual Communities.*

42. Clem Brooks, "Civil Rights Liberalism and the Suppression of a Republican Political Realignment in the United States, 1972 to 1996," *American Sociological Review* 65 (2000): 483–505.

43. George Chauncey et al., "Amicus brief in support of the petitioners in Lawrence v. Texas" (2003).

44. Arnett, *Emerging Adulthood;* Duane F. Alwin, "From Obedience to Autonomy: Changes in Traits Desired in Children, 1924–1978," *Public Opinion Quarterly* 52, no. 1 (1988): 33–52; John Demos, "Child Abuse in Context: An Historian's Perspective," in *Past, Present and Personal: The Family and the Life Course in American History* (New York: Oxford University Press, 1986), pp. 68–91; Joseph F. Kett, *Rites of Passage: Adolescence in America 1790 to the Present* (New York: Basic Books, 1977).

45. Griswold v. Connecticut, 381 U.S. 479 (1965); Robert H. Bork, *The Tempting of America: The Political Seduction of the Law* (New York: Simon & Schuster, 1991); Loving v. Virginia; Eisenstadt v. Baird, 405 U.S. 438 (1972); Roe v. Wade, 410 U.S. 113 (1973); Lawrence v. Texas; Koppelman, *The Gay Rights Question in Contemporary American Law;* Laurence H. Tribe, *Abortion: The Clash of Absolutes* (New York: W. W. Norton, 1992).

2. Family Government

1. Edmund S. Morgan, *The Puritan Family: Religion and Domestic Relations in Seventeenth-Century New England* (New York: Harper, [1944] 1966).

2. Morgan, *The Puritan Family;* David Hackett Fischer, *Albion's Seed: Four British Folkways in America* (New York: Oxford University Press, 1989).

3. Nancy F. Cott, *Public Vows: A History of Marriage and the Nation* (Cambridge, Mass.: Harvard University Press, 2000); Michael Grossberg, *Governing the Hearth: Law and the Family in Nineteenth-Century America* (Chapel Hill: University of North Carolina Press, 1985); Claude Lévi-Strauss, *The Elementary Structures of Kinship,* trans. James Harle Bell and John Richard von Sturmer (Boston: Beacon Press, 1969); Richard Godbeer, *Sexual Revolution in Early America* (Baltimore, Md.: Johns Hopkins University Press, 2002).

4. Morton Hunt, *The Natural History of Love* (New York: Anchor Books, 1994).

5. John Demos, *A Little Commonwealth: Family Life in Plymouth Colony* (London: Oxford University Press, 2000); Godbeer, *Sexual Revolution in Early America;* Grossberg, *Governing the Hearth;* Morgan, *The Puritan Family.* Although the view of strong family government over young adults in the colonies is the dominant scholarly view, there are dissenters; see Carole Shammas, *A History of Household Government in America* (Charlottesville: University of Virginia Press, 2002). Since the currently available census microdata extend back only to

1850, all assumptions about family life in the United States before 1850 are necessarily based on fragmentary data. Some colonial American observers believed that marriages were made without much consideration of parental wishes, but this misses the point: the structure of colonial life constrained mate selection in ways that young people would usually not have been aware of.

6. Demos, *A Little Commonwealth;* Fischer, *Albion's Seed;* Grossberg, *Governing the Hearth;* Morgan, *The Puritan Family.*

7. Fischer, *Albion's Seed;* Barry Levy, *Quakers and the American Family: British Settlement in the Delaware Valley* (New York: Oxford University Press, 1988).

8. Fischer, *Albion's Seed,* p. 485.

9. Shammas, *A History of Household Government in America,* p. 105.

10. Edmund S. Morgan, *Virginians at Home: Family Life in the Eighteenth Century* (Williamsburg, Va.: William Byrd Press, 1952); Fischer, *Albion's Seed.*

11. Fischer, *Albion's Seed.*

12. Grossberg, *Governing the Hearth.*

13. Godbeer, *Sexual Revolution in Early America.*

14. Grossberg, *Governing the Hearth,* p. 66.

15. Ibid., p. 68.

16. John D'Emilio and Estelle Freedman, *Intimate Matters: A History of Sexuality in America* (New York: Harper and Row, 1988); Morgan, *The Puritan Family.*

17. Joseph F. Kett, *Rites of Passage: Adolescence in America 1790 to the Present* (New York: Basic Books, 1977).

18. Fischer, *Albion's Seed.*

19. More than half of the white European immigrants to the English colonies in North America in the eighteenth century arrived in the colonies as indentured servants. See Steven Mintz, *Huck's Raft: A History of American Childhood* (Cambridge, Mass.: Harvard University Press, 2004), p. 33.

20. Philippe Ariès, *Centuries of Childhood: A Social History of Family Life,* trans. Robert Baldick (New York: Vintage, 1962); Kett, *Rites of Passage;* Edward Shorter, *The Making of the Modern Family* (New York: Basic Books, 1975).

21. Demos, *A Little Commonwealth.*

22. Godbeer, *Sexual Revolution in Early America.*

23. Ibid.

24. Fischer, *Albion's Seed.*

25. Morgan, *The Puritan Family*.
26. Arthur W. Calhoun, *A Social History of the American Family: Colonial Period*, vol. 1 (New York: Barnes and Noble, [1917] 1960).
27. Roger Thompson, *Sex in Middlesex: Popular Mores in a Massachusetts County, 1649–1699* (Amherst: University of Massachusetts Press, 1986), p. 10.
28. Fischer, *Albion's Seed*.
29. Morgan, *The Puritan Family*, pp. 148–149.
30. Carole Shammas, "Anglo-American Household Government in Comparative Perspective," *William and Mary Quarterly* 52, no. 1 (1995): 104–144.
31. Calhoun, *A Social History of the American Family: Colonial Period*, p. 248.
32. According to historian George Fredrickson, the colonists' desire to conquer the native peoples west of the Mississippi and take their land, combined with the English crown's unwillingness to permit the abrogation of treaties with the native peoples, meant that the colonists needed to be independent of England in order to pursue their goals of territorial expansion. This, according to Fredrickson, was the primary reason for the American Revolution. See George M. Fredrickson, *White Supremacy: A Comparative Study in American and South African History* (Oxford: Oxford University Press, 1981).
33. William J. Goode, *World Revolution and Family Patterns* (New York: Free Press, [1963] 1970); Frank F. Furstenberg, Jr., "Industrialization and the American Family: A Look Backward," *American Sociological Review* 31, no. 3 (1966): 326–337; Godbeer, *Sexual Revolution in Early America*.
34. Alexis de Tocqueville, *Democracy in America*, vol. 1, trans. Henry Reeve, Francis Bowen, and Phillips Bradley (New York: Vintage, [1835] 1945).
35. For a modern re-appreciation of Tocqueville's ideas of independence in American life, see Robert N. Bellah et al., *Habits of the Heart: Individualism and Commitment in American Life* (New York: Harper and Row, 1985).
36. Noel Ignatiev, *How the Irish Became White* (New York: Routledge, 1995); Kett, *Rites of Passage*.
37. Daniel Scott Smith and Michael S. Hindus, "Premarital Pregnancy in America, 1640–1971: An Overview and Interpretation," *Journal of Interdisciplinary History* 5, no. 4 (1975): 537–570.
38. Kett, *Rites of Passage*.

39. John Demos, "The Rise and Fall of Adolescence," in *Past, Present, and Personal: The Family and the Life Course in American History* (New York: Oxford University Press, 1986), pp. 92–113, quotation from p. 102.

40. Grossberg, *Governing the Hearth.* On the other hand, other scholars wonder if "republicanism's love of small government tend[ed] to favor household solutions to social problems"; Shammas, "Anglo-American Household Government in Comparative Perspective," p. 106.

41. Historian Carole Shammas notes that white male patriarchy in the colonies had limits inherited from English law: the father could not take more than one wife, he could not sell his servants, and he could not force marriage upon his children. See Shammas, "Anglo-American Household Government in Comparative Perspective."

42. The white men who made the American Revolution used a universal language of rights, but in reality they had only white male rights in mind, so some scholars have argued that the spirit of republicanism had no effect on the rights of women, minors, or blacks. Some of the northern states that had small numbers of slaves emancipated their slaves after independence, but the influence of slavery deepened in the South. In the North, indentured servitude continued unabated. See Shammas, "Anglo-American Household Government in Comparative Perspective."

43. Grossberg, *Governing the Hearth.*

44. In colonial times, sodomy had generally been illegal (and continued to be illegal in some states until the 2003 Supreme Court decision in Lawrence v. Texas) but homosexuality was unknown, that is, there was no language of different sexual orientations. The term "homosexuality" was a creation of the late nineteenth century. Michel Foucault, *The History of Sexuality: An Introduction* (New York: Vintage, [1976] 1990); D'Emilio and Freedman, *Intimate Matters.*

45. Carroll Smith-Rosenberg, "The Abortion Movement and the AMA, 1850–1880," in *Disorderly Conduct: Visions of Gender in Victorian America* (New York: Oxford University Press, 1985), pp. 217–244.

46. D'Emilio and Freedman, *Intimate Matters;* Anna Louise Bates, *Weeder in the Garden of the Lord: Anthony Comstock's Life and Career* (Lanham, Md: University Press of America, 1995); James Q. Wilson, "Crime and American Culture," *The Public Interest* 70, no. Winter (1983): 22–48.

47. Bates, *Weeder in the Garden of the Lord;* Nicola Beisel, *Imperiled Innocents: Anthony Comstock and Family Reproduction in Victorian America* (Princeton, N.J.: Princeton University Press, 1997).

48. Nancy F. Cott, *The Bonds of Womanhood: "Woman's Sphere" in New England, 1780–1835* (New Haven, Conn.: Yale University Press, 1997).

49. Ibid., Carroll Smith-Rosenberg, "Beauty, the Beast and the Militant Woman: A Case Study in Sex Roles and Social Stress in Jacksonian America," in *Disorderly Conduct: Visions of Gender in Victorian America* (New York: Oxford University Press, 1985), pp. 109–128.

50. Lillian Faderman, *Odd Girls and Twilight Lovers: A History of Lesbian Life in Twentieth-Century America* (New York: Penguin, 1991), p. 13.

51. Arthur W. Calhoun, *A Social History of the American Family: From 1865 to 1919*, vol. 3 (New York: Barnes and Noble, [1919] 1960), p. 93.

52. Carroll Smith-Rosenberg, "The Female World of Love and Ritual: Relations between Women in Nineteenth-Century America," in *Disorderly Conduct: Visions of Gender in Victorian America* (New York: Oxford University Press, 1985), pp. 53–76; Lillian Faderman, *Surpassing the Love of Men: Romantic Friendship and Love between Women from the Renaissance to the Present* (New York: Harper Collins, [1981] 1998).

53. Faderman, *Surpassing the Love of Men.*

54. Faderman, *Odd Girls and Twilight Lovers*, p. 4.

55. Faderman, *Surpassing the Love of Men.*

56. Faderman, *Odd Girls and Twilight Lovers*, p. 42.

57. Smith-Rosenberg, "The Female World of Love and Ritual."

58. Ibid., p. 57.

59. Faderman, *Surpassing the Love of Men*, pp. 190–203.

60. Eugene D. Genovese, *Roll, Jordan, Roll: The World the Slaves Made* (New York: Vintage, 1976). Kenneth Stampp points out that slave weddings, even when celebrated jointly by master and slave at the master's expense, were not so much joint celebrations as staged amusements in which the illiteracy and simple customs of the slaves were entertainment for the masters. Kenneth M. Stampp, *The Peculiar Institution: Slavery in the Ante-Bellum South* (New York: Vintage Books, [1956] 1989), p. 329.

61. Wilma King, *Stolen Childhood: Slave Youth in Nineteenth-Century America* (Bloomington: Indiana University Press, 1995); Stampp, *The Peculiar Institution;* Genovese, *Roll, Jordan, Roll.*

62. Mintz, *Huck's Raft*, p. 103; Frederick Douglass, *Narrative of the Life of Frederick Douglass, An American Slave, Written by Himself* (New Haven, Conn.: Yale University Press, [1845] 2001); Stampp, *The Peculiar Institution.*

63. Mintz, *Huck's Raft;* King, *Stolen Childhood;* Douglass, *Narrative.*

64. Lee Rainwater and William L. Yancey, *The Moynihan Report and the Politics of Controversy* (Cambridge, Mass.: MIT Press, 1967); J. E. Gold-

thorpe, *Family Life in Western Societies: A Historical Sociology of Family Relationships in Britain and North America* (Cambridge: Cambridge University Press, 1987).

65. Daniel Patrick Moynihan, in a famous report on the black family that he prepared for President Lyndon Johnson, argued that the black family of the 1960s was a damaged institution (with low marriage rates, high divorce rates, and too many woman-headed families) because of the harm slavery had done. Herbert Gutman, in a scholarly response, argued that slavery's impact on black families was far less than was usually assumed and that low black marriage rates in the twentieth century could not be attributed to slavery. Critics, including James Q. Wilson, replied that Gutman had glossed over the harm that slavery did to black families. See Hebert G. Gutman, *The Black Family in Slavery and Freedom, 1750–1925* (New York: Vintage, 1976); Rainwater and Yancey, *The Moynihan Report;* Genovese, *Roll, Jordan, Roll;* Goldthorpe, *Family Life in Western Societies;* James Q. Wilson, *The Marriage Problem: How Our Culture Has Weakened Families* (New York: Harper Collins, 2002).

66. Winthrop D. Jordan, *White over Black: American Attitudes toward the Negro, 1550–1812* (Chapel Hill: University of North Carolina Press, 1968); Stampp, *The Peculiar Institution;* Genovese, *Roll, Jordan, Roll;* Godbeer, *Sexual Revolution in Early America.*

67. Godbeer, *Sexual Revolution in Early America;* Joseph J. Ellis, "Jefferson: Post-DNA," *William and Mary Quarterly* 57, no. 1 (2000): 125–138; Annette Gordon-Reed, "Engaging Jefferson: Blacks and the Founding Father," *William and Mary Quarterly* 57, no. 1 (2000): 171–182. Thomas Jefferson's will freed Sally Hemings's children, but while Jefferson was alive they remained slaves.

68. There were exceptions of course: some writers assumed Jefferson was a hypocrite from the start. See Ellis, "Jefferson: Post-DNA"; Jordan, *White over Black.*

69. The evidence of Jefferson's paternity of Sally Hemings's children comes not only from DNA evidence (which could equally implicate Thomas Jefferson's son as the father of Sally Hemings's children) but also from the timing of birth of Hemings's six children born at Monticello, coming always nine months after Jefferson's return to Monticello. See Fraser D. Neiman, "Coincidence or Causal Connection? The Relationship between Thomas Jefferson's Visits to Monticello and Sally Hemings's Conceptions," *William and Mary Quarterly* 57, no. 1 (2000): 198–210. Taken together, the DNA evidence and the timing evidence have eradicated any reasonable doubts about Jefferson's paternity of Hemings's children.

70. Ellis, "Jefferson: Post-DNA."
71. Stampp, *The Peculiar Institution;* Douglass, *Narrative.*
72. James West Davidson and Mark Hamilton Lytle, *After the Fact: The Art of Historical Detection* (New York: McGraw-Hill, 1999), pp. 147–177.
73. Ellis, "Jefferson: Post-DNA"; Peter S. Onuf, "Every Generation Is an 'Independent Nation': Colonization, Miscegenation, and the Fate of Jefferson's Children," *William and Mary Quarterly* 57, no. 1 (2000): 153–170.
74. Ignatiev, *How the Irish Became White;* Stampp, *The Peculiar Institution.*
75. Martha Hodes, *White Women, Black Men: Illicit Sex in the 19th Century* (New Haven, Conn.: Yale University Press, 1997).
76. Rachel Moran, *Interracial Intimacy: The Regulation of Race and Romance* (Chicago: University of Chicago Press, 2001); Peter Wallenstein, *Tell the Court I Love My Wife: Race, Marriage, and Law—An American History* (New York: Palgrave Macmillan, 2002). The word "miscegenation" was invented during the U.S. presidential campaign of 1864 by pro-slavery newspaper editors in New York; see Sidney Kaplan, "The Miscegenation Issue in the Election of 1864," *Journal of Negro History* 34, no. 3 (1949): 274–343.
77. Calhoun, *A Social History of the American Family: From 1865 to 1919.*
78. Neil J. Smelser, *Social Change in the Industrial Revolution: An Application of Theory to the British Cotton Industry, 1770–1840* (Chicago: University of Chicago Press, 1959).
79. Peter Laslett, *The World We Have Lost: England before the Industrial Age* (New York: Charles Scribner's Sons, [1965] 1971); Peter Laslett, *Family Life and Illicit Love in Earlier Generations* (Cambridge: Cambridge University Press, 1977).
80. Beth L. Bailey, *From Front Porch to Back Seat: Courtship in Twentieth-Century America* (Baltimore, Md.: Johns Hopkins University Press, 1988), p. 17.
81. Ibid.
82. Ibid., p. 18
83. Bates, *Weeder in the Garden of the Lord,* p. 200.
84. D'Emilio and Freedman, *Intimate Matters;* Paula S. Fass, *The Damned and the Beautiful: American Youth in the 1920's* (New York: Oxford University Press, 1977).
85. Cott, *Public Vows.*
86. Glen H. Elder, Jr., *Children of the Great Depression: Social Change in Life Experience* (Chicago: University of Chicago Press, 1974).
87. Kingsley Davis and Pietronella van den Oever, "Age Relations and Public Policy in Advanced Industrial Societies," *Population and Development Review* 7, no. 1 (1981): 1–18.

88. Allan Bérubé, *Coming Out under Fire: The History of Gay Men and Women in World War Two* (New York: Free Press, 1990); John D'Emilio, *Sexual Politics, Sexual Communities: The Making of a Homosexual Minority in the United States, 1940–1970* (Chicago: University of Chicago Press, 1998); D'Emilio and Freedman, *Intimate Matters.*

89. Bérubé, *Coming Out under Fire.*

90. Elizabeth Lapovsky Kennedy and Madeline D. Davis, *Boots of Leather, Slippers of Gold: The History of a Lesbian Community* (New York: Routledge, 1993); Faderman, *Odd Girls and Twilight Lovers,* pp. 118–138.

91. Randy Shilts, *Conduct Unbecoming: Gays and Lesbians in the U.S. Military* (New York: Fawcett Columbine, 1993); Bérubé, *Coming Out under Fire.*

92. Beth Bailey, *Sex in the Heartland* (Cambridge, Mass.: Harvard University Press, 1999).

93. Ibid.

94. Ibid., David Riesman, Nathan Glazer, and Reuel Denney, *The Lonely Crowd: A Study of the Changing American Character* (New Haven, Conn.: Yale University Press, [1950] 2001).

95. Douglas S. Massey and Nancy A. Denton, *American Apartheid: Segregation and the Making of the Underclass* (Cambridge, Mass.: Harvard University Press, 1993); Arnold R Hirsch, *Making the Second Ghetto: Race and Housing in Chicago, 1940–1960* (Cambridge: Cambridge University Press, 1983).

96. Gunnar Myrdal, Richard Sterner, and Arnold Rose, *An American Dilemma: The Negro Problem and Modern Democracy* (New York: Harper, 1944).

97. Emory S. Bogardus, "Measurement of Personal-Group Relations," *Sociometry* 10, no. 4 (1947): 306–311.

98. Hirsch, *Making the Second Ghetto.*

99. Massey and Denton, *American Apartheid;* Hirsch, *Making the Second Ghetto.*

100. Julie DaVanzo and M. Omar Rahman, "American Families: Trends and Correlates," *Population Index* 59 (1993): 350–386.

101. Ruby Jo Reeves Kennedy, "Premarital Residential Propinquity and Ethnic Endogamy," *American Journal of Sociology* 48, no. 5 (1943): 580–584; Maurice R. Davie and Ruby Jo Reeves, "Propinquity of Residence before Marriage," *American Journal of Sociology* 44, no. 4 (1939): 510–517; Alfred C. Clarke, "An Examination of the Operation of Residential Propinquity as a Factor in Mate Selection," *American Sociological Review* 17 (1952): 17–22; James H. S. Bossard, "Residential Propinquity as a Factor in Marriage Selection," *American Journal of*

Sociology 38, no. 2 (1932): 219–224; Joseph R. Marches and Gus Tur-
beville, "The Effect of Residential Propinquity on Marriage Selection," *American Journal of Sociology* 58, no. 6 (1953): 592–595.

102. Bossard, "Residential Propinquity as a Factor in Marriage Selection."
103. Kennedy, "Premarital Residential Propinquity and Ethnic En-
     dogamy."
104. Massey and Denton, *American Apartheid*.
105. D'Emilio, *Sexual Politics, Sexual Communities;* George Chauncey, *Gay
     New York: Gender, Urban Culture and the Making of the Gay Male World,
     1890–1940* (New York: Basic Books, 1994); Kennedy and Davis, *Boots
     of Leather, Slippers of Gold*.
106. D'Emilio, *Sexual Politics, Sexual Communities*.
107. Ibid., Chauncey, *Gay New York;* Claude Fischer, "Toward a Subcul-
     tural Theory of Urbanism," *American Journal of Sociology* 80, no. 6
     (1975): 1319–1341; Louis Wirth, "Urbanism as a Way of Life," *Amer-
     ican Journal of Sociology* 44, no. 1 (1938): 1–24.
108. Betty Friedan, *The Feminine Mystique* (New York: Dell, 1974); Ken-
     nedy and Davis, *Boots of Leather, Slippers of Gold*.
109. Bérubé, *Coming Out under Fire;* Renee C. Romano, *Race Mixing: Black-
     White Marriage in Postwar America* (Cambridge, Mass.: Harvard Uni-
     versity Press, 2003); John D'Emilio, "Capitalism and Gay Identity," in
     The Lesbian and Gay Studies Reader, ed. Henry Abelove, Michele Aina
     Barale, and David M. Halperin (New York: Routledge, 1993), pp. 467–
     478.
110. Bérubé, *Coming Out under Fire*.
111. Ibid., p. 6.
112. Romano, *Race Mixing*.
113. Goode, *World Revolution and Family Patterns*, p. 32.

3. The Independent Life Stage

1. Larry L. Bumpass, "What's Happening to the Family? Interactions between Demographic and Institutional Change," *Demography* 27, no. 4
   (1990): 483–498; Andrew J. Cherlin, *Marriage, Divorce, Remarriage*
   (Cambridge, Mass.: Harvard University Press, 1992); Julie DaVanzo
   and M. Omar Rahman, "American Families: Trends and Correlates,"
   Population Index 59 (1993): 350–386; Frank F. Furstenberg, Jr., "Divorce and the American Family," *Annual Review of Sociology* 16 (1990):
   379–403; Frank F. Furstenberg, Jr., "Family Change and Family Diversity," in *Diversity and Its Discontents: Cultural Conflict and Common
   Ground in Contemporary American Society,* ed. Neil J. Smelser and Jef-

frey C. Alexander (Princeton, N.J.: Princeton University Press, 1999);
William J. Goode, *World Revolution and Family Patterns* (New York:
The Free Press, [1963] 1970); Tom W. Smith, "The Emerging 21st
Century American Family," *General Social Survey Social Change Report*
No. 42 (1999).

2. Arthur W. Calhoun, *A Social History of the American Family: From 1865
to 1919,* vol. 3 (New York: Barnes and Noble, [1919] 1960), pp. 323–
332.

3. Karl Marx and Friedrich Engels, *The Marx-Engels Reader,* trans.
Robert C. Tucker (New York: W. W. Norton, 1978).

4. Lewis A. Coser, *Masters of Sociological Thought* (Fort Worth, Tex.: Harcourt Brace Jovanovich, 1977); Frédéric Le Play, *On Family, Work,
and Social Change,* trans. Catherine Bodard Silver (Chicago: University of Chicago Press, 1982).

5. Peter Laslett, *The World We Have Lost: England before the Industrial Age*
(New York: Charles Scribner's Sons, [1965] 1971); John Hajnal, "European Marriage Patterns in Perspective," in *Population in History: Essays in Historical Demography,* ed. D. V. Glass and D. E. C. Eversley
(Chicago: Aldine, 1965), pp. 101–143.

6. Peter Laslett and Richard Wall, eds., *Household and Family in Past
Time* (Cambridge: Cambridge University Press, [1972] 1977). Laslett's influential assertions about the premodern family have been
challenged on several grounds. For critiques, see Lutz K. Berkner,
"The Use and Misuse of Census Data for the Historical Analysis of
Family Structure," *Journal of Interdisciplinary History* 5, no. 4 (1975):
721–738; David I. Kertzer, "Household History and Sociological
Theory," *Annual Review of Sociology* 17 (1991): 155–179; Steven Ruggles, "The Transformation of the American Family Structure," *American Historical Review* 99, no. 1 (1994): 103–128. Whether the premodern family was really a nuclear family, as Laslett argued, or
whether stem families and complex families were common depends
on historical period, specific geography, and each researcher's interpretation of the limited data that does exist. Technically, a stem
family is a family formed when one adult child who lives with his or
her parents brings his or her spouse into the parental home.

7. The finding of population turnover in preindustrial towns is from
Laslett's study of the parish records for the English towns of Clay-
worth and Cogenhoe, reprinted in Peter Laslett, *Family Life and Illicit
Love in Earlier Generations* (Cambridge: Cambridge University Press,
1977).

8. Laslett, *The World We Have Lost;* Laslett, *Family Life and Illicit Love in Earlier Generations.* Around the same time as Laslett was first publishing his influential work on the pre-industrial family, several American sociologists also become skeptical of the supposed influence of the industrial revolution on the family. See Frank F. Furstenberg, Jr., "Industrialization and the American Family: A Look Backward," *American Sociological Review* 31, no. 3 (1966): 326–337; Goode, *World Revolution and Family Patterns.*

9. U.S. Bureau of the Census, *Historical Statistics of the United States, Colonial Times to 1970, Bicentennial Edition, Part 1* (Washington, D.C.: U.S. Government Printing Office, 1975); Michael J. Rosenfeld, "Young Adulthood as a Factor in Social Change in the United States," *Population and Development Review* 32, no. 1 (2006).

10. Paul H. Jacobson, *American Marriage and Divorce* (New York: Rinehart and Company, 1959); Cherlin, *Marriage, Divorce, Remarriage.*

11. Michael B. Katz, *Reconstructing American Education* (Cambridge, Mass.: Harvard University Press, 1987); Joseph F. Kett, *Rites of Passage: Adolescence in America, 1790 to the Present* (New York: Basic Books, 1977); Samuel Bowles and Herbert Gintis, *Schooling in Capitalist America: Educational Reform and the Contradictions of Economic Life* (New York: Basic Books, 1976).

12. Calhoun, *A Social History of the American Family: From 1865 to 1919;* Anna Louise Bates, *Weeder in the Garden of the Lord: Anthony Comstock's Life and Career* (Lanham, Md.: University Press of America, 1995).

13. Ellen Rothman, *Hands and Hearts: A History of Courtship in America* (New York: Basic Books, 1984). Additional historical literature that emphasizes the independence of young adult whites from family government during the industrial revolution includes Nan Enstad, *Ladies of Labor, Girls of Adventure: Working Women, Popular Culture, and Labor Politics at the Turn of the Twentieth Century* (New York: Columbia University Press, 1999); Christine Stansell, *City of Women: Sex and Class in New York 1789–1860* (Urbana: University of Illinois Press, 1982); Howard P. Chudacoff, *The Age of the Bachelor: Creating an American Subculture* (Princeton, N.J.: Princeton University Press, 1999). For a historical argument about the rise of youthful independence in the 1920s, see Paula S. Fass, *The Damned and the Beautiful: American Youth in the 1920's* (New York: Oxford University Press, 1977).

14. Berkner, "The Use and Misuse of Census Data for the Historical Analysis of Family Structure."

15. Steven Ruggles et al., "Integrated Public Use Microdata Series: Version 3.0," in *Historical Census Projects* (Minneapolis: University of Minnesota, 2004), http://www.ipums.org.

16. U.S. census microdata for 1930 is not yet available, because the census bureau did not produce public use microdata from the 1930 census, and the anonymity-preserving seventy-two-year embargo on the original census files has only recently expired.

17. In 1980, 1990, and 2000, the U.S. Census Bureau sent a census form to every household in the United States. A random subset of households received a longer, more detailed form. The 5 percent census microdata is derived from the full set of responses to the long form. The weights in the census microdata are the inverse of the sampling probability, so weights average 100 in the 1-in-100 samples, and weights average 20 in the 1-in-20 samples. Usage of the weights yields reliable population totals and unbiased population proportions. In the 1980–2000 censuses, but especially in 2000, some individual weights are higher and some are lower than the average of 20. The variability of the weights is designed to correct for response rates to the census long form, which vary across subpopulations. Compared with response rates for the short form, which is legally obligatory, blacks for instance have lower response rates to the census long form. To compensate for this lower response rate to the census long form, blacks have slightly higher weights in the 5 percent microdata.

18. Hyman Alterman, *Counting People: The Census in History* (New York: Harcourt, Brace and World, 1969); Ruggles et al., "Integrated Public Use Microdata Series: Version 3.0."

19. U.S. Bureau of the Census, "Technical Note on Same-Sex Unmarried Partner Data from the 1990 and 2000 Censuses," (2001), http://landview.census.gov/population/www/cen2000/samesex.html (accessed February 7, 2004).

20. Alterman, *Counting People.*

21. Furstenberg, "Industrialization and the American Family."

22. The definition of metropolitan areas changes from census to census, so some caution must be exercised in interpreting Figure 3.1. In a few censuses (most notably 2000), a large proportion of individual records have missing metropolitan and central city status, which is why Figure 3.1 does not report a value for suburban percentage for 2000.

23. Jacob A. Riis, *How the Other Half Lives: Studies Among the Tenements of New York* (New York: C. Scribner's Sons, 1906).

24. Stansell, *City of Women.*
25. Bates, *Weeder in the Garden of the Lord;* Nicola Beisel, *Imperiled Innocents: Anthony Comstock and Family Reproduction in Victorian America* (Princeton, N.J.: Princeton University Press, 1997), Stansell, *City of Women.*
26. Calhoun, *A Social History of the American Family: From 1865 to 1919;* Beisel, *Imperiled Innocents.*
27. Tamara Hareven, *Family Time and Industrial Time: The Relationship between the Family and Work in a New England Industrial Community.* (Cambridge: Cambridge University Press, 1982).
28. Louise A. Tilly and Joan W. Scott, *Women, Work, and Family* (New York: Routledge, 1987); Neil J. Smelser, *Social Change in the Industrial Revolution: An Application of Theory to the British Cotton Industry 1770–1840* (Chicago: University of Chicago Press, 1959); E. P. Thompson, *The Making of the English Working Class* (London: Camelot Press, 1963).
29. Tilly and Scott, *Women, Work, and Family.*
30. Smelser, *Social Change in the Industrial Revolution.*
31. Figures 3.1 and 3.2 include only U.S.-born persons. The inclusion of immigrants does not change the shape of these figures.
32. The greatest difference between mortality risk in the nineteenth century and today is the decline of infant mortality. Life expectancy at birth in Massachusetts in 1850 was only thirty-nine years, but those who reached age twenty were expected to live to about age sixty. In contrast, whites born in the United States in 1950 had a life expectancy at birth of about seventy years (women a few years more, men a few years less), and those who were already twenty years of age could also expect to live to roughly seventy (women a few years more). U.S. Bureau of the Census, *Historical Statistics of the United States, Colonial Times to 1970,* p. 56.
33. Ruggles, "The Transformation of the American Family Structure"; U.S. Bureau of the Census, *Historical Statistics of the United States, Colonial Times to 1970;* Susan Cotts Watkins, Jane A. Menken, and John Bongaarts, "Demographic Foundations of Family Change," *American Sociological Review* 52 (1987): 346–358. The debate over the demographic limits to multigenerational co-residence is an important debate, because Laslett and his colleagues claimed that the paucity of multigenerational households in preindustrial western Europe meant that the western European family system had never been a multigenerational system, whereas critics claimed that high mortality meant that multigenerational households would have been rare even

if couples with children preferred to live with their parents. For critical discussion see Michael Anderson, *Approaches to the History of the Western Family 1500–1914* (London: Macmillan Press, 1980); Berkner, "The Use and Misuse of Census Data for the Historical Analysis of Family Structure"; Marion J. Levy, Jr., "Aspects of the Analysis of Family Structure," in *Aspects of the Analysis of Family Structure*, ed. Ansley J. Coale, et al. (Princeton, N.J.: Princeton University Press, 1965), pp. 1–63. For competing simulation studies of the effects of demographic limits on multigenerational households, see Steven Ruggles, *Prolonged Connections: The Rise of the Extended Family in Nineteenth-Century England and America* (Madison: University of Wisconsin Press, 1987); Kenneth W. Wachter, Eugene A. Hammel, and Peter Laslett, *Statistical Studies of Historical Social Structure* (New York: Academic Press, 1978).

34. John Modell and Tamara Hareven, "Urbanization and the Malleable Household: An Examination of Boarding and Lodging in American Families," *Journal of Marriage and the Family* 35, no. 3 (1973): 467–479; Stansell, *City of Women.*

35. Kett, *Rites of Passage;* Edmund S. Morgan, *The Puritan Family: Religion and Domestic Relations in Seventeenth-Century New England* (New York: Harper, [1944] 1966).

36. Modell and Hareven, "Urbanization and the Malleable Household."

37. Morgan, *The Puritan Family.*

38. It is also interesting to note that whereas young men had more residential autonomy from their parents in the beginning of the twentieth century, by the end of the twentieth century young women were less likely than young men to live with their parents. The independent life stage has been especially empowering to women, who were especially constrained by the previously dominant patriarchal family forms.

39. John Modell, Frank F. Furstenberg, Jr., and Theodore Hershberg, "Social Change and Transitions to Adulthood in Historical Perspective," in *The American Family in Social-Historical Perspective*, ed. Michael Gordon (New York: St. Martin's Press, 1978), pp. 192–219.

40. Cherlin, *Marriage, Divorce, Remarriage;* DaVanzo and Rahman, "American Families: Trends and Correlates."

41. See Jeffrey Jensen Arnett, *Emerging Adulthood: The Winding Road from the Late Teens through the Early Twenties* (Oxford: Oxford University Press, 2004); John Modell, *Into One's Own: From Youth to Adulthood in the United States, 1920–1975* (Berkeley: University of California Press, 1989); Marlis Buchmann, *The Script of Life in Modern Society: Entry*

into Adulthood in a Changing World (Chicago: University of Chicago Press, 1989); Richard A. Setterstein, Jr., Frank F. Furstenberg, Jr., and Rubén G. Rumbaut, eds., *On the Frontier of Adulthood: Theory, Research, and Public Policy* (Chicago: University of Chicago Press, 2005); Jeffrey Jensen Arnett and Susan Taber, "Adolescence Terminable and Interminable: When Does Adolescence End?" *Journal of Youth and Adolescence* 23, no. 5 (1994): 517–537.

42. The *New York Times* is especially responsible for this misperception. See for instance Tamar Lewin, "For More People in 20's and 30's, Home Is Where the Parents Are," *New York Times,* December 22, 2003, B:1; Dale Buss, "Sure, Come Back to the Nest. Here are the Rules," *New York Times,* January 23, 2005, 3:8; Abby Ellin, "You Earned Your Wings, So Return to the Nest," *New York Times,* June 16, 2002, 3:10.

43. According to Table 3.1, the percentage of all young women (including married and single women) who were both single and living with their parents went up between 1960 and 2000, from 12.4 percent to 21.1 percent, but the reason for this change is simply that marriage itself was declining in this age group.

44. Peter Applebome, "Parting Wisdom: Don't Worry, but Don't Rent Out My Room," *New York Times,* June 5, 2005, A:37.

45. Frances K. Goldscheider and Calvin Goldscheider, *Leaving Home before Marriage: Ethnicity, Familism, and Generational Relationships* (Madison: University of Wisconsin Press, 1993); Frances K. Goldscheider and Calvin Goldscheider, *The Changing Transition to Adulthood: Leaving and Returning Home* (Thousand Oaks, Calif.: Sage Publications, 1999).

46. Robert F. Schoeni and Karen E. Ross, "Material Assistance from Families during the Transition to Adulthood," in *On the Frontier of Adulthood,* ed. Richard A. Setterstein, Jr., Frank F. Furstenberg, Jr., and Rubén G. Rumbaut (Chicago: University of Chicago Press, 2005), pp. 396–416.

47. College attendance percentages are the author's tabulations from weighted census microdata. The year 1940 was the first for which the U.S. census recorded the educational attainment of all household members.

48. Steven Mintz, *Huck's Raft: A History of American Childhood* (Cambridge, Mass.: Harvard University Press, 2004), p. 59.

49. Kett, *Rites of Passage.*

50. Ibid.

51. Beth L. Bailey, *From Front Porch to Back Seat: Courtship in Twentieth-*

Century America (Baltimore, Md.: Johns Hopkins University Press, 1988).

52. John D'Emilio, *Making Trouble: Essays on Gay History, Politics, and the University* (New York: Routledge, 1992); Thomas Frank, *What's the Matter with Kansas? How Conservatives Won the Heart of America* (New York: Henry Holt, 2004).

53. Jon Weiner, "A Review of *The Common-Sense Guide to American Colleges 1991–1992,* Edited by Charles Horner," *The Nation,* February 24, 1992, 236–240; Frank, *What's the Matter with Kansas?*

54. The story of the Free Speech Movement and its implications is from the documentary film by Mark Kitchell, *Berkeley in the Sixties* (First Run Feature Films, 1990).

55. Ibid.

56. Ibid.

57. Ibid.

58. For a different perspective on the moral crisis of universities after 1960 (with special reference to Clark Kerr and the University of California), see Katz, *Reconstructing American Education,* pp. 160–183.

59. Enstad, *Ladies of Labor, Girls of Adventure.*

60. Kett, *Rites of Passage;* John Demos, *A Little Commonwealth: Family Life in Plymouth Colony* (London: Oxford University Press, 2000).

61. Robert Staughton Lynd and Helen Merrell Lynd, *Middletown: A Study in Contemporary American Culture* (New York: Harcourt, Brace, 1929), p. 26.

62. Betty Friedan, *The Feminine Mystique* (New York: Dell, 1974); Carroll Smith-Rosenberg, "Hearing Women's Words: A Feminist Reconstruction of History," in *Disorderly Conduct: Visions of Gender in Victorian America* (New York: Oxford University Press, 1985), pp. 11–52.

63. My calculation of the median age at first marriage from census records includes all individuals, whether they eventually marry or not, and therefore differs slightly (by about half a year) from the more standard calculations of age at first marriage, which usually exclude persons who remain unmarried at age fifty from the calculation. The standard method assumes that persons unmarried at fifty will never marry (one increasingly tenuous assumption), and the standard method must also must apply what demographers call the stationary population assumption (a second potentially problematic assumption) in order to apply older cohorts' percentages of unmarried persons at age fifty to more recent birth cohorts; see Catherine A. Fitch and Steven Ruggles, "Historical Trends in Marriage Formation: The United States, 1850–1990," in *The Ties That*

Bind: Perspectives on Marriage and Cohabitation, ed. Linda J. Waite et al. (New York: Aldine de Gruyter, 2000), pp. 59–90; Henry S. Shryock and Jacob S. Siegel, *The Methods and Materials of Demography* (Washington, D.C.: U.S. Bureau of the Census, 1975); John Hajnal, "Age at Marriage and Proportions Marrying," *Population Studies* 7, no. 2 (1953): 111–136. Fitch and Ruggles's calculations of median age at first marriage for U.S.-born whites from census microdata (their Figure 4.1) take the same shape as my figure, but their median ages are slightly lower than mine because they exclude the modest percentage of people they estimate will never marry. For examples of age at marriage from reconstructed parish records, see Philip J. Greven, Jr., *Four Generations: Population, Land and Family in Colonial Andover, Massachusetts* (Ithaca, N.Y.: Cornell University Press, 1970); Laslett, *The World We Have Lost;* Laslett, *Family Life and Illicit Love in Earlier Generations.*

64. For a variety of perspectives on the age at first marriage and its measurement with data from the United States, see Cherlin, *Marriage, Divorce, Remarriage;* Fitch and Ruggles, "Historical Trends in Marriage Formation"; Walt Saveland and Paul C. Glick, "First-Marriage Decrement Tables by Color and Sex for the United States in 1958–60," *Demography* 6, no. 3 (1969): 243–260; Paul C. Glick and Emanuel Landau, "Age as a Factor in Marriage," *American Sociological Review* 15, no. 4 (1950): 517–529; Paul C. Glick and Robert Parke, Jr., "New Approaches in Studying the Life Cycle of the Family," *Demography* 2 (1965): 187–202; DaVanzo and Rahman, "American Families: Trends and Correlates"; Thomas J. Espenshade, "Marriage Trends in America: Estimates, Implications, and Underlying Causes," *Population and Development Review* 11, no. 2 (1985): 193–245; Margaret Mooney Marini, "Measuring the Effects of the Timing of Marriage and First Birth," *Journal of Marriage and the Family* 43, no. 1 (1981): 19–26; Arland Thornton and Deborah Freedman, "The Changing American Family," *Population Index* 38 (1983): 1–43.

65. Cherlin, *Marriage, Divorce, Remarriage;* DaVanzo and Rahman, "American Families: Trends and Correlates"; Thornton and Freedman, "The Changing American Family."

66. Laslett, *The World We Have Lost;* Greven, *Four Generations.* In Greven's case the median age of marriage (all marriages, not just first marriages) is not provided but can be estimated from the tables (p. 121, Table 11) if one also knows how many individuals remained unmarried.

67. Greven, *Four Generations.*

68. Barry Levy, *Quakers and the American Family: British Settlement in the Delaware Valley* (New York: Oxford University Press, 1988).

69. Author's calculations from weighted census data.

70. Valerie Kinckaid Oppenheimer, "A Theory of Marriage Timing," *American Journal of Sociology* 94 (1988): 563–591.

71. Enstad, *Ladies of Labor, Girls of Adventure;* Fass, *The Damned and the Beautiful;* Stansell, *City of Women;* Calhoun, *A Social History of the American Family: From 1865 to 1919,* Rothman, *Hands and Hearts;* Chudacoff, *The Age of the Bachelor;* Mintz, *Huck's Raft;* Steven Mintz and Susan Kellogg, *Domestic Revolutions: A Social History of American Family Life* (New York: Free Press, 1988).

4. The Rise of Alternative Unions

1. Sections of transcribed interviews appear in this and in subsequent chapters. I interviewed twenty-eight couples in their homes in the San Francisco Bay Area between 2001 and 2004, usually with both partners together. Interviews lasted between ninety minutes and five hours, with an average of two and a half hours. Interviews were wide open and free form, but every interview started with a version of the same question: "Tell me about where you grew up, what your family was like, and what you can remember learning about race and gender roles."

2. Michael J. Rosenfeld, "Measures of Assimilation in the Marriage Market: Mexican Americans 1970–1990," *Journal of Marriage and the Family* 64 (2002): 152–162; Frank D. Bean and Marta Tienda, *The Hispanic Population of the United States* (New York: Russell Sage, 1987).

3. Rachel Moran, *Interracial Intimacy: The Regulation of Race and Romance* (Chicago: University of Chicago Press, 2001). But see also Zhenchao Qian, "Breaking the Racial Barriers: Variations in Interracial Marriage between 1980 and 1990," *Demography* 34 (1997): 263–276; Rosenfeld, "Measures of Assimilation in the Marriage Market: Mexican Americans 1970–1990"; Stanley Lieberson and Mary C. Waters, *From Many Strands: Ethnic and Racial Groups in Contemporary America* (New York: Russell Sage Foundation, 1988).

4. Guillermina Jasso and Mark R. Rosenzweig, *The New Chosen People: Immigrants in the United States* (New York: Russell Sage Foundation, 1990).

5. Michael J. Rosenfeld and Byung-Soo Kim, "The Independence of Young Adults and the Rise of Interracial and Same-Sex Unions," *American Sociological Review* 70, no. 4 (2005): 541–562.

6. The potential value of the 1990 and 2000 censuses for exploring the social demography of same-sex couples has been largely unrealized, with few exceptions. Exceptions include Marieka M. Klawitter and Victor Flatt, "The Effects of State and Local Antidiscrimination Policies on Earnings for Gays and Lesbians," *Journal of Policy Analysis and Management* 17, no. 4 (1998): 658–686; Gary J. Gates and Jason Ost, *The Gay and Lesbian Atlas* (Washington, D.C.: Urban Institute Press, 2004); Dan Black et al., "Demographics of the Gay and Lesbian Population in the United States: Evidence from Available Systematic Data Sources," *Demography* 37, no. 2 (2000): 139–154; Lisa K. Jepsen and Christopher A. Jepsen, "An Empirical Analysis of the Matching Patterns of Same-Sex and Opposite-Sex Couples," *Demography* 39, no. 3 (2002): 435–453.

7. Elizabeth Lapovsky Kennedy and Madeline D. Davis, *Boots of Leather, Slippers of Gold: The History of a Lesbian Community* (New York: Routledge, 1993); George Chauncey, *Gay New York: Gender, Urban Culture and the Making of the Gay Male World, 1890–1940* (New York: Basic Books, 1994).

8. The official published figures for same-sex couples from the census summary tapes, which are based on the census short form that was mailed out to every household in the United States, were 145,000 in 1990 and 593,000 in 2000. The census summary tapes provide better estimates for total population size, but researchers use the microdata because the microdata (unlike the summary tape files) can be studied at the individual level. Since most of the detailed statistics and the data analysis in the book can only be produced by using the census microdata, I rely on the census microdata for all the population statistics in order to be consistent. For the 2000 total of same-sex cohabiting couples from 100 percent summary tape files, see U.S. Bureau of the Census, *Statistical Abstract of the United States* (Washington, D.C.: U.S. Government Printing Office, 2003), p. 62, table 69.

9. U.S. Bureau of the Census, "Technical Note on Same-Sex Unmarried Partner Data from the 1990 and 2000 Censuses" (2001), http://landview.census.gov/population/www/cen2000/samesex.html (accessed February 7, 2004); Rosenfeld and Kim, "The Independence of Young Adults and the Rise of Interracial and Same-Sex Unions." The census technical note suggests that the 1990 and 2000 same-sex partner data simply cannot be compared. I argue that the 2000 same-sex partner data can be adjusted to be more compatible (though not perfectly compatible) with the 1990 data. For a detailed descrip-

tion of the adjustment procedure and its validity, see the supplement to the August 2005 American Sociological Review at http://www2.asanet.org/journals/asr/contents.html, or see my own Web site http://www.stanford.edu/~mrosenfe.

10. U.S. Bureau of the Census, "Technical Note on Same-Sex Unmarried Partner Data from the 1990 and 2000 Censuses."

11. Even though the adjusted sample of same-sex couples in 2000 is only about half as large as the full sample, both samples yield the same key empirical results. Using the more compatible adjusted data for same-sex couples in 2000 yields a growth rate of 108 percent in same-sex couples from 1990 to 2000, which is still an astonishing rate of growth and more reasonable than the 270 percent growth rate implied by the unadjusted published data; see Rosenfeld and Kim, "The Independence of Young Adults and the Rise of Interracial and Same-Sex Unions."

12. More important than the question of undercount of same-sex couples in the 1990 census is the question of bias. Black et al. argue that the 1990 sample of same-sex cohabiting couples is unbiased compared with other data sources, including the geographical distribution of persons who died of AIDS in 1990. Badgett and Rogers claim that the 2000 census sample of same-sex cohabiters is biased toward higher socioeconomic status compared with two small ($N =$ 174 and $N = 90$) convenience samples of gay couples. M. V. Lee Badgett and Marc A. Rogers, "Left Out of the Count: Missing Same-Sex Couples in Census 2000" (Amherst, Mass.: Institute for Gay and Lesbian Strategic Studies, 2003). The limitations of the other data sources on gays in the United States make evaluations of potential bias in the census rather difficult.

13. John Boswell, *Christianity, Social Tolerance and Homosexuality* (Chicago: University of Chicago Press, 1980).

14. See, for instance, Laumann's description of why conservative politicians were unwilling to fund their research; Edward O. Laumann et al., *The Social Organization of Sexuality: Sexual Practices in the United States* (Chicago: University of Chicago Press, 1994), p. 286. See also Eve Kosofsky Sedgwick, "Epistemology of the Closet," in *The Lesbian and Gay Studies Reader,* ed. Henry Abelove, Michele Aina Barale, and David M. Halperin (New York: Routledge, 1993), pp. 45–61.

15. Alfred C. Kinsey, Wardell B. Pomeroy, and Clyde E. Martin, *Sexual Behavior in the Human Male* (Philadelphia: W. B. Saunders, 1948); Chauncey, *Gay New York;* John D'Emilio, "Capitalism and Gay Identity," in *The Lesbian and Gay Studies Reader,* ed. Henry Abelove,

Michele Aina Barale, and David M. Halperin (New York: Routledge, 1993), pp. 467–478; John D'Emilio, *Sexual Politics, Sexual Communities: The Making of a Homosexual Minority in the United States, 1940–1970* (Chicago: University of Chicago Press, 1998); John D'Emilio and Estelle Freedman, *Intimate Matters: A History of Sexuality in America* (New York: Harper and Row, 1988); Laumann et al., *The Social Organization of Sexuality.*

16. Kinsey, Pomeroy, and Martin, *Sexual Behavior in the Human Male,* pp. 650–651.

17. William G. Cochran, Frederick Mosteller, and John W. Tukey, "Statistical Problems of the Kinsey Report," *Journal of the American Statistical Association* 48 (1953): 673–716; W. Allen Wallis, "Statistics of the Kinsey Report," *Journal of the American Statistical Association* 44 (1949): 463–484; Laumann et al., *The Social Organization of Sexuality.*

18. James Howard Jones, *Alfred Kinsey: A Public/Private Life* (New York: W. W. Norton, 1997); Laumann et al., *The Social Organization of Sexuality.*

19. Laumann et al., *The Social Organization of Sexuality,* p. 294.

20. D'Emilio, "Capitalism and Gay Identity."

21. If one assumes that the United States is a closed society with respect to sexual partners (that is, that none or very few of the Americans' sexual partners live outside the United States), and one further assumes that every act of heterosexual sexual congress involves exactly one person from each gender group, then the total number of heterosexual partners for men and for women in any given amount of time must be the same. This is true even if the distributions are uneven, say if one woman had a thousand sexual partners whereas a thousand men had only one partner each. The equality of total heterosexual partners constitutes what economists call an accounting identity. In a truly representative survey, the total number (and therefore also the average) of heterosexual partners for men and for women should be nearly equal. There are difficulties, of course. For one thing, the most important people to capture in a survey that quantifies sex are the people with the greatest number of partners (such as commercial sex workers) who are also among the least likely to respond to the survey. And then there are the social factors. As Americans found out in the aftermath of the Bill Clinton scandals, not everyone agrees about what constitutes "sex." Finally, different populations feel differently about sexual norms, faithfulness to partners, and promiscuity, and they overreport or underreport their sexual experience accordingly.

22. Richard C. Lewontin, "Sex, Lies, and Social Science," *The New York Review of Books,* April 20 1995; Laumann et al., *The Social Organization of Sexuality.*

23. Sedgwick, "Epistemology of the Closet."

24. For a study of the different ways gays in the United States manage disclosure and nondisclosure, see Wayne H. Brekhus, *Peacocks, Chameleons, Centaurs: Gay Suburbia and the Grammar of Social Identity* (Chicago: University of Chicago Press, 2003).

25. D'Emilio, "Capitalism and Gay Identity."

26. Michael Grossberg, *Governing the Hearth: Law and the Family in Nineteenth-Century America* (Chapel Hill: University of North Carolina Press, 1985).

27. Lillian Faderman, *Odd Girls and Twilight Lovers: A History of Lesbian Life in Twentieth-Century America* (New York: Penguin, 1991); Lillian Faderman, *Surpassing the Love of Men: Romantic Friendship and Love between Women from the Renaissance to the Present* (New York: Harper Collins, [1981] 1998); D'Emilio and Freedman, *Intimate Matters.*

28. In the 1970s, the U.S. Census Bureau introduced a new and unwieldy phrase for this theoretically unwieldy mixture of partners and roommates: "People of the Opposite Sex Sharing Living Quarters," or POSSLQ. In order to qualify as a cohabiting couple in Figure 4.2, the male householder and his female roommate or partner must have been unrelated by blood, both unmarried, both living apart from their parents, and of similar ages (both 20 to 39 years of age). The male householders were all U.S. born (so as to exclude international immigrants separated from their partners), and all were living in private homes or apartments rather than in group quarters.

29. Elijah Anderson, *Streetwise: Race, Class, and Change in an Urban Community* (Chicago: University of Chicago Press, 1990).

30. For a thoroughly iconoclastic, typically intelligent, and highly controversial treatment of Little Rock, race, rights, and intermarriage (so controversial that the *Dissent* editors prefaced her article with a broad disclaimer and followed it with two hostile rejoinders), see Hannah Arendt, "Reflections on Little Rock," *Dissent* 6, no. 4 (1959): 45–56.

31. Elliot Aronson, *The Jigsaw Classroom* (Beverly Hills, Calif.: Sage Press, 1978).

32. Mark Twain, *The Adventures of Huckleberry Finn (Tom Sawyer's Comrade): Scene, the Mississippi Valley: Time, Forty to Fifty Years Ago* (London: Chatto and Windus, 1884).

33. If r is the probability that any one couple is in the specified nontrad-

itional group, *N* is the number of couples in the social circle, and *P* is the probability that at least one out of *N* couples will be nontraditional, then $(1 - r)$ is the probability that any given couple is not in the specified nontraditional group. For *N* couples, the probability that none will be in the specified nontraditional group is $(1 - r)^N$ (that's where the assumption of independence comes in). The converse probability, that at least one of the *N* couples will be in the specified nontraditional group is $P = 1 - (1 - r)^N$. When *N* and *r* are both small, this probability approximates $P \approx rN$.

34. For an evaluation of the this assumption, see Joshua Goldstein, "Kinship Networks That Cross Racial Lines: The Exception or the Rule?" *Demography* 36, no. 3 (1999): 399–407.

35. D'Emilio, "Capitalism and Gay Identity"; D'Emilio, *Sexual Politics, Sexual Communities;* D'Emilio and Freedman, *Intimate Matters;* Faderman, *Surpassing the Love of Men.*

5. Alternative Unions and the Independent Life Stage

1. Douglas S. Massey and Nancy A. Denton, *American Apartheid: Segregation and the Making of the Underclass* (Cambridge, Mass.: Harvard University Press, 1993).

2. Claude Fischer, "Ever More Rooted Americans" (The Survey Research Center, University of California–Berkeley, 2000). Cited with permission. There was a dramatic rise in interstate mobility for young U.S.-born persons between 1940 and 1970, followed by a modest decline from 1970 to 1980. Geographic mobility for young adults was relatively flat from 1980 to 2000; see Michael J. Rosenfeld and Byung-Soo Kim, "The Independence of Young Adults and the Rise of Interracial and Same-Sex Unions," *American Sociological Review* 70, no. 4 (2005): 541–562. In other words, the rise of nontraditional unions from 1980 to 2000 cannot be due to a general increase in geographic mobility alone because geographic mobility was not generally increasing during this period. Residential independence of young adults increased from 1980 to 2000, age at marriage increased, women's labor force participation increased, and educational attainment increased (see Chapter 3), but geographic mobility did not increase from 1980 to 2000. I suspect that the young adults use geographic mobility selectively. For young adults who need to put distance between themselves and their communities of origin, geographic mobility is an increasingly available option. For young adults who have traditional heterosexual partners, proximity

to community of origin is more valuable now than it used to be because both husbands and wives have careers, and therefore the potential value of the extended family to provide free child care was more valuable in 2000 than it was in 1980.

3. Larry L. Bumpass, "What's Happening to the Family? Interactions between Demographic and Institutional Change," *Demography* 27, no. 4 (1990): 483–498.

4. If P_1 is a probability, the odds are $P_1/(1 - P_1)$. When comparing two percentages, one generates the odds from both percentages and then takes the ratio of the two, or odds ratio = $[P_2/(1 - P_2)] / [P_1/(1 - P_1)]$. The odds take into account the fact that 100 percent is the maximum for population percentages. One cannot generate a population percentage that is twice as much as 51 percent, but one can always double the odds, or triple the odds, and so on. The odds ratio has a variety of useful features, including the fact that the natural logarithm of the odds ratio is normally distributed if samples are large enough. See Alan Agresti, *Categorical Data Analysis* (New York: John Wiley, 1990).

5. Collapsing the ethno-racial groups into one dimension is fairly typical in the intermarriage literature. See Zhenchao Qian, "Breaking the Racial Barriers: Variations in Interracial Marriage between 1980 and 1990," *Demography* 34 (1997): 263–276. For data from the 2000 census, I put the small percentage of multiracial persons in the residual "all other" category. In the census questionnaire, Hispanicity is a separate category from race. Researchers usually refer to Hispanics in the United States as an ethnic group rather than as a race, to emphasize that the social barriers between Hispanics and non-Hispanics have usually been more flexible than the social barriers between whites and blacks or between whites and Asians. See Frank D. Bean and Marta Tienda, *The Hispanic Population of the United States* (New York: Russell Sage, 1987); Michael J. Rosenfeld, "Measures of Assimilation in the Marriage Market: Mexican Americans 1970–1990," *Journal of Marriage and the Family* 64 (2002): 152–162. Laws against racial intermarriage in the United States usually specified that only intermarriages between whites and blacks, or sometimes between whites and Asians or whites and Native Americans were illegal; see Rachel Moran, *Interracial Intimacy: The Regulation of Race and Romance* (Chicago: University of Chicago Press, 2001). Mexican Americans, the largest Hispanic group in the United States, have usually been considered racially white in the U.S. courts if not in every-

day U.S. social interactions; see Ian F. Haney López, *White by Law: The Legal Construction of Race* (New York: New York University Press, 1996).

6. $[.591/(1 - .591)] / [.481/(1 - .481)] = 1.56$. Table 5.1 compares the percentage of geographically mobile couples across five different kinds of couples. One could just as easily compare the percentage of geographic movers and geographic stayers who belong to each of the five couple types. For instance, in 2000, among the 2 million geographically mobile young couples, 66.5 percent were heterosexual same-race married couples, whereas 0.69 percent were same-sex cohabiting couples. Among the 2.2 million young couples living in the birth state of both partners, 70.3 percent were heterosexual same-race married couples whereas 0.31 percent were same-sex cohabiting couples. This presentation of the data appears different from Table 5.1, but it conveys the same information, that is, same-sex couples make up a higher percentage of the movers (0.69 percent) than the stayers (0.31 percent) (author's tabulation from census microdata, same source as Table 5.1). As in Table 5.1, all couples were composed of individuals born in the United States, ages twenty to twenty-nine at the time of the census. The key point is that alternative unions are associated with geographic mobility. The tables make no distinction as to the causal direction of the correlation, that is, whether the formation of alternative unions causes geographic mobility or whether geographic mobility leads to the formation of alternative unions. The census data and the ethnographic interviews each provide evidence for both causal directions. In fact, one can reproduce the same odds ratios as in Table 5.1, starting with the percentages of movers and stayers that belong to each couple type and treating the couple types two at a time. The reason is that the odds ratio is a symmetric measure of the relationship between two variables. See Agresti, *Categorical Data Analysis*.

7. For a recent quantitative study of geographic mobility and other distinguishing sociodemographic factors of gays and lesbians, see Esther D. Rothblum and Rhonda Factor, "Lesbians and Their Sisters as a Control Group: Demographic and Mental Health Factors," *Psychological Science* 12, no. 1 (2001): 63–69.

8. For instance, Massachusetts passed the Banishment Act in 1778, which ordered that those who were banished and returned without approval were subject to death.

9. John Modell, Frank F. Furstenberg, Jr., and Theodore Hershberg,

"Social Change and Transitions to Adulthood in Historical Perspective," in *The American Family in Social-Historical Perspective,* ed. Michael Gordon (New York: St. Martin's Press, 1978), pp. 192–219.

10. Rosenfeld, "Measures of Assimilation in the Marriage Market: Mexican Americans 1970–1990"; David Montejano, *Anglos and Mexicanos in the Making of Texas, 1836–1986* (Austin: University of Texas Press, 1987); López, *White by Law;* Stanley Lieberson and Mary C. Waters, *From Many Strands: Ethnic and Racial Groups in Contemporary America* (New York: Russell Sage Foundation, 1988).

11. Asian-Asian and Asian-white couples were left out of Figure 5.1 to improve readability, but the results are similar: Asian-white couples were more geographically mobile than endogamous Asian and endogamous white couples across all census years. Asian-white couples were even more geographically mobile than black-white couples in 2000.

12. Louis Wirth, "Urbanism as a Way of Life," *American Journal of Sociology* 44, no. 1 (1938): 1–24; Claude Fischer, "Toward a Subcultural Theory of Urbanism," *American Journal of Sociology* 80, no. 6 (1975): 1319–1341.

13. On the issue of social control in colonial America, see John Demos, *A Little Commonwealth: Family Life in Plymouth Colony* (London: Oxford University Press, 2000); Philip J. Greven, Jr., *Four Generations: Population, Land, and Family in Colonial Andover, Massachusetts* (Ithaca, N.Y.: Cornell University Press, 1970); Edmund S. Morgan, *The Puritan Family: Religion and Domestic Relations in Seventeenth-Century New England* (New York: Harper, [1944] 1966).

14. Peter Laslett, *The World We Have Lost: England before the Industrial Age* (New York: Charles Scribner's Sons, [1965] 1971).

15. John D'Emilio and Estelle Freedman, *Intimate Matters: A History of Sexuality in America* (New York: Harper and Row, 1988).

16. Because urban residence is available in the 1990 1 percent microdata but not the 5 percent microdata, sample sizes are smaller and there are insufficient numbers of same-sex interracial couples to allow for a reasonable estimate of their urban-ness.

17. For the essential urban character of gay life in the United States, see George Chauncey, *Gay New York: Gender, Urban Culture, and the Making of the Gay Male World, 1890–1940* (New York: Basic Books, 1994). For a study of the geography of same-sex couples using the 2000 census, see Gary J. Gates and Jason Ost, *The Gay and Lesbian Atlas* (Washington, D.C.: Urban Institute Press, 2004). Laumann and

his colleagues suggested that self-identified lesbians were much less likely to be urban than self-identified gay men, but their survey had small samples of both populations (about forty gay men and twenty-five lesbians); see Edward O. Laumann et al., *The Social Organization of Sexuality: Sexual Practices in the United States* (Chicago: University of Chicago Press, 1994), p. 305. In the 1990 and 2000 U.S. censuses, there was no significant difference in the rate of urban living between young gay male couples and young lesbian couples, the type of couples in Table 5.2 (the sample size of young same-sex couples from the 1 percent sample of the 1990 census data was sixty-nine gay male couples and fifty-two lesbian couples; the sample size from the 5 percent sample of the 2000 census was 826 gay male couples and 844 lesbian couples). Among U.S.-born gay couples of all ages from the 5 percent sample of the 2000 census whose urban status could be determined (gay male couples $N = 8,107$, lesbian couples $N = 8,538$), there was a significant difference in urban residence: 39.5 percent of the gay male couples lived in a city, whereas 30.5 percent of the lesbian couples lived in a city, compared with an urban residence rate of 15.3 percent for same-race heterosexual married couples of all ages.

18. D'Emilio and Freedman, *Intimate Matters;* Elizabeth Lapovsky Kennedy and Madeline D. Davis, *Boots of Leather, Slippers of Gold: The History of a Lesbian Community* (New York: Routledge, 1993).

19. For the definitive history of the early homophile organizations, see John D'Emilio, *Sexual Politics, Sexual Communities: The Making of a Homosexual Minority in the United States, 1940–1970* (Chicago: University of Chicago Press, 1998).

20. Ibid.; Allan Bérubé, *Coming Out under Fire: The History of Gay Men and Women in World War Two* (New York: Free Press, 1990); Randy Shilts, *The Mayor of Castro Street: The Life and Times of Harvey Milk* (New York: St. Martin's Press, 1982).

21. Shilts, *The Mayor of Castro Street;* Martin Duberman, *Stonewall* (New York: Plume, 1993).

22. Shilts, *The Mayor of Castro Street.*

23. If one uses the adjusted census data from 2000, which excludes dual marital status recodes, the association between geographic mobility and same-sex unions is stronger and similarly stable regardless of which controls are entered into the models.

24. Rosenfeld and Kim, "The Independence of Young Adults and the Rise of Interracial and Same-Sex Unions."

25. Rafael M. Díaz, *Latino Gay Men and HIV* (New York: Routledge, 1998); Martin F. Manalansan IV, *Global Divas: Filipino Gay Men in the Diaspora* (Durham, N.C.: Duke University Press, 2003).

26. William N. Eskridge, Jr., *Gaylaw: Challenging the Apartheid of the Closet* (Cambridge, Mass.: Harvard University Press, 1999); Rhonda R. Rivera, "Sexual Orientation and the Law," in *Homosexuality: Research Implications for Public Policy,* ed. John C. Gonsiorek and James D. Weinrich (Newbury Park, Calif.: Sage, 1991), pp. 81–100.

27. Guillermina Jasso and Mark R. Rosenzweig, *The New Chosen People: Immigrants in the United States* (New York: Russell Sage, 1990); Andrew Reding, "Sexual Orientation and Human Rights in the Americas" (New York: World Policy Institute, 2003); Human Rights Watch, "Locked Doors: The Human Rights of People Living with HIV/AIDS in China" (New York: Human Rights Watch, 2003); Human Rights Watch, "Future Forsaken: Abuses against Children Affected by HIV/AIDS in India" (New York: Human Rights Watch, 2004).

28. Manalansan, *Global Divas.*

29. Ibid., p. 101.

30. Díaz, *Latino Gay Men and HIV.*

31. Manalansan, *Global Divas.*

32. Héctor Carrillo, "Sexual Migration, Cross-Cultural Sexual Encounters, and Sexual Health," *Sexuality Research and Social Policy* 1, no. 3 (2004): 58–70.

33. F. James Davis, *Who Is Black? One Nation's Definition* (University Park: Pennsylvania State University Press, 1991).

34. Jasso and Rosenzweig, *The New Chosen People.*

35. Joane Nagel, *Race, Ethnicity, and Sexuality: Intimate Intersections, Forbidden Frontiers* (New York: Oxford University Press, 2003), pp. 177–199; Renee C. Romano, *Race Mixing: Black-White Marriage in Postwar America* (Cambridge, Mass.: Harvard University Press, 2003).

36. Michael J. Rosenfeld, "The Salience of Pan-National Hispanic and Asian Identities in U.S. Marriage Markets," *Demography* 38 (2001): 161–175; Yen Le Espiritu, *Asian American Panethnicity: Bridging Institutions and Identities* (Philadelphia, Pa.: Temple University Press, 1992).

37. Yen Le Espiritu, "Gender and Labor in Asian Immigrant Families," in *Gender and U.S. Immigration: Contemporary Trends,* ed. Pierrette Hondagneu-Sotelo (Berkeley: University of California Press, 2003), pp. 81–100; Patricia R. Pessar, "Engendering Migration Studies: The Case of New Immigrants in the United States," in *Gender and U.S. Immigration,* ed. Hondagneu-Sotelo, pp. 20–42.

38. Espiritu, "Gender and Labor in Asian Immigrant Families"; Pessar, "Engendering Migration Studies."

39. Nagel, *Race, Ethnicity, and Sexuality;* Pessar, "Engendering Migration Studies."

40. Emilio A. Parrado and Chenoa A. Flippen, "Migration and Gender among Mexican Women," *American Sociological Review* 70, no. 4 (2005): 606–632.

41. Milton Gordon, *Assimilation in American Life: The Role of Race, Religion, and National Origin* (New York: Oxford University Press, 1964).

42. Howard Schuman et al., *Racial Attitudes in America: Trends and Interpretations* (Cambridge, Mass.: Harvard University Press, 1997).

43. Mary R. Jackman, "General and Applied Tolerance: Does Education Increase Commitment to Racial Integration?" *American Journal of Political Science* 22, no. 2 (1978): 302–324; Mary R. Jackman and Michael J. Muha, "Education and Intergroup Attitudes: Moral Enlightenment, Superficial Democratic Commitment, or Ideological Refinement?" *American Sociological Review* 49, no. 6 (1984): 751–769.

44. The association between interracial couples and college education is due not so much to unions between U.S. native whites and U.S. native blacks (since U.S. native blacks are underrepresented in higher education), but rather to unions between whites and Asians, and interracial unions between U.S.-born and foreign-born persons.

45. One popular theory of race, education, and social class is the exchange theory, first proposed by sociological giants Kingsley Davis and Robert Merton in 1941. See Kingsley Davis, "Intermarriage in Caste Societies," *American Anthropologist* 43 (1941): 376–395; Robert K. Merton, "Intermarriage and the Social Structure: Fact and Theory," *Psychiatry,* no. 4 (1941): 361–374. Merton and Davis were struggling to understand why a white person would choose to marry a black person given the terrible disadvantages of being black in the United States in 1941. Merton and Davis each theorized that interracial marriages would be based on an exchange—the theory predicted that the black spouse would have to have much higher education or social class than their white spouse in order to compensate the white spouse for throwing his or her lot in with black society. Merton and Davis had no data to substantiate their theory, and subsequent empirical studies have had divergent results. I have surveyed the data and the literature on this subject and found that there has never been any hard evidence for exchange theory; black-white intermarried couples tend to be homogamous with respect to class

and education just exactly the way other couples are. See Michael J. Rosenfeld, "A Critique of Exchange Theory in Mate Selection," *American Journal of Sociology* 110, no. 5 (2005): 1284–1325.

46. Excluding the dual marital status recodes from the 2000 data yields a similar result.

47. My tabulations of data from the General Social Survey show that tolerance for homosexual rights is consistently about 15 percent lower for blacks than for whites. See also Díaz, *Latino Gay Men and HIV*; Benoit Denizet-Lewis, "Double Lives on the Down Low," *New York Times Magazine*, August 3, 2003.

48. Kennedy and Davis, *Boots of Leather, Slippers of Gold*.

49. Same-sex couples had significantly higher rates of interraciality than heterosexual couples in both 1990 and 2000. Although heterosexual cohabiting couples had the highest rates of interraciality in 2000, the young heterosexual married couples outnumber the heterosexual cohabiters by 3.4 to 1 in 2000 (and by 6.4 to 1 in 1990). If we combine the heterosexual cohabiters with the heterosexual married couples into a single heterosexual category, the resulting rate of interraciality would be close to the rate for heterosexual married couples alone since the married couples predominate among heterosexual couples. The rate of interraciality for all young heterosexual couples combined was 6.21 percent in 1990 and 10.19 percent in 2000, both significantly lower than the rates of interraciality for same-sex cohabiting couples.

50. Unfortunately, reliance on the 1980 census excludes an analysis of cohabitation since the U.S. census did not begin to distinguish unmarried partners from roommates until 1990.

51. Glenn Firebaugh and Kenneth E. Davis, "Trends in Antiblack Prejudice, 1972–1984: Region and Cohort Effects," *American Journal of Sociology* 94, no. 2 (1988): 251–272; Schuman et al., *Racial Attitudes in America*.

52. Joyner and Kao found no association between age at marriage and interracial marriage using data gathered two decades later; see Kara Joyner and Grace Kao, "Interracial Relationships and the Transition to Adulthood," *American Sociological Review* 70, no. 4 (2005): 563–581.

53. Firebaugh and Davis, "Trends in Antiblack Prejudice, 1972–1984"; Schuman et al., *Racial Attitudes in America*.

54. Mark Granovetter, "Economic Action and Social Structure: The Problem of Embeddedness," *American Journal of Sociology* 91, no. 3 (1985): 481–510.

55. For the a theoretical statements of the influence of exposure on intermarriage, see Peter M. Blau, *Inequality and Heterogeneity: A Primitive Theory of Social Structure* (New York: Free Press, 1977); Peter M. Blau and Joseph E. Schwartz, *Crosscutting Social Circles: Testing a Macrostructural Theory of Intergroup Relations* (Orlando, Fla.: Academic Press, 1984).

56. The felicitous phrase "field of eligible candidates" is due to Robert F. Winch, *Mate-Selection: A Study of Complementary Needs* (New York: Harper and Brothers, 1958).

57. Morton Hunt, *The Natural History of Love* (New York: Anchor Books, 1994); Edward Shorter, *The Making of the Modern Family* (New York: Basic Books, 1975).

58. For one interesting example of a quantitative test of the theory of geographic mobility for nontraditional unions, see Rothblum and Factor, "Lesbians and Their Sisters as a Control Group: Demographic and Mental Health Factors."

59. Bérubé, *Coming Out under Fire;* Chauncey, *Gay New York;* John D'Emilio, "Capitalism and Gay Identity," in *The Lesbian and Gay Studies Reader,* ed. Henry Abelove, Michele Aina Barale, and David M. Halperin (New York: Routledge, 1993), pp. 467–478; D'Emilio and Freedman, *Intimate Matters.*

60. Louise A. Tilly and Joan W. Scott, *Women, Work and Family* (New York: Routledge, 1987), p. 191; Romano, *Race Mixing,* p. 14.

61. Morgan, *The Puritan Family;* Demos, *A Little Commonwealth;* Greven, *Four Generations.*

62. See Elizabeth Bott, *Family and Social Network: Roles, Norms, and External Relationships in Ordinary Urban Families* (London: Tavistock, 1957).

63. Davis, *Who Is Black?*

0. Childhood

1. For one classic comparison of child rearing in two very different societies, see Urie Bronfenbrenner, *Two Worlds of Childhood: U.S. and U.S.S.R.* (New York: Touchstone, 1972). For comparisons of child-rearing styles between social classes in the United States, see Urie Bronfenbrenner, "Socialization and Social Class through Time and Space," in *Readings in Social Psychology,* ed. Eleanor E. Maccoby, Theodore M. Newcomb, and Eugene L. Hartley (New York: Holt, 1958), pp. 400–425; Annette Lareau, *Unequal Childhoods: Class, Race,*

and Family Life (Berkeley: University of California Press, 2003); Melvin L. Kohn, *Class and Conformity: A Study in Values* (Chicago: University of Chicago Press, 1977).

2. Jeffrey Jensen Arnett and Susan Taber, "Adolescence Terminable and Interminable: When Does Adolescence End?" *Journal of Youth and Adolescence* 23, no. 5 (1994): 517–537. In this chapter I contrast the authoritarian parenting style that was recommended in the past to the more permissive and tolerant style of parenting that is normative in the middle class in the post–1960 United States. The literature on child psychology recognizes more distinct types of parent-child relationships. Maccoby and Martin (using terminology derived from the work of Diana Baumrind) discuss four basic categories of parent-child relationships, including authoritarian, permissive, and authoritative. In Diana Baumrind's formative work on parenting styles, "permissive" parents have too little involvement in their children's day-to-day lives, while "authoritative" parents strike a more appropriate balance between involvement without too much arbitrary discipline. See Eleanor E. Maccoby and John A. Martin, "Socialization in the Context of the Family: Parent-Child Interaction," in *Handbook of Child Psychology,* vol. 4, ed. Paul H. Mussen and E. Mavis Hetherington (New York: John Wiley, 1983), pp. 1–101; Diana Baumrind, "The Discipline Encounter: Contemporary Issues," *Aggression and Violent Behavior* 2, no. 4 (1997): 321–335; Diana Baumrind and Ross A. Thompson, "The Ethics of Parenting," in *Handbook of Parenting,* ed. Marc H. Bornstein (Mahwah, N.J.: Lawrence Erlbaum and Associates, 2002), pp. 3–34; Diana Baumrind, "Effects of Authoritative Parental Control on Child Behavior," *Child Development* 37, no. 4 (1966): 887–907. I use a simplified typology of parenting styles (permissive vs. authoritarian) in this chapter to accommodate the lack of historically consistent data on the actual interactions between parents and children, therefore, my use of the term "permissive" is more general and less pejorative than the way the term is used in the child development literature.

3. Maccoby and Martin, "Socialization in the Context of the Family: Parent-Child Interaction."

4. John Demos, "Child Abuse in Context: An Historian's Perspective," in *Past, Present and Personal: The Family and the Life Course in American History* (New York: Oxford University Press, 1986), pp. 68–91; C. Henry Kempe et al., "The Battered-Child Syndrome," *Journal of the American Medical Association* 181, no. 1 (1962): 17–24; Marilyn Heins,

"The 'Battered Child' Revisited," *Journal of the American Medical Association* 251, no. 24 (1984): 3295–3300.

5. David Riesman, Nathan Glazer, and Reuel Denney, *The Lonely Crowd: A Study of the Changing American Character* (New Haven, Conn.: Yale University Press, [1950] 2001); Arnett and Taber, "Adolescence Terminable and Interminable: When Does Adolescence End?"; Christopher Lasch, *Haven in a Heartless World: The Family Besieged* (New York: W. W. Norton, 1977); Benjamin Spock and Steven J. Parker, *Dr. Spock's Baby and Child Care* (New York: Pocket Books, 1998).

6. Philippe Ariès, *Centuries of Childhood: A Social History of Family Life*, trans. Robert Baldick (New York: Vintage, 1962); Joseph F. Kett, *Rites of Passage: Adolescence in America, 1790 to the Present* (New York: Basic Books, 1977); Morton Hunt, *The Natural History of Love* (New York: Anchor Books, 1994); Edward Shorter, *The Making of the Modern Family* (New York: Basic Books, 1975).

7. Samuel X. Radbill, "Children in a World of Violence: A History of Sexual Abuse," in *The Battered Child*, ed. C. Henry Kempe and Ray E. Helfer (Chicago: University of Chicago Press, 1980), pp. 3–20; Lloyd deMause, "The Evolution of Childhood," in *The History of Childhood*, ed. Lloyd deMause (New York: Peter Bedrick Books, 1988), pp. 1–73.

8. David Hackett Fischer, *Albion's Seed: Four British Folkways in America* (New York: Oxford University Press, 1989), p. 100.

9. Cotton Mather, *A Family Well-Ordered: An Essay to Render Parents and Children Happy in One Another* (Boston: Green and Allen, 1699), p. 24. At another time, Mather wrote more ambiguously about physical discipline: "I would never come to give a child a blow except in case of obstinacy or some gross enormity." Philip J. Greven, Jr., *Spare the Child: The Religious Roots of Punishment and the Psychological Impact of Physical Abuse* (New York: Vintage Books, 1990), p. 84.

10. Julia Grant, *Raising Baby by the Book: The Education of American Mothers* (New Haven, Conn.: Yale University Press, 1998).

11. Mather, *A Family Well-Ordered*, p. 11.

12. One reason Linda Pollock does not find preindustrial diaries to be overflowing with parental admissions and childhood anguish over the cruelty of spanking, whipping, and the beating of children is that the physical corrections were usually applied in a way that the parents, children, and community would all have recognized as normal or appropriate. See Linda A. Pollock, *Forgotten Children: Parent-Child Relations from 1500 to 1900* (Cambridge: Cambridge University Press, 1983).

13. Fischer, *Albion's Seed;* Barry Levy, *Quakers and the American Family: British Settlement in the Delaware Valley* (New York: Oxford University Press, 1988).

14. Linda Gordon, *Heroes of Their Own Lives: The Politics and History of Family Violence* (New York: Viking, 1988).

15. Demos, "Child Abuse in Context: An Historian's Perspective," p. 71.

16. Ann Hulbert, *Raising America: Experts, Parents and a Century of Advice about Children* (New York: Vintage, 2003).

17. G. Stanley Hall, *Adolescence: Its Psychology and Its Relations to Physiology, Anthropology, Sociology, Sex, Crime, Religion and Education* (New York: D. Appleton and Company, 1904); Hulbert, *Raising America*, p. 79.

18. Nancy Pottishman Weiss, "Mother, the Invention of Necessity: Dr. Benjamin Spock's Baby and Child Care," *American Quarterly* 29, no. 5 (1977): 519–546.

19. U.S. Children's Bureau and Mrs. Max West, *Infant Care* (Washington, D.C: U.S. Government Printing Office, 1914), p. 59.

20. John Bowlby in England and Mary Ainsworth in the United States were the pioneers of the attachment school. See Robert Karen, *Becoming Attached: First Relationships and How They Shape Our Capacity to Love* (New York: Oxford University Press, 1998).

21. Karen, *Becoming Attached;* Spock and Parker, *Dr. Spock's Baby and Child Care.* The irony of attachment theory is that for centuries women were home with their children and were advised not to spoil them with too much attention. Now that the formal labor market is open to women and women have to balance work and family, experts have discovered that children nurtured lovingly and individually are more likely to thrive. Feminists have been critical of attachment theory precisely because the theory suggests that mothers should be staying home with their children rather than going off to work.

22. Martha Wolfenstein, "Fun Morality: An Analysis of Recent American Child-Training Literature," in *Childhood in Contemporary Cultures*, ed. Margaret Mead and Martha Wolfenstein (Chicago: University of Chicago Press, 1955), pp. 168–178; U.S. Children's Bureau, *Infant Care* (Washington, D.C.: U.S. Government Printing Office, 1921); U.S. Children's Bureau and West, *Infant Care* (1914).

23. U.S. Children's Bureau and West, *Infant Care* (1914), p. 62.

24. U.S. Children's Bureau, *Infant Care* (1921), p. 42.

25. See U.S. Children's Bureau and West, *Infant Care* (1914).

26. Benjamin Spock, *The Common Sense Book of Baby and Child Care* (New York: Deull, Sloan and Pearce, 1946).

27. Spock and Parker, *Dr. Spock's Baby and Child Care,* p. 438. See also the first edition, Spock, *The Common Sense Book of Baby and Child Care,* pp. 269–272; Greven, *Spare the Child.*

28. Weiss, "Mother, the Invention of Necessity"; Hulbert, *Raising America.*

29. The most well known of the modern conservative Christian child-rearing manuals is James Dobson, *Dare to Discipline* (New York: Bantam Doubleday, 1980). For a survey of Dobson's competitors, see John P. Bartkowski and Christopher G. Ellison, "Divergent Models of Childrearing in Popular Manuals: Conservative Protestants vs. the Mainstream Experts," *Sociology of Religion* 56, no. 1 (1995): 21–34.

30. Theodore Roszak, *The Making of a Counter Culture* (Berkeley: University of California Press, [1968] 1995); Christopher Jencks, "Is It All Dr. Spock's Fault?" *New York Times Magazine,* May 28 1968.

31. Hulbert, *Raising America.*

32. Spock and Parker, *Dr. Spock's Baby and Child Care,* p. 456 (1998).

33. Hulbert, *Raising America.*

34. Spock and Parker, *Dr. Spock's Baby and Child Care,* p. 38 (1998).

35. Ibid., p. 40.

36. Hulbert, *Raising America.*

37. Ibid.; Bartkowski and Ellison, "Divergent Models of Childrearing in Popular Manuals."

38. Hulbert, *Raising America;* Dobson, *Dare to Discipline.*

39. Mather, *A Family Well-Ordered;* Dobson, *Dare to Discipline;* Hulbert, *Raising America;* Greven, *Spare the Child;* Bartkowski and Ellison, "Divergent Models of Childrearing in Popular Manuals."

40. Hulbert, *Raising America,* p. 258.

41. Ibid.

42. See the 1998 edition, Spock and Parker, *Dr. Spock's Baby and Child Care,* p. 1.

43. Lasch, *Haven in a Heartless World.*

44. John Demos, *A Little Commonwealth: Family Life in Plymouth Colony* (London: Oxford University Press, 2000); Fischer, *Albion's Seed.*

45. Maccoby and Martin, "Socialization in the Context of the Family: Parent-Child Interaction," p. 84.

46. Spock and Parker, *Dr. Spock's Baby and Child Care;* Weiss, "Mother, the Invention of Necessity."

47. The data on rooms per home extends back only to 1960, but the available census data on household size extends back to 1850. My tabulations of the data show that household size has been steadily declining since 1850 (except for the baby boom of the 1950s). To extend Column A of Table 6.1, the number of children (at the time

of the census) per household in households with a U.S.-born head
and at least one child, the corresponding totals were 3.29 in 1850,
2.85 in 1880, 2.61 in 1910, and 2.21 in 1940.

48. Bronfenbrenner, "Socialization and Social Class through Time and
Space"; Lareau, *Unequal Childhoods.*

49. Bronfenbrenner, "Socialization and Social Class through Time and
Space."

50. Kohn, *Class and Conformity.* See also Robert Staughton Lynd and
Helen Merrell Lynd, *Middletown: A Study in Contemporary American
Culture* (New York: Harcourt, Brace and Company, 1929).

51. Hulbert, *Raising America,* p. 264.

52. Middletown of sociological fame was a pseudonym for Muncie, Indiana. Muncie, Indiana, is not particularly cosmopolitan, and it is
rarely confused for San Francisco or New York. The Lynds chose
Muncie precisely because it was a typical parochial Midwestern town;
any social change measured in Muncie was likely present in many
other towns across the country. Theodore Caplow et al., *Middletown
Families: Fifty Years of Change and Continuity* (Minneapolis: University
of Minnesota Press, 1982), p. 3N.

53. Lynd and Lynd, *Middletown.*

54. Caplow et al., *Middletown Families.*

55. Duane F. Alwin, "From Obedience to Autonomy: Changes in Traits
Desired in Children, 1924–1978," *Public Opinion Quarterly* 52, no. 1
(1988): 33–52.

56. The Lynds also noted that the more affluent parents put less emphasis on childhood obedience, presumably because they imagined
that their children were destined to professional careers in which initiative and internal motivation were expected to be more important
than obedience.

7. The Rise of Tolerance

1. T. W. Adorno et al., *The Authoritarian Personality* (New York: W. W.
Norton, [1950] 1982); Erik H. Erikson, *Childhood and Society* (New
York: W. W. Norton, [1950] 1963); Alex Inkeles and Daniel J. Lev-
inson, "National Character: The Study of Modal Personality and So-
ciocultural Systems," in *Handbook of Social Psychology,* vol. 2, ed.
Gardner Lindzey (Reading, Mass.: Addison-Wesley, 1954).

2. Adorno et al., *The Authoritarian Personality,* pp. 256–266. For a more
strident view of the potential harm of authoritarian parenting styles,
see Alice Miller, *For Your Own Good: Hidden Cruelty in Child-Rearing*

and the Roots of Violence, trans. Hildegarde Hannum and Hunter Hannum (New York: Farrar, Straus and Giroux, 1983).

3. Adorno and his colleagues wrote *The Authoritarian Personality* to attempt to explain the rise of Nazism. They argued, in part, that authoritarian child rearing explained the susceptibility of Germans to fascism. Unfortunately for the theory, contemporary child-rearing norms were also authoritarian in the United States and Britain and many other of the democracies that fought against the Nazis. Adorno and his colleagues did not even attempt to show that child rearing in Germany was *unusually* authoritarian (compared with other countries) in the late nineteenth and early twentieth centuries, when the future Nazis were children. No data existed that would have allowed for standardized empirical comparisons of child-rearing practices between countries. Because the meaning and impact of parenting practices is subtle and subjective (to say nothing of the meaning of "national character"), it is hard to imagine that nationally representative standardized data could (even in theory) be gathered in a way that would allow for empirical tests of the theory that national differences in child rearing determine differences in national character or political behavior. Modern academic psychology has moved away from the sweeping historical theories of Freud and Adorno because they are difficult to test empirically. For critiques of *The Authoritarian Personality* from various perspectives, see Richard Christie and Marie Jahoda, eds., *Studies in the Scope and Method of "The Authoritarian Personality"* (Glencoe, Ill.: Free Press, 1954).

4. Eleanor E. Maccoby and John A. Martin, "Socialization in the Context of the Family: Parent-Child Interaction," in *Handbook of Child Psychology,* vol. 4, ed. Paul H. Mussen and E. Mavis Hetherington (New York: John Wiley, 1983), pp. 1–101; Judith Rich Harris, *The Nurture Assumption: Why Children Turn Out the Way They Do* (New York: Touchstone, 1998).

5. For a biographical and intellectual history of the attachment school, see Robert Karen, *Becoming Attached: First Relationships and How They Shape Our Capacity to Love* (New York: Oxford University Press, 1998).

6. Michael Rutter, "Nature, Nurture, and Development: From Evangelism through Science toward Policy and Practice," *Child Development* 73, no. 1 (2002): 1–21; Sandra Scarr, "Developmental Theories for the 1990s: Development and Individual Differences," *Child Development* 63, no. 1 (1992): 1–19.

7. Richard J. Gelles and Murray A. Straus, *Intimate Violence* (New York:

Simon and Schuster, 1988); Philip J. Greven, Jr., *Spare the Child: The Religious Roots of Punishment and the Psychological Impact of Physical Abuse* (New York: Vintage Books, 1990).

8. Scarr, "Developmental Theories for the 1990s."

9. Diana Baumrind, "The Average Expectable Environment Is Not Good Enough: A Response to Scarr," *Child Development* 64, no. 5 (1993): 1299–1317.

10. Harris, *The Nurture Assumption*, p. 335.

11. David Riesman, Nathan Glazer, and Reuel Denney, *The Lonely Crowd: A Study of the Changing American Character* (New Haven, Conn.: Yale University Press, [1950] 2001). *The Lonely Crowd* sold more than 1 million copies and is reputed to be the best-selling book ever by an academic American sociologist; see Herbert J. Gans, "Best-Sellers by Sociologists: An Exploratory Study," *Contemporary Sociology* 26, no. 2 (1997): 131–135.

12. Riesman, Glazer, and Denney, *The Lonely Crowd*, p. 159; Dennis Wrong, "*The Lonely Crowd* Revisited," *Sociological Forum* 7, no. 2 (1992): 381–389.

13. Wrong, "*The Lonely Crowd* Revisited."

14. Howard Schuman et al., *Racial Attitudes in America: Trends and Interpretations* (Cambridge, Mass.: Harvard University Press, 1997); Reynolds Farley, "Racial Trends and Differences in the United States 30 Years after the Civil Rights Decade," *Social Science Research* 26 (1997): 235–262.

15. David O. Sears, "Symbolic Racism," in *Eliminating Racism: Profiles in Controversy,* ed. Phyllis A. Katz and Dalmas A. Taylor (New York: Plenum Press, 1988).

16. Sears, "Symbolic Racism"; Mary R. Jackman, "General and Applied Tolerance: Does Education Increase Commitment to Racial Integration?" *American Journal of Political Science* 22, no. 2 (1978): 302–324; Mary R. Jackman and Michael J. Muha, "Education and Intergroup Attitudes: Moral Enlightenment, Superficial Democratic Commitment, or Ideological Refinement?" *American Sociological Review* 49, no. 6 (1984): 751–769.

17. Renee C. Romano, *Race Mixing: Black-White Marriage in Postwar America* (Cambridge, Mass.: Harvard University Press, 2003).

18. Sears, "Symbolic Racism." But see also Larry Bobo's response to Sears; Lawrence Bobo, "Group Conflict, Prejudice, and the Paradox of Contemporary Racial Attitudes," in *Eliminating Racism: Profiles in Controversy,* ed. Phyllis A. Katz and Dalmas A. Taylor (New York: Plenum, 1988).

19. Sears, "Symbolic Racism."

20. Clem Brooks, "Civil Rights Liberalism and the Suppression of a Republican Political Realignment in the United States, 1972 to 1996," *American Sociological Review* 65 (2000): 483–505.

21. Robert Staughton Lynd and Helen Merrell Lynd, *Middletown: A Study in Contemporary American Culture* (New York: Harcourt, Brace, 1929).

22. Baker v. State 170 Vt. 194 (1999).

23. David Moats, *Civil Wars: A Battle for Gay Marriage* (Orlando, Fla. Harcourt, 2004), p. 16.

24. Tom W. Smith, "Attitudes toward Sexual Permissiveness: Trends, Correlates, and Behavioral Connections," in *Sexuality across the Life Course,* ed. Alice S. Rossi (Chicago: University of Chicago Press, 1994), pp. 63–97.

25. Seymour Martin Lipset, *Continental Divide: The Values and Institutions of the United States and Canada* (New York: Routledge, 1991); Wayne Baker, *America's Crisis of Values: Reality and Perception* (Princeton, N.J.: Princeton University Press, 2005). Lipset notes that Canada offers national health care and a more general social safety net than the United States offers its citizens. In 2005, Canada (six months after a dozen U.S. states passed or reinforced their bans on same-sex marriage) began offering marriage equality to same-sex couples as a matter of national policy, expanding rights that were previously offered only in a few Canadian provinces. See Clifford Krauss, "Gay Marriage Is Extended Nationwide in Canada," *New York Times,* June 29, 2005, A:4.

26. Tom W. Smith, "Timely Artifacts: A Review of Measurement Variation in the 1972–1989 GSS," paper presented at the 1990 meetings of the American Statistical Association, Anaheim, Calif.; James Allan Davis, Tom W. Smith, and Peter V. Marsden, *General Social Surveys, 1972–2002: Cumulative Codebook* (Ann Arbor, Mich.: Inter-university Consortium for Political and Social Research, 2003).

27. Alan S. Yang, "Trends: Attitudes toward Homosexuality," *Public Opinion Quarterly* 61, no. 3 (1997): 477–507; Jeni Loftus, "America's Liberalization in Attitudes toward Homosexuality, 1973 to 1998," *American Sociological Review* 66 (2001): 762–782.

28. For a brief review of the literature on predictors of tolerance and liberalism toward homosexuals, see Loftus, "America's Liberalization in Attitudes toward Homosexuality, 1973 to 1998."

29. $[0.926/(1 - .926)]/[.518/(1 - .518)] = 11.64.$

30. Gary S. Becker, *A Treatise on the Family* (Cambridge, Mass.: Harvard University Press, 1991).

31. Paula S. Fass, *The Damned and the Beautiful: American Youth in the 1920's* (New York: Oxford University Press, 1977), p. 90.

32. Philip J. Greven, Jr., *Four Generations: Population, Land, and Family in Colonial Andover, Massachusetts* (Ithaca, N.Y.: Cornell University Press, 1970); Louise A. Tilly and Joan W. Scott, *Women, Work, and Family* (New York: Routledge, 1987).

33. U.S. Children's Bureau and Mrs. Max West, *Infant Care* (Washington, D.C.: U.S. Government Printing Office, 1914).

34. Having a large family, that is, twelve or more children, is (in the post-1960 era) strongly correlated with biblical literalism. If "attitudes toward the Bible" is entered into the multivariate model, the number of siblings ceases to be a significant predictor of tolerance toward gay rights. The problem is that "attitude toward the Bible" was not asked in the GSS until 1984, and in order to use "attitude toward the Bible" in the models, all the GSS data from 1973 to 1982 has to be discarded from the analysis.

35. Researchers subdivide historical effects into "cohort" effects (historical forces that have a special effect on one age group) and "period" effects (historical effects that affect all ages in a similar way). The Great Depression was clearly a period effect (since it affected nearly everyone), but the Great Depression also had a distinctive cohort effect on the generation of young adults who came of age in the 1930s. Some researchers argue that the post–World War II baby boom was simply the delayed fertility of the generation that came of age during the Great Depression. Andrew Cherlin has shown, by comparing the fertility of different birth cohorts, that the baby boom of the 1950s was the result of high fertility from all parental birth cohorts, not only the parental cohorts that came of age during the Great Depression. In Cherlin's view, the baby boom of the 1950s was a period effect, not a cohort effect. See Glen H. Elder, Jr., "Age Differentiation in the Life Course," *Annual Review of Sociology* 1 (1975): 165–190; Glen H. Elder, Jr., *Children of the Great Depression: Social Change in Life Experience* (Chicago: University of Chicago Press, 1974); Andrew J. Cherlin, *Marriage, Divorce, Remarriage* (Cambridge, Mass.: Harvard University Press, 1992); Norman B. Ryder, "The Cohort in the Study of Social Change," *American Sociological Review* 30 (1965): 843–861.

36. Ryder, "The Cohort in the Study of Social Change."

37. Ronald Inglehart, *Culture Shift in Advanced Industrial Society* (Princeton, N.J.: Princeton University Press, 1990).

8. Privacy and the Law

1. For birth control access, see Griswold v. Connecticut, 381 U.S. 479 (1965); Eisenstadt v. Baird, 405 U.S. 438 (1972). For abortion rights, see Roe v. Wade, 410 U.S. 113 (1973). For racial intermarriage, see Loving v. Virginia, 388 U.S. 1 (1967). For removal of the anti-sodomy laws, see Lawrence v. Texas, 539 U.S. 558 (2003).

2. Robert H. Bork, *The Tempting of America: The Political Seduction of the Law* (New York: Simon and Schuster, 1991).

3. John D'Emilio and Estelle Freedman, *Intimate Matters: A History of Sexuality in America* (New York: Harper and Row, 1988).

4. Rachel Moran, *Interracial Intimacy: The Regulation of Race and Romance* (Chicago: University of Chicago Press, 2001); Carroll Smith-Rosenberg, "The Abortion Movement and the AMA, 1850–1880," in *Disorderly Conduct: Visions of Gender in Victorian America* (New York: Oxford University Press, 1985), pp. 217–244.

5. See the unanimous decision in Loving v. Virginia. Rejected in that decision were the traditionalist arguments of Attorney General of Virginia, "Brief on Behalf of Appellee in Loving v. Virginia" (Westlaw 93641, 1967); Attorney General of North Carolina, "Amicus Brief in Loving v. Virginia" (Westlaw 93614, 1967).

6. Jeffrey Jensen Arnett, *Emerging Adulthood: The Winding Road from the Late Teens through the Early Twenties* (Oxford: Oxford University Press, 2004).

7. Alan S. Yang, "Trends: Attitudes toward Homosexuality," *Public Opinion Quarterly* 61, no. 3 (1997): 477–507; David O. Sears, "Symbolic Racism," in *Eliminating Racism: Profiles in Controversy*, ed. Phyllis A. Katz and Dalmas A. Taylor (New York: Plenum Press, 1988).

8. Jeni Loftus, "America's Liberalization in Attitudes toward Homosexuality, 1973 to 1998," *American Sociological Review* 66 (2001): 762–782.

9. Kingsley Davis and Pietronella van den Oever, "Age Relations and Public Policy in Advanced Industrial Societies," *Population and Development Review* 7, no. 1 (1981): 1–18; Göran Therborn, *Between Sex and Power: Family in the World, 1900–2000* (London: Routledge, 2004); David John Frank and Elizabeth H. Mceneaney, "The Individualization of Society and the Liberalization of State Policies on Same-Sex Relations, 1984–1995," *Social Forces* 77, no. 3 (1999): 911–943; Edward Shorter, *The Making of the Modern Family* (New York: Basic Books, 1975); Morton Hunt, *The Natural History of Love* (New York: Anchor Books, 1994).

10. Frank and Mceneaney, "The Individualization of Society and the Liberalization of State Policies on Same-Sex Relations, 1984–1995."

11. Max Weber, *The Protestant Ethic and the Spirit of Capitalism*, trans. Stephen Kalberg (Los Angeles: Roxbury, [1905] 2001).

12. Because most nominees to the U.S. Supreme Court have achieved their nomination through distinguished careers in the law or in public service, justices tend to be older than the general population. Chief Justice Earl Warren was born in 1891 and joined the Supreme Court in 1953. Earl Warren's successor as chief justice, Warren Burger, was born in 1907 and became chief justice in 1969. When Burger retired in 1986, William Rehnquist (born in 1924) became chief justice. John Roberts (born in 1955), who replaced Rehnquist in 2005, is the first chief justice of the U.S. Supreme Court who came of age after 1960.

13. Bork, *The Tempting of America*; Andrew Koppelman, *The Gay Rights Question in Contemporary American Law* (Chicago: University of Chicago Press, 2002).

14. Griswold v. Connecticut, 381 U.S. 479 (1965); Nicola Beisel, *Imperiled Innocents: Anthony Comstock and Family Reproduction in Victorian America* (Princeton, N.J.: Princeton University Press, 1997).

15. Griswold v. Connecticut at 485.

16. Griswold v. Connecticut at 508.

17. Eisenstadt v. Baird, 405 U.S. 438 (1972).

18. Eisenstadt v. Baird, 405 U.S. 438 (1972) at 453.

19. Moran, *Interracial Intimacy*, p. 91.

20. Eisenstadt v. Baird, 405 U.S. 438 (1972) at 471.

21. Roe v. Wade, 410 U.S. 113 (1973).

22. Smith-Rosenberg, "The Abortion Movement and the AMA, 1850–1880."

23. Roe v. Wade, 410 U.S. 113 (1973) at 153.

24. Roe v. Wade, 410 U.S. 113 (1973) at 174.

25. Ruth Bader Ginsburg, "Speaking in a Judicial Voice," *New York University Law Review* 67 (1992): 1185–1209.

26. Ibid.; Kristin Luker, *Abortion and the Politics of Motherhood* (Berkeley: University of California Press, 1984); Neal Devins, "Book Review Essay: Through the Looking Glass: What Abortion Teaches Us about American Politics," *Columbia Law Review* 94 (1994): 293–330; Laurence H. Tribe, *Abortion: The Clash of Absolutes* (New York: W. W. Norton, 1992).

27. Mary Ann Glendon, *Rights Talk: The Impoverishment of Political Discourse* (New York: Free Press, 1993).

28. Therborn, *Between Sex and Power*: United Nations, *The World's Women 2000: Trends and Statistics*, vol. 16 (New York: United Nations, 2000); United Nations, *The World's Women, 1970–1990: Trends and Statistics*, vol. 8 (New York: United Nations, 1991).

29. Peter Wallenstein, *Tell the Court I Love My Wife: Race, Marriage and Law—An American History* (New York: Palgrave Macmillan, 2002); Koppelman, *The Gay Rights Question in Contemporary American Law.*

30. Loving v. Virginia, 388 U.S. 1 (1967).

31. Loving v. Virginia, 388 U.S. 1 (1967) at 12.

32. Wallenstein, *Tell the Court I Love My Wife.*

33. Ibid., Moran, *Interracial Intimacy;* Robert J. Sickels, *Race, Marriage and the Law* (Albuquerque: University of New Mexico Press, 1972).

34. Wallenstein, *Tell the Court I Love My Wife.*

35. Sickels, *Race, Marriage and the Law.*

36. Bork, *The Tempting of America;* Tribe, *Abortion.*

37. Bowers v. Hardwick, 478 U.S. 186 (1986).

38. Griswold v. Connecticut, 381 U.S. 479 (1965) at 499.

39. For an overview of the biblical and legal antecedents of sodomy laws, see John Boswell, *Christianity, Social Tolerance, and Homosexuality* (Chicago: University of Chicago Press, 1980).

40. Koppelman, *The Gay Rights Question in Contemporary American Law,* p. 40.

41. Bowers v Hardwick, 478 U.S. 186 (1986) at 196.

42. Lawrence v. Texas, 539 U.S. 558 (2003).

43. Ibid. at 558.

44. Justice O'Connor did not agree with the majority in Lawrence v. Texas that Bowers v. Hardwick had been wrongly decided. She, of course, had voted against Mr. Hardwick in 1986. O'Connor's concurring opinion in Lawrence v. Texas was not that sodomy was protected under the new personal rights, but that Texas's sodomy law violated the equal protection clause of the Constitution because it applied only to homosexual couples. Georgia's anti-sodomy law had not been specific to acts of sodomy between same-sex couples and would, in O'Connor's view, be constitutional.

45. The communitarians are also critics of the way personal freedoms dominate our political discourse. Mary Ann Glendon and Amitai Etzioni argue that the new personal freedoms are problematic because they create too much expectation of individual rights at the expense of obligations to the community. See Glendon, *Rights Talk;* Amitai Etzioni, *The Spirit of Community: The Reinvention of American Society* (New York: Simon and Schuster, 1993).

46. Koppelman, *The Gay Rights Question in Contemporary American Law*, p. 39.

9. Same-Sex Marriage and the Future of the American Family

1. Rachel Moran, *Interracial Intimacy: The Regulation of Race and Romance* (Chicago: University of Chicago Press, 2001); Robert J. Sickels, *Race, Marriage and the Law* (Albuquerque: University of New Mexico Press, 1972).

2. William N. Eskridge, Jr., *Equality Practice: Civil Unions and the Future of Gay Rights* (New York: Routledge, 2002); Andrew Koppelman, *The Gay Rights Question in Contemporary American Law* (Chicago: University of Chicago Press, 2002).

3. Attorney General of Virginia, "Brief on Behalf of Appellee in Loving v. Virginia" (Westlaw 93641, 1967).

4. Leonard W. Levy, *Original Intent and the Framers' Constitution* (New York: Macmillan, 1988). Of all Americans, James Madison was in the best position to bolster legal and constitutional arguments with evidence of the original intent of the Constitution's framers, because he was one of the chief framers and he had taken the best notes of the constitutional convention. Yet in Madison's prominent career in the early American republic, he hardly relied on his privileged knowledge of original intent. The constitutional convention had a secrecy agreement in order to ensure that their debates would not color later discussion of the Constitution. The constitutional convention took place in 1787, but Madison did not exactly hurry his notes of the convention to press: Madison died in 1836 and his notes were not published until 1840. In other words, Madison's personal original intent is not consistent with original intent theory as currently advocated. See also Jack N. Rackove, *Original Meanings: Politics and Ideas in the Making of the Constitution* (New York: Alfred A. Knopf, 1996).

5. Laurence H. Tribe, *American Constitutional Law* (Mineola, N.Y.: Foundation Press, 1978); Levy, *Original Intent and the Framers' Constitution;* Laurence H. Tribe, *Abortion: The Clash of Absolutes* (New York: W. W. Norton, 1992).

6. Marbury v. Madison, 5 U.S. 137 (1803). Legal scholars like Robert Bork who are critical of the principle of judicial review necessarily take issue not only with modern judicial decisions but also with the entire history of the Supreme Court back to 1803. In other words, complaints against the principle of judicial review contradict not

only the principle of original intent, but the principle of tradition-alism as well. Robert H. Bork, *The Tempting of America: The Political Seduction of the Law* (New York: Simon and Schuster, 1991); Levy, *Original Intent and the Framers' Constitution;* Tribe, *American Constitutional Law;* Koppelman, *The Gay Rights Question in Contemporary American Law.*

7. Michael Banton, *Racial Theories* (Cambridge: Cambridge University Press, 1998); Tomás Almaguer, *Racial Fault Lines: The Historical Origins of White Supremacy in California* (Berkeley: University of California Press, 1994); Stephen Jay Gould, *The Mismeasure of Man* (New York: W. W. Norton, 1996).

8. Attorney General of North Carolina, "Amicus Brief in Loving v. Virginia" (Westlaw 93614, 1967).

9. Ibid., 5.

10. Attorney General of Virginia, "Brief on Behalf of Appellee in Loving v. Virginia," 26.

11. Moran, *Interracial Intimacy,* p. 95.

12. The nineteenth-century temperance movement was framed as an effort to prevent drunken parents from harming or neglecting their children, and Anthony Comstock's campaigns against vice were generally framed as an effort to guard vulnerable children from the predations and corruptions of the city; see Nicola Beisel, *Imperiled Innocents: Anthony Comstock and Family Reproduction in Victorian America* (Princeton, N.J.: Princeton University Press, 1997).

13. Attorney General of Virginia, "Brief on Behalf of Appellee in Loving v. Virginia," 29. Citing Albert Isaac Gordon, *Intermarriage: Interfaith, Interracial, Interethnic* (Boston: Beacon Press, 1964), pp. 334–335.

14. Renee C. Romano, *Race Mixing: Black-White Marriage in Postwar America* (Cambridge, Mass.: Harvard University Press, 2003).

15. For an interesting historical argument that early Christians celebrated same-sex unions in a fashion tantamount to gay marriage, see John Boswell, *Same-Sex Unions in Premodern Europe* (New York: Vintage, 1994). For a critique and discussion of Boswell's use of the early Christian manuscripts, see Brent D. Shaw, "A Groom of One's Own?" *The New Republic,* July 18, 1994, 33. See also subsequent exchange between Shaw and Hexter in the October 3, 1994, edition of the same journal.

16. Massachusetts's brief in Goodridge v. Department of Public Health made several of these points, including that the issue of same-sex marriage was best left to the legislature, that same-sex marriage was counter to centuries of tradition and common law, and that same-

sex marriage was potentially injurious to children. See Attorney General of Massachusetts, "Brief of Defendants—Appellees on Appeal from a Final Judgment of the Superior Court in Goodridge v. Department of Public Health" (Boston, 2004). See also the very similar earlier brief, Attorney General of Vermont, "Motion to Dismiss Baker v State, Vermont Superior Court" (Montpelier, 1997). For a sharply written opinion article on the miscegenation analogy for prejudice against same-sex marriage, see Eric Zorn, "Marriage Issue Just as Plain as Black and White," *Chicago Tribune,* May 19, 1996, C:1. For further commentary on the analogy from a legal and public policy perspective, see Evan Wolfson, *Why Marriage Matters: America, Equality, and Gay People's Right to Marry* (New York: Simon and Schuster, 2004); Mark Strasser, "Family, Definitions, and the Constitution: On the Antimiscegenation Analogy," *Suffolk University Law Review* 25 (1991): 981–1034; Koppelman, *The Gay Rights Question in Contemporary American Law;* Eskridge, *Equality Practice.*

17. The past religious arguments against racial intermarriage and the current religious arguments against gay marriage are similar but not identical. One difference is that the Bible's view of interracial and interethnic marriage is varied, whereas the biblical injunctions against homosexuality are more emphatic, though of course the interpretations of the Bible vary widely. For example, Leviticus 20:13 states, "If a man also lie with mankind, as he lieth with a woman, both of them have committed an abomination: they shall surely be put to death; their blood shall be upon them." See also John Boswell, *Christianity, Social Tolerance and Homosexuality* (Chicago: University of Chicago Press, 1980); Alliance of Baptists et al., "Amicus Brief in Lawrence v. Texas" (2003).

18. Eskridge, *Equality Practice;* Carlos A. Ball and Janice Farrel Pea, "Warring with Wardle: Morality, Social Science, and Gay and Lesbian Parents," *University of Illinois Law Review* (1998): 253–339; Lynn D. Wardle, "The Potential Impact of Homosexual Parenting on Children," *University of Illinois Law Review* (1997): 833–920.

19. Wardle, "The Potential Impact of Homosexual Parenting on Children."

20. Ball and Pea, "Warring with Wardle."

21. Wardle, "The Potential Impact of Homosexual Parenting on Children."

22. Ball and Pea, "Warring with Wardle."

23. U.S. Bureau of the Census, "Technical Note on Same-Sex Unmarried Partner Data from the 1990 and 2000 Censuses" (2001), http://landview.census.gov/population/www/cen2000/samesex.html (ac-

cessed February 7, 2004); Michael J. Rosenfeld and Byung-Soo Kim, "The Independence of Young Adults and the Rise of Interracial and Same-Sex Unions," *American Sociological Review* 70, no. 4 (2005): 541–562.

24. For discussion of the federal Defense of Marriage Act, see Koppelman, *The Gay Rights Question in Contemporary American Law;* Eskridge, *Equality Practice.*

25. Koppelman, *The Gay Rights Question in Contemporary American Law;* Eskridge, *Equality Practice.*

26. Baehr v. Lewin, 852 P.2d Hawaii 44 (1993). During the years of hearings, appeals, and retrials, Lawrence Miike replaced John Lewin as director of Hawaii's Department of Health, and the case was renamed Baehr v. Miike.

27. Baehr v. Miike, WL 694235 Hawaii Circuit Court (1996).

28. Attorney General of Hawaii, "State of Hawaii's Pre-trial Memorandum in Baehr v. Miike" (Honolulu: 1996); Baehr v. Miike.

29. See Judge Chang's opinion, quoting from defense witnesses Dr. Pruett (at page 4) and Dr. Eggebeen (at page 5) in Baehr v. Miike.

30. The witness was Dr. Richard Williams. See Judge Chang's decision at page 6 in Baehr v. Miike.

31. This is a point on which Wardle agrees with Ball and Pea. Wardle explains Hawaii's defeat at trial by arguing that the state had not made its case enthusiastically enough. Ball and Pea, "Warring with Wardle," Wardle, "The Potential Impact of Homosexual Parenting on Children."

32. Attorney General of Vermont, "Brief Arguing that the Superior Court Decision in Baker v. State Be Affirmed" (Montpelier: 1998).

33. Baker v. State, 170 Vermont 194 (1909).

34. American Psychiatric Association, *Diagnostic and Statistical Manual of Mental Disorders* (Washington, D.C.: American Psychiatric Association, 1952). The 1952 version of the *DSM* clearly categorized homosexuality as a personality disorder, but the second edition of the *DSM,* published in 1968, was equivocal. The third edition of the *DSM,* published in 1978, eliminated homosexuality entirely.

35. Evelyn Hooker, "The Adjustment of the Male Overt Homosexual," *Journal of Projective Techniques* 21 (1957): 17–31.

36. Ibid.

37. John C. Gonsiorek, "The Empirical Basis for the Demise of the Illness Model of Homosexuality," in *Homosexuality: Research Implications for Public Policy,* ed. John C. Gonsiorek and James D. Weinrich (Beverly Hills, Calif.: Sage, 1991).

38. Ronald Bayer, *Homosexuality and American Psychiatry: The Politics of Diagnosis* (Princeton, N.J.: Princeton University Press, 1987); American Psychological Association et al., "Amicus Brief in Support of Petitioners in Lawrence v. Texas" (Washington, D.C.: 2003).

39. Bayer, *Homosexuality and American Psychiatry;* Charles Silverstein, "Psychological and Medical Treatments of Homosexuality," in *Homosexuality: Research Implications for Public Policy,* ed. John C. Gonsiorek and James D. Weinrich (Newbury Park, Calif.: Sage, 1991), pp. 101–114.

40. American Psychiatric Association, "Position Statement on Homosexuality and Civil Rights," *American Journal of Psychiatry* 131 (1973): 497. Some of the leading psychiatrists continued to believe that homosexuality, like alcoholism, could be (and ought to be) cured through intensive therapy. These psychiatric traditionalists were appalled by the new APA statement on homosexuality, and they demanded that the issue be put before the entire APA membership in a referendum. In 1974, 58 percent of APA members endorsed the decision to remove homosexuality from the list of mental disorders in the organization's forthcoming revision of their official *Diagnostic and Statistical Manual.* See Bayer, *Homosexuality and American Psychiatry;* Charles W. Socarides, *Homosexuality* (New York: Jason Aronson, 1978).

41. American Psychological Association et al., "Amicus Brief in Support of Petitioners in Lawrence v. Texas," 11.

42. Dean E. Murphy, "San Francisco Married 4,037 Same-Sex Pairs from 46 States," *New York Times,* March 18, 2004, A:1; Dean E. Murphy, "San Francisco Mayor Exults in Move on Gay Marriage," *New York Times,* February 19, 2004, A:14.

43. Murphy, "San Francisco Married 4,037 Same-Sex Pairs from 46 States"; Murphy, "San Francisco Mayor Exults in Move on Gay Marriage."

44. Dean E. Murphy and Carolyn Marshall, "California Court Rules Gay Unions Have No Standing," *New York Times,* August 13, 2004, A1; Lockyer v. City and County of San Francisco, CA S122923 (2004).

45. Goodridge v. Department of Public Health Massachusetts, SJC-08860 (2003).

46. Eskridge, *Equality Practice.*

47. Pam Belluck, "Massachusetts Rejects Bill to Eliminate Gay Marriage," *New York Times,* September 15, 2005, A:14.

48. David Moats, *Civil Wars: A Battle for Gay Marriage* (Orlando, Fla.: Harcourt, 2004).

49. Lawrence v. Texas, 539 U.S. 558 (2003, Scalia dissenting) at 602.

50. Doug McAdam, *Political Process and the Development of Black Insurgency,*

1930–1970 (Chicago: University of Chicago Press, 1982); Frances Fox Piven and Richard Cloward, *Poor People's Movements: How They Succeed, How They Fail* (New York: Pantheon, 1977).

51. Mark Lacey and Laurie Goodstein, "African Anglican Leaders Outraged over Gay Bishop in U.S.," *New York Times*, November 4, 2003, A:1. There was substantial division among Episcopalians within the United States as well; see Jane Gordon, "Meetings, and a Schism, Continue," *New York Times*, April 24, 2005, 14:1.

52. Laurie Goodstein, "Church Is Rebuked on Same-Sex Unions," *New York Times*, October 19, 2004, A:13.

53. Peter Wallenstein, *Tell the Court I Love My Wife: Race, Marriage, and Law—An American History* (New York: Palgrave Macmillan, 2002).

54. Koppelman, *The Gay Rights Question in Contemporary American Law*.

55. Ibid.

56. For an optimistic view of the future of same-sex marriage, in light of historical trends in gay rights and gay life in the United States, see George Chauncey, *Why Marriage? The History Shaping Today's Debate* (New York: Basic Books, 2004).

57. Arthur W. Calhoun, *A Social History of the American Family: From Independence through the Civil War*, vol. 2 (New York: Barnes and Noble, [1918] 1960); Richard Godbeer, *Sexual Revolution in Early America* (Baltimore, Md.: Johns Hopkins University Press, 2002).

58. Godbeer, *Sexual Revolution in Early America;* Michael Grossberg, *Governing the Hearth: Law and the Family in Nineteenth-Century America* (Chapel Hill: University of North Carolina Press, 1985).

59. Carroll Smith-Rosenberg, "The Abortion Movement and the AMA, 1850–1880," in *Disorderly Conduct: Visions of Gender in Victorian America* (New York: Oxford University Press, 1985), pp. 217–244; John D'Emilio and Estelle Freedman, *Intimate Matters: A History of Sexuality in America* (New York: Harper and Row, 1988).

60. Murphy, "San Francisco Married 4,037 Same-Sex Pairs from 46 States"; Murphy, "San Francisco Mayor Exults in Move on Gay Marriage"; Thomas Crampton, "Court Says New Paltz Mayor Can't Hold Gay Weddings," *New York Times*, June 8, 2004, B:6; Thomas Crampton, "Issuing Licenses, Quietly, to Couples in Asbury Park," *New York Times*, March 10, 2004, B:5; Matthew Preusch, "Oregonians Look to One Suit to Settle Gay Marriage Issue," *New York Times*, March 25, 2004, A:16.

61. Pam Belluck, "Hundreds of Same-Sex Couples Wed in Massachusetts," *New York Times*, May 18, 2004, A:1; Goodridge v. Department of Public Health Massachusetts, SJC-08860 (2004).

62. For a thorough discussion of comparative marriage rights with data

that is just a few years out of date, see Eskridge, *Equality Practice*. For more up-to-date information, see http://www.lambdalegal.org.

63. Renwick McLean, "Spanish Parliament Gives Approval to Bill to Legalize Same-Sex Marriages," *New York Times*, April 22, 2005, A:12; Clifford Krauss, "Gay Marriage Is Extended Nationwide in Canada," *New York Times*, June 29, 2005, A:4.

64. Jeffrey Jensen Arnett, *Emerging Adulthood: The Winding Road from the Late Teens through the Early Twenties* (Oxford: Oxford University Press, 2004); Richard A. Setterstein, Jr., Frank F. Furstenberg, Jr., and Rubén G. Rumbaut, eds., *On the Frontier of Adulthood: Theory, Research, and Public Policy* (Chicago: University of Chicago Press, 2005); John Modell, Frank F. Furstenberg, Jr., and Theodore Hershberg, "Social Change and Transitions to Adulthood in Historical Perspective," in *The American Family in Social-Historical Perspective*, ed. Michael Gordon (New York: St. Martin's Press, 1978), pp. 192–219.

65. Edward Shorter, *The Making of the Modern Family* (New York: Basic Books, 1975).

66. Lenore Weitzman, *The Marriage Contract: Spouses, Lovers, and the Law* (New York: Free Press, 1981).

67. Shorter, *The Making of the Modern Family;* Anthony Giddens, *The Transformation of Intimacy: Sexuality, Love, and Eroticism in Modern Societies* (Cambridge: Polity Press, 1992); Morton Hunt, *The Natural History of Love* (New York: Anchor Books, 1994); Ron Lesthaeghe, "A Century of Demographic and Cultural Change in Western Europe: An Exploration of Underlying Dimensions," *Population and Development Review* 9 (1983): 411–435.

68. Ulrich Beck and Elisabeth Beck-Gernsheim, *The Normal Chaos of Love,* trans. Mark Ritter and Jane Wiebel (Cambridge: Polity Press, 1995); James Q. Wilson, *The Marriage Problem: How Our Culture Has Weakened Families* (New York: Harper Collins, 2002); Christopher Lasch, *Haven in a Heartless World: The Family Besieged* (New York: W. W. Norton, 1977).

69. For communitarian critiques of the new individualism, see Amitai Etzioni, *The Spirit of Community: The Reinvention of American Society* (New York: Simon and Schuster, 1993); Mary Ann Glendon, *Rights Talk: The Impoverishment of Political Discourse* (New York: Free Press, 1993).

70. Wilson, *The Marriage Problem;* Linda J. Waite and Maggie Gallagher, *The Case for Marriage: Why Married People Are Happier, Healthier, and Better Off Financially* (New York: Doubleday, 2000); James Dobson, *Dare to Discipline* (New York: Bantam Doubleday, 1980). For a colonial perspective on the importance of family order, see Cotton

Mather, *A Family Well-Ordered: An Essay to Render Parents and Children Happy in One Another* (Boston: Green and Allen, 1699); Edmund S. Morgan, *The Puritan Family: Religion and Domestic Relations in Seventeenth-Century New England* (New York: Harper, [1944] 1966).

71. William F. Ogburn and N. F. Nimkoff, *Technology and the Changing Family* (Westport, Conn.: Greenwood Press, 1955).

72. Sickels, *Race, Marriage and the Law;* Loving v. Virginia, 388 U.S. 1 (1967); Moran, *Interracial Intimacy.*

73. Romano, *Race Mixing.*

Index

Abortion, 28, 158, 160–161
Adorno, Theodor, 141
Age at first marriage, 62–64, 193, 224–225n63; and interraciality, 114–118
Ainsworth, Mary, 141
Alwin, Duane, 135–136
American Civil Liberties Union (ACLU), 163
American Medical Association, 28, 160
American Psychiatric Association (APA), 177–178
Anderson, Elijah, 78–79
Antimiscegenation laws. *See* Loving v. Virginia
Attachment theory, 141–142
Authoritarian Personality, The (Adorno et al.), 141, 245n3

Baby boom, the, 62–64
Baehr v. Miike, 174–176, 178, 182–183
Bailey, Beth, 35, 37
Baker v. State, 144, 175–176, 178
Baumrind, Diana, 240n2
Becker, Gary, 150
Bérubé, Allan, 40
Birth control, 158–160, 188
Bogardus, Emory, 37
"Boomerang effect," 56
Bork, Robert, 166–167, 252–253n6
"Boston marriages," 31
Bott, Elizabeth, 120

Bowers v. Hardwick, 164–166
Bowlby, John, 141
Brown University, 27

Calhoun, Arthur, 42–45
Caplow, Theodore, 135
Census, U.S., 4–8, 12–14, 16, 45–103, 107, 110, 114, 116, 117, 120, 133, 151, 173–174, 192–202; explanation of, 45–48; changing treatment of same-sex unions, 68–72, 227n6, 227n8, 227–228n9, 228n11, 228n12; definitions of geographic mobility, 88–91; operational definition of interracial couples, 91. *See also* Figures; Tables
Chicago: segregation and neighborhood violence, 37–38
Childhood: abuse of children, 125–128; colonial times, 126–127; nineteenth century, 127–128; physical privacy, 132–134; and social class, 134
Civil rights movement, 8–15, 116, 143–147, 162, 181–182
Cities. *See* Urban areas
Closet, the, 11, 33, 50, 68, 73–76, 101, 122, 177, 185
Cohabitation, heterosexual: numbers of, 70, 76–77, 81; exposure to, 80–82; and geographic mobility, 89, 92; and urban areas, 96–97, 198–199; and ed-